CAMARGO GUARNIERI, BRAZILIAN COMPOSER

Camargo Guarnieri,

INDIANA UNIVERSITY PRESS

Bloomington and Indianapolis

Brazilian Composer

A STUDY OF HIS CREATIVE LIFE AND WORKS

MARION VERHAALEN

With a Preface by José Marie Neves

This book is a publication of

Indiana University Press
601 North Morton Street
Bloomington, IN 47404-3797 USA

http://iupress.indiana.edu

Telephone orders	800-842-6796
Fax orders	812-855-7931
Orders by e-mail	iuporder@indiana.edu

The paper used in this publication meets the minimum requirements of
American National Standard for Information Sciences—Permanence of
Paper for Printed Library Materials, ANSI Z39.48-1984.

MANUFACTURED IN THE UNITED STATES OF AMERICA

Library of Congress Cataloging-in-Publication Data

Verhaalen, Marion.
  Camargo Guarnieri, Brazilian composer : a study of his creative life and
works / Marion Verhaalen ; with a preface by José Maria Neves.
    p. cm.
  Includes bibliographical references and index.
  ISBN 0-253-34475-1 (cloth)
  1. Guarnieri, Camargo, 1907—Criticism and interpretation. I. Neves,
José Maria. II. Title.
  ML410.G9462V47 2005
  780'.92—dc22

                                        2004018687

1 2 3 4 5 10 09 08 07 06 05

CONTENTS

PREFACE

No one would say that Mozart Camargo Guarnieri is a composer unknown to those who have had contact with what is called *erudite* Brazilian music. Guarnieri has merited references and praise from critics, and chapters have been dedicated to him in books on the history of Brazilian music. Although many of his works appear frequently on concert programs and in recordings, nonetheless until now he has lacked a systematic and exhaustive study of his life and his works. Finally this study has appeared, the fruit of long and dedicated work of the pianist and professor of music Marion Verhaalen.

The origin of this immense project was a doctoral thesis on the piano works of the composer (and those of Francisco Mignone), defended in 1971 at Teachers College, Columbia University in New York City. In truth, since 1969 Marion Verhaalen has given a great part of her time to the study of the music of this composer. In many trips to Brazil, particularly in two longer periods in 1969–70 and again in 1988, with grants from the Organization of American States and the Fulbright Foundation, respectively, the author collected abundant documentation on the composer, establishing a complete catalog of his works, which were also analyzed. She examined concert programs, critical articles, and musicological studies on the composer and his works. Dr. Robert Pace of Columbia University observed that she brought special gifts to this study: she was both a pianist and a composer with a solid background. Another important circumstance was that she established a deep friendship with Camargo Guarnieri and his family. She was a guest in their home in São Paulo while she pursued her research. With all of this, it is no exaggeration to say that few people would be able to bring a deeper understanding and background to this study. The author probably knows more about the works of Guarnieri than the composer himself—a point to which he himself attested.

What is the importance of Camargo Guarnieri, objectively speaking, to the panorama of Brazilian music in the twentieth century? First, he represents the best concretization and example of Modern Nationalism. In fact, Guarnieri had a very special relationship to the Modernist ideas of Mário

First published in *Camargo Guarnieri, Expressões de uma Vida*, in 2001 by the University of São Paulo Press.

de Andrade, the defender of technical and aesthetic solutions of Modern Nationalism. On the occasion of the 1922 Week of Modern Art, Heitor Villa-Lobos was already an established composer and, because of this, perhaps less influenced by the new Modern Nationalism. Still, Villa-Lobos's works during the next twenty years showed the effects of these new ideas. Francisco Mignone, on the contrary, was literally conquered by Mário de Andrade. One can easily detect the difference in his musical posture before and after his contact with Modernism. Guarnieri approached composition under the influence of de Andrade, who, in effect, assumed the responsibility of orienting Guarnieri, in both music and culture. The composer himself in an article published in 1943 in the *Revista Brasileira de Música* related that, in the house of de Andrade, "literature, sociology, philosophy, art, and the devil were discussed! For me it was as rich as taking courses at a university."

The ideas of Modern Nationalism were completely absorbed by the young composer, and, as he refined his technique, he remained faithful to them. On the other hand, Guarnieri became a teacher of composition involved with the formation of hundreds of students. In fact, of all the composition teachers in Brazil, Guarnieri seems to have been the only one who truly established a "school" of composition, with all the consequences that flow from this.

This book of Marion Verhaalen's is the most complete study of the life and works of Camargo Guarnieri, a reference work covering all the works of the composer until his death in January 1993. Beginning with an excellent biography, there follows an examination of the aesthetic ideas and technical solutions of the Brazilian National Movement as derived from the Modernist Movement. The author then gives a general stylistic description of all of Guarnieri's works, divided into seven large categories. One cannot but underline the richness of information offered in this text with citations from critics and musicologists who wrote about the composer. The author has demonstrated her extensive knowledge of the Brazilian musical bibliography, and she has known how to utilize it to substantiate the conclusions reached throughout the study.

Marion Verhaalen merits our compliments and our thanks for her work. With this book Brazilian musicology is much richer. Students of music, lovers of Brazilian music—here and in the United States—will know more about Camargo Guarnieri and about this most important phase of Brazilian music. It is a stranger who has come to guide us, who loves and understands Brazil and its cultural reality.

José Maria Neves (+2002)
Professor, University of Rio de Janeiro
Doctorate in Musicology, University of Paris–Sorbonne
Rio de Janeiro, 1999

ACKNOWLEDGMENTS

Acknowledgment is made for permission to use citations from *The Port-land Press Herald, The Boston Herald,* and *The Cleveland Plain Dealer*

My thanks also go to the musicians who participated in the recording of Guarnieri's music for the accompanying CD:

Dr. Cristina Capparelli Gerling and Dr. Ney Fialkow, Federal University of Rio Grande do Sul in Porto Alegre, Brazil

Dr. Tadeu Coelho, North Carolina School of the Arts

Lawrence Blind, University of New Mexico

Dr. James Przygocki and Dr. Theresa Bogard, University of Wyoming

William Helmers, Milwaukee Symphony Orchestra

Frederick Moyer, Lee, New Hampshire

Marlee Sabo, Braden Flanagan-Zitoun, and Dr. Michael Thiele, Wisconsin Conservatory of Music

The São Paulo Symphony Orchestra, John Neschling, conductor.

INTRODUCTION

Some decisions become life-changing. My decision to study Brazilian music for a doctoral dissertation was such a decision. Seeking initial information for selection of a topic was like looking into a dark mouse hole: there was very little to see! I was experiencing what Juan Orrego Salas of Indiana University had said some years earlier: "Brazilians do not write; we know very little about the history of their arts." (A brief look at the bibliography in this book will attest to that.) The only pertinent book in English, Nicholas Slonimsky's 1945 *Music of Latin America,* had only one brief paragraph on Villa-Lobos, one on Francisco Mignone, and another, shorter one on Camargo Guarnieri. Thinking that most people knew of Villa-Lobos, although I did not realize that no major study of him in English had yet been published, I chose the other two composers. Both had written a considerable amount of music for piano. With a refurbishing of my Portuguese and a grant from the Organization of American States, the venture began in 1969.

Dividing the year between Rio de Janeiro and São Paulo, the respective homes to the two composers, I began casting a little light into those mouse holes of information. Mercedes Reis Pequeno, head of the Music Division of the Biblioteca Nacional in Rio, was a treasure. She had organized decades of clippings from newspaper reviews on the composers and was most helpful in pointing me to other resources which, though limited, were to be found. Most other people could not imagine what I was about. What became clear was that the discipline of musical research in Brazil had not yet been born. I was paddling out to the crest of a brand new wave of research.

In both Rio and São Paulo, I established a cyclic routine of interviews with the composers, analysis of their works, and listening to their music at concerts or on the radio. The samba throbbed at night in the hills in Rio and rounded out my musical education in many ways. The two men, Mignone and Guarnieri, well represented the different cultures of their two cities. The affable Mignone reflected sunny Rio, and Guarnieri was energetic São Paulo in person. Guarnieri immediately offered me whatever assistance I needed. Twice weekly I recorded our interviews and then went home with a satchel of his precious manuscripts. Analysis of the music and transcription of the interviews would raise questions for the next meeting a few days later. This went on for four months on my first sojourn in the country. Guarnieri was so organized and generous with his time and materials that, in those four months, I was able to study his entire output, not just the music for piano. Many subsequent trips allowed me to update the information as he continued composing. By our last meeting in 1990, he was already not well, and virtually nothing more came from his pen after that.

It was insightful to know Guarnieri as a friend and see him live his daily life as a composer, conductor, and teacher. I was able to witness the demands placed on him and understand his struggle to keep all the facets of his life together. Being accepted by his family as a friend and frequent guest over the years has also provided a unique perspective for this study. My deepest thanks go to his wife, Vera Silvia, for her welcome, her friendship, and her help. She translated into Portuguese the original, more detailed edition of my study for publication in 2001 by the University of São Paulo, *Camargo Guarnieri: Expressions of a Life,* and she has continued to assist my efforts.

My sincere thanks go to Lori Reinhall, who persevered with me through the rewriting of this work for a new American edition. Also deserving of thanks for their inestimable contributions are the music critics who regularly wrote reviews of Guarnieri's music over the years: Mário de Andrade, João Itiberê da Cunha, Caldeira Filho, Eurico Nogueira França, Vasco Mariz, Andrade Muricy, and others. Without their efforts, an entire period of Brazilian music history would have been lost to the world.

Looking back on what has happened over the past thirty years since I first ventured to Brazil is nothing short of astounding. What Brazilians term *erudite music* is every bit as vital now as the popular and folk music tradition was then. Graduate and doctoral programs at Brazilian universities have proliferated, and Brazilians are both studying and teaching all over the world. More than a dozen doctoral studies on Guarnieri have been written in the United States alone. Brazilian research organizations and the government are supportive of their youthful talent. Musical composition is flourishing amazingly well, and hundreds of young composers have taken their places in the world arena of music.

Brazil used to be called a "sleeping giant." It is still an impressive giant, but it is no longer sleeping. It is awake and well, riding the current of a vital musical wave. Young Brazilian musicians have some wonderful models to emulate, and among them Camargo Guarnieri is one of the most distinguished. He did eminently well what was his to do, and now it is their turn. All translations from the Portuguese in this book are my own.

ABBREVIATIONS

AMP   Associated Music Publishers, New York
RA   Ricordi Americana, Buenos Aires, Argentina
RB   Ricordi Brasileira, São Paulo, Brazil

CAMARGO GUARNIERI, BRAZILIAN COMPOSER

ONE

The Man

On the evening of March 18, 1928, Mário de Andrade was waiting for Antonio Munhoz to stop by with the young composer Camargo Guarnieri. Andrade's apartment on Rua Lopez Chaves, no. 106, in São Paulo had become a gathering place for young intellectuals of the city, but this was the first time that Guarnieri was to meet Andrade. Guarnieri recalled the occasion:

> With that delicacy and cordiality which were such a part of his spirit (and which contributed much to calming my nervousness), Mário invited us in, and we began to talk. After a short time he asked me to play some things. He listened with great attention and interest. What I can honestly say is that, from that moment, Mário de Andrade placed himself in defense of my works, helping me in every way possible.[1]

Andrade, a professor of history and aesthetics at the São Paulo Conservatory of Drama and Music, had become the spokesman for a whole new national movement in the arts in Brazil. He had been exploring the national elements in music for some time in his own thinking and teaching. He had finally given his ideas national exposure in the 1922 Week of Modern Art in São Paulo, six years before Guarnieri's meeting with him. His published essay of 1928 *Ensaio Sôbre a Música Brasileira* (Essay on Brazilian Music) laid the basis for an aesthetic orientation that artists and composers were to follow if they intended to produce works of a truly national character. This was the first of his many writings on the subject. Meeting Andrade at this propitious time was to have a lasting effect on Guarnieri. It initiated a quantum leap in his journey to becoming one of Brazil's most important composers of the twentieth century.

EARLY YEARS

Despite his Italian name and partial ancestry, Guarnieri's first pieces that Andrade heard in 1928 left no doubt that the young composer was solidly rooted in his Brazilian culture. His Italian grandfather had emigrated from Caltanisetta, Sicily, with wife and family, as did so many other Italians in the late nineteenth century. When the family landed in Santos, Brazil, in 1895, a careless stroke of an immigration official's pen added an "i" to the name, severing the nominal connection with the Cremona Guarneri of violin-making fame. The composer's father, Miguel, was eleven at this time. Though a temporary home was made in the growing city of São Paulo, a new power plant in nearby Paranaíba offered hope of better employment, so Guarnieri's grandfather resettled his family there.

After a few years in Paranaíba, Miguel joined his older brother in Tietê, a small town located about sixty-five miles northwest of São Paulo. Here they established a small barbershop. Thus it was in Tietê that Miguel met and subsequently married Gessia Arruda Camargo Penteado, daughter of a wealthy family whose ancestry can be traced back to the marriage of a Spanish adventurer and an Indian woman some four hundred years earlier. Guarnieri commented that, in the course of those four hundred years, the family genetic strain also absorbed the Black culture along with the predominant Portuguese blood. Gessia's marriage in 1905 to Miguel, a barber, was a disappointment to her family, but it turned into a solid union that brought forth ten children.

Miguel was a lover of opera and a fairly good musician in his own right, able to play the piano, flute, and string bass. As his family grew, he couldn't resist naming his boys after his favorite composers. Mozart Camargo was the oldest, born February 1, 1907. When he was old enough to realize the significance of his own name, he dropped it "so as not to offend a master."[2] He later retained only the initial "M." before Camargo. There were three other boys: Rossine, Bellini, and Verdi, who died at the age of two. Bellini did not pursue an artistic career, but Rossine became a well-known writer and poet; many of his verses can be found among Camargo's songs. Among the six girls were Alice, a poet and library technician, Maria Cecilia, who was an artist, and Rosa, a lawyer. With so many children who had successful professional careers, it is no wonder that Miguel and Gessia were held in high esteem in the small town of Tietê.

Camargo began two years of primary school in Tietê when he was seven, his only early formal education. He was to feel this minimum of formal education deeply as the years passed. Because he was the oldest son, he had to leave school and help his father in the barbershop, while his younger brothers and his sisters were able to remain in elementary school. There he had gained initial skills in reading and writing, although he recalled that his interests were anything but academic at the time. His preferences were "for planting things, chasing butterflies, experimenting with insects."[3] He remembered that these years were, in many ways, very happy ones, filled with the sounds of the folk music and dancing from around his home.

The young student had no interest whatsoever in a music theory class in which his father had enrolled him. A local clarinetist could not seem to make the tracing of quarter and half notes very interesting. Guarnieri related:

> The first week, Benedito Flora taught us how to draw a whole note, and we spent the class drawing whole notes. The next week we learned the quarter note. Such difficult work! The fourth week he mixed them up. I never returned to class, but during the class time I would play in a large garden near his house. He didn't bother about my absence. This went on until my father stopped by one day to ask how I was doing, and Flora said he didn't know.[4]

In an attempt to use a different approach with his son, Miguel rented a small piano, and his wife, Gessia, gave the youth lessons. It was a small French keyboard which Guarnieri soon outgrew, so Miguel arranged to have him practice across the street in a club, within hearing distance of the home. Guarnieri practiced, but he spent more time improvising, an activity his father did not fully appreciate at first. Actually, this was the beginning of his creative development, and it had a permanent influence on his music.

The improvisation flowered into Guarnieri's first written piece in 1918: *Sonho de Artista* (An Artist's Dream). It was inspired by a young friend his sister brought home, his first awakening to girls, as he recalled. Miguel endured a mixture of surprise, confusion, and excitement at this event, and in his overzealous way he borrowed money to have the piece engraved in São Paulo in 1920. It bore a dedication from Camargo to Virginio Dias, a piano teacher in Tietê with whom he had just started to study. Dias was enraged at Miguel's presumption. Angry words, futile predictions that the boy would never be a composer, and counterpredictions by the father severed this relationship and ended the lessons. For the next two years young Guarnieri's musical education was on his own.

This episode and the events leading up to it suggest the image of a devoted father who fostered, protected, and pushed a gifted son who might just achieve what the father could not accomplish personally. The hope that urged Miguel to invest his energies in this son also made him decide to uproot the entire family in 1922. They all moved to São Paulo in order to find better music teachers for Camargo.

Sonho de Artista, the piano waltz printed by Casa Mignon in São Paulo two years earlier, had come to the attention of local music critics, who gave it reviews in various papers. Guarnieri saved these unidentified clippings. An anonymous critic in one of them wrote, "There has come from Tietê a beautiful *Valsa Lenta* [Slow Waltz], a composition of Mozart Guarnieri. The composer is still a boy of only thirteen. Even at that, he appears to be precocious, and if he continues, he will be an artist. We offer our good wishes to Mozart Guarnieri." Another noted, "With an extraordinary vocation for music, he is already achieving great things. Being only thirteen, he has composed an expressive and admirable piece, giving it all the necessary color. He appears to be a master. It is enough to hear the *Sonho de Artista* to know how much promise there is in the young Mozart Guarnieri." A third anonymous article extolled the qualities of genius and then concluded, "His music discovers intimate situations: in shimmering emotions each phrase reveals feelings of poetry. It is a beautiful page of inspiration, so rare, suggestive and playable that it predicts a future of praise and glory for the talented youth. To young Mozart, our congratulations and expectations of more happy products." All this referred to a thirteen-year-old.

These early years in the life of Camargo Guarnieri reveal his great struggle, determination, and extreme effort to find his own way. His first published piece also suggests his deep emotional power and musical expressiveness. One might marvel at the thought of this young boy growing up in a small village, surrounded by natural beauty, and carrying within himself the tremendous musical giftedness which he honed in relative isolation. He heard and absorbed the music and dances of the people around him—the folk songs, the Sunday band concerts, the popular music of pre-Lenten carnival—and he explored his own abilities to improvise and create. His two years of primary school in Tietê, however, were hardly a basis for his continuing studies, a realization that created a shyness and certain insecurity in him as a person. His early isolation from the formal music world was a blessing, in that his own talent was free of outside influences. But it was also a bane to the extent that he lacked the contacts and exchanges with others of similar interests. He was a very bright, highly sensitive youth. His father recognized his talent, and Camargo himself began to realize that he needed a more formal education and experience in order to continue developing. As he grew into a young man, he continued to feel keenly this lack of formal education and spoke of it at times. These early experiences left indelible marks on his personality and shaped him as a person and a composer.

SÃO PAULO

Camargo was fifteen when the family moved to São Paulo in 1922. While showing him around the city upon their arrival, his uncle took him past the São Paulo Conservatory of Drama and Music, an experience which stirred in him the desire to be one of the students there. As the eldest son, however, he was expected to help his father support the family. He found several jobs which earned some money, one of which was at Casa di Franco, a music store that maintained a pianist to demonstrate music for potential customers. Camargo did this every afternoon from one o'clock to half past five. One customer who heard him play asked with whom he studied.

When Guarnieri answered that he did not have a teacher, the man recommended Ernani Braga. He and his father went to visit Braga, who agreed to give him lessons. Braga would accept no payment for his services. In addition to the piano lessons, Guarnieri also studied flute with his father.

Every evening he would be at the Teatro Recreio on Avenida Rio Branco, playing for the silent movies with his father until midnight. Miguel usually played bass, sometimes the flute, and the younger Guarnieri was at the piano. From here he would go to a cabaret, where he would play until three or four in the morning. A few hours sleep until nine o'clock were all he could afford before rising to practice.

Guarnieri was dismissed by Casa di Franco after several months because he preferred to read through the shelves of classical music instead of demonstrate the more popular music which the proprietor was eager to sell. Part of his job was to keep the music organized. He not only did that, but he played through all the solo literature up to "S" before he was dismissed. In these few months, he had the invaluable experience of coming to know the major keyboard works of Bach, Beethoven, Chopin, Mozart, Rachmaninoff, and others "up to S."

Guarnieri's piano studies with Ernani Braga continued for about three years. Braga was a fine musician who had studied in Rio de Janeiro and Paris and later founded a conservatory in Pernambuco. He left a small collection of his own compositions. Guarnieri gradually felt the need for a new teacher and contacted Antônio Sá Pereira. About this same time Miguel sold his barbershop for a more lucrative sales position. This allowed the young Guarnieri to discontinue some of his jobs and concentrate on his musical studies.

In the course of his lessons with Sá Pereira, Guarnieri shared some of his own pieces. Sá Pereira liked them and took Guarnieri to meet Agostino Cantú, an Italian teacher friend in the city. When Cantú looked at one of the pieces, he said with irritation, "There is a mistake!"[5] The eighteen-year-old calmly replied that if he were perfect he would not be looking for a teacher. This unpleasant encounter and their complete contrast in temperaments did not lead to a productive time. After a few discouraging lessons, Guarnieri discontinued them.

The composer remembered that the following year, 1926, was decisive in his life. He had read in the paper of the arrival in São Paulo of Lamberto Baldi, a fine Italian conductor. After one of the first concerts, Guarnieri went backstage to talk to Baldi, who could not speak Portuguese. Guarnieri managed to convey that he wanted an appointment, which they arranged. Guarnieri took his father along, as well as some of his pieces. Baldi was impressed and agreed to take him on as a student. He told Miguel, "Your son needs a teacher, and, frankly, I need some pupils. I hope that I am the

Mário de Andrade, Lamberto Baldi, and Camargo Guarnieri (1920s).
Photo courtesy of the University of São Paulo IEB archives.

teacher he needs and that he will be the student that I expect him to be."[6] When the father asked about the cost of lessons, Baldi said that they could speak of that later. Five years later, Baldi still refused to speak of the matter of payment.

The five years with Lamberto Baldi (1926–31) provided Guarnieri with a firm, extensive musical formation. He recalled:

> Baldi was a tremendous person, a man of great intelligence. His manner of teaching was so integrated. I was studying harmony, counterpoint, fugue, and orchestration simultaneously, all from the music literature itself, and my own composing was entirely free. He never put obstacles in my way. He would only check a passage and say, "I don't like this; correct it." One of the first things he did was to have me play in the orchestra. I had to play all the keyboard instruments—piano, xylophone, and celesta. I spent the entire day studying or rehearsing with the orchestra, and at night I would go to have the evening meal with him, and then he would teach me. There were eight of us who studied with him in this way.[7]

This orchestral experience was particularly valuable to Guarnieri. Baldi was not only an excellent conductor, but he also introduced many contemporary compositions to Brazilian audiences, giving the young man a first-hand experience with new and valuable models from some of the world's finest composers. For example, many of Stravinsky's pieces were given their first Latin American performances under Baldi in São Paulo. This performing experience inspired Guarnieri to write his own first pieces for orchestra: the *Suite Infantil* (Children's Suite) of 1929 and an orchestration of his 1928 piano solo *Dança Brasileira* (Brazilian Dance).

Sá Pereira was very pleased with Guarnieri's progress under Baldi. He appreciated the way in which Baldi guided him. Sá Pereira wrote in the *Diário de São Paulo* in 1929, after the publication of the First Piano Sonatina:

> It happens that a teacher of composition, even a competent one, being unfamiliar, can without intending to, stifle a talent in formation, simply by not comprehending the new spirit of the environment in which one lives and which offers new problems and demands new solutions. I see in Maestro Baldi a great superiority in the way in which he knew how to submit his student to the severe discipline of counterpoint without tyrannizing the spirit with a tourniquet of sterile idolatry for certain methods, inciting him on the contrary to find a new solution, a personal style, taking advantage of and supporting the national tendencies which were already so pronounced in his student.[8]

By this time Guarnieri had spent six years in São Paulo. They were hard years in which he was learning in the school of life as a practicing musician. And he was getting some solid musical guidance. These experiences, though important, were no substitute for the formal training, especially academic, which others with more means could obtain for themselves. While this lack continued to feed his sense of insecurity, it also increased his appreciation and deep affection for the fine teachers who continued to guide him in these formative years. He was able to continue honing his unique gifts without any artificial restrictions being imposed upon him. He was also building confidence which prepared him for the year 1928, which would become a momentous one for him.

FIRST WORKS AND
A NATIONAL THRUST

After taking a piano lesson with Sá Pereira, Guarnieri had the habit of stopping to talk with his young pianist friend Antônio Munhoz, who happened to live in the same apartment as Sá Pereira. It was through Munhoz that Guarnieri first came into contact with Mário de Andrade in 1928. By this time Guarnieri, at twenty-one, had written under Professor Baldi, not only the *Dança Brasileira* for piano which was dedicated to Munhoz and the

First Piano Sonatina, but a sheaf of songs as well. Andrade was stunned by the degree of national consciousness which these first pieces revealed. For example, the piano sonatina not only breathed the flavor of the Brazilian folk forms, but the directions to the performer were given in Portuguese rather than the customary Italian—a real innovation. The second movement was clearly a guitar-like serenade. The Brazilian flavor of the *Dança Brasileira* was unmistakable, and the craftsmanship nearly perfect. Andrade was able immediately to identify this music with his own theories of nationalism, and thus he began to support the young composer, with both helpful criticism and encouragement.

Shortly after this first meeting, Andrade contacted Baldi and made a pact with him: Baldi was to continue Guarnieri's technical foundation, and Andrade would school him in the areas of aesthetics and general culture. With their agreement, a whole new era began for Guarnieri, who hungered by this time to fill the gap following the two years in primary school in Tietê. One can understand his devotion to these two men to whom he attributed so much of his formation. He also began taking courses at the School of Philosophy of São Bento in São Paulo this same year. In the two years he spent there between 1928 and 1930, he became familiar with Thomistic philosophy. The discipline of philosophy continued to shape his thinking for the rest of his life.

Along with Guarnieri, there were two other young men Andrade tutored on Thursday evenings, both of them writers: Fernando Mendes de Almeida and the poet Ferreira Prestes. They would have dinner and then go to his study, where he would begin to question them on aesthetics, on the books he had given them to read, or on any other topic. Guarnieri remembered Andrade as a pragmatist in his teaching. He would purposely throw out all types of questions to challenge the young men, to force them to develop their own theories, and to learn how to defend them. In an interview with Vasco Mariz on his eightieth birthday, Guarnieri said, "We discussed literature, sociology, philosophy, art, and the devil! For me that was equivalent to studying in a university."[9] It was Andrade who helped Guarnieri to discover his own way, "pointing with his prodigious intuition to a weak spot in a work which he had heard, or disagreeing with an idea and being very critical only to awaken his spirit of confidence in defending an opinion."[10]

Guarnieri recalled that they had marvelous discussions. Realizing that this was the same year that Andrade published his *Essay on Brazilian Music,* one can imagine the caliber of their exchanges. After several hours of this kind of repartee, Andrade would give each student an armful of new books to read for the following week. It was in this way that Guarnieri received his foundation, not only in aesthetics, but also in literature and history.

Guarnieri's work with Lamberto Baldi continued to produce a flow of new compositions. It was a very rich time for the young composer, a period in which he was able to experience his own creative potential under expert guidance and to synthesize his own aesthetic position as well. Andrade's regular columns in the *O Estado de São Paulo* kept Guarnieri's name very much in the public eye. Eurico Nogueira França wrote, "With his prestige as a critic, Mário de Andrade launched Guarnieri as a composer with the publication of his *Dança Brasileira* and gave him reviews, both constructive and praising, protecting him with the impartiality of his observations, but always helpful, while personally strengthening him in long discussions which he had with him on the problems of musical creation."[11]

In 1927 Guarnieri became a teacher of piano and conducting at the São Paulo Conservatory of Drama and Music. He was named an adjunct professor of piano in 1932. Federal law prohibited a double assignment, so his conducting was transferred in 1938 to the Department of Culture in the city. It was a rather unusual procedure that someone who had not had formal Conservatory training would be given a teaching position at this institution. His lack of a diploma also almost prevented his securing a scholarship for study in Paris a few years later. Finally in 1941, the remaining question of his Conservatory status as a faculty member was resolved when the school conferred on him an honorary degree, which enabled him to teach classes in other disciplines. Then in 1957, after thirty years, he was unanimously elected director of this same Conservatory, a position he resigned the following year, unable to deal with the politics involved in his administrative responsibilities.

THE 1930S

In 1931 Professor Baldi left São Paulo for Montevideo, Uruguay, where he became the Director of the Serviço Official Difusão Radio Electric, the official cultural organization of Montevideo. Guarnieri then also assumed the class that Baldi had taught at the Conservatory.

Baldi's departure left Guarnieri with some rather desperate feelings, but Baldi reassured him that he no longer needed a teacher: "All you need to do is write, write, write!"[12] Guarnieri depended very much on Andrade's critiques after Baldi left. It is difficult to realize the impact that these two men had on Guarnieri. Maria Abreu noted that Andrade looked upon Guarnieri as another self, the composer he wished he could have been, a musician who was an extension of the writer that he was himself.[13] Guarnieri was always very moved when speaking of Andrade, who was one of those rare persons who gifted Guarnieri's life—intelligent, creative, compassionate, and loyal. Guarnieri recalled:

I owe all of my humanistic formation to Mário de Andrade. He was to me an example of character, honesty, and goodness. When I first met him, my own knowledge was very elementary. He traced for me a plan of cultural development, even at a time when I was not able to afford to buy any books. From him I learned to love books, to respect the knowledge they contained, to be honest with myself, frank and loyal. This has been the guiding force of my life; the best example of all those things that I ever knew to be good could be found in Mário de Andrade.[14]

Getúlio Vargas had taken power as dictator in Brazil in 1930. His style of governing was particularly oppressive to the Paulistans, and they resisted. Finally on July 9, 1932, São Paulo incited a Constitutional Revolution, which ultimately deposed Vargas. Guarnieri served on a local civil defense team for some months, usually from midnight to six o'clock in the morning. The situation caused a general state of alert in São Paulo, and many schools were closed. After six months of intensive resistance, Vargas entered the city and quelled the revolution.

Amid the revolutionary spirit of 1930, Guarnieri took his own large first step into marriage to Lavinia Viotti, a pianist who had frequently performed in the home of Mário de Andrade. He was twenty-three at the time of the marriage but, as he acknowledged in retrospect, was not really ready for the responsibility. A son, Mário, named after Andrade, was born to them, but they separated after two years. Mário grew up to have his own son, also named Mário, who for a time studied composition with his grandfather.

In 1930 there were already signs in his music that Guarnieri was searching for a more intense and less obvious musical language, probably stemming from his study of the scores of contemporary composers. He spent many hours analyzing the scores of Arnold Schoenberg, Alois Hába, Alban Berg, and Paul Hindemith, which he borrowed from Andrade's library. His own compositions began to reflect these influences as he entered upon what he called his "period of being enamored with atonalism." Even though he had his own and Baldi's students and, in 1932, additional responsibilities as head of the piano department at the Conservatory, he still enjoyed leisure provided by the city's restricted activities.

How far and fast he had moved was brought home to him one evening early in 1930 when he performed for a commission composed of Dona Olivia Guedes Penteado, Dr. Freitas Valle, and Dr. Sampaio Viana. Dona Olivia was wealthy and had been instrumental in forming the commission with the purpose of awarding scholarships to worthy young artists. Guarnieri was invited to perform for them, and Professor Baldi was also invited to be present. After the performance, Dr. Valle called Baldi aside and asked him about the young boy who didn't seem to have his head in the right place. The music had sounded completely cacophonic to him.

Despite this one adverse reaction, Guarnieri was awarded a pension which would have allowed him to study in Europe. Because of the unstable political situation in São Paulo, however, the commission was disbanded, and the scholarship never materialized. Guarnieri was not completely discouraged because he was contemplating his marriage to Lavinia at that time. Regarding the hoped-for pension, the journalist Flávio Silva clarified that the state of São Paulo had established a Pensionata Artística in April 1912, but that it was canceled on April 11, 1931, as a result of the political upheaval.[15] The following year, however, another decree reinstated artistic pensions for study in world centers for three years, from which Guarnieri would benefit within a few years.

Guarnieri's music of the early 1930s also disturbed Mário de Andrade at times, but for very different reasons. Andrade was at first concerned about the great facility Guarnieri evidenced, fearing the superficiality that could result. Guarnieri's use of folk elements—not folk themes but the spirit of the song and dance forms—seemed to Andrade to be a potential limitation. Following a performance of the *Toada* (a lazy, melancholy kind of song) for piano in September 1930, Andrade wrote:

> This work pleased me very much, but it still didn't leave me completely peaceful. It seems to me that the musical talent of Camargo Guarnieri is beyond doubt, but the orientation that this talent is taking in the pursuit of our traditions bothers me. Having acquired this or that habit of composing, it seems to me that Guarnieri is resisting in this very act, convinced that, here in Brazil, it is enough to want to create. Unhappily that has been enough in the past, but this repose in facility is not worthy of Guarnieri or of the destiny that he could have.
>
> It seems to me that he is too complacent. He does not analyze enough, does not have enough firmness with his own creations, and does not see that he is repeating himself, and it seems incontestable to me that Guarnieri is repeating himself. To repeat in art does not mean to write the same things; it means falling back on certain essentials of artistic construction.
>
> This phenomenon I find in his works, that is, an absence of the curiosity to surpass, which is the font of all progress in art.[16]

A more vigorous, less obvious style can be noted in several pieces from 1930–31, including the *Choro Torturado* for piano, the First Violin Sonata, and the First Cello Sonata. In the two sonatas in particular, one senses a certain stringency in the construction of melodic lines and harmonic movement. These pieces perhaps were not as immediately appealing, yet the composer's intent was clear. This change of direction would have been noted quickly by Andrade, and he was not completely happy with it.

One day at the Conservatory, where they were both teaching in 1934, Guarnieri was carrying the manuscript of his Violin Sonata no. 2, written in 1933. Andrade wanted to see it. As Guarnieri put it, "He scribbled words of destruction all over several pages!"[17] There followed three critical letters from Andrade which led to a standoff of opinion. When this piece was part of a 1940 concert of Guarnieri's works in Rio de Janeiro, Andrade embraced the composer after the performance with highest praise for the piece, forgetting that he had formerly torn this very work to shreds. It was this kind of experience that caused Andrade to reflect and comment many times that the music of Guarnieri is difficult to comprehend only with the eyes, and that an actual hearing of what one sees can give an entirely different impression.

Flávio Silva discussed this incident regarding the Violin Sonata no. 2 in a January 2003 article.[18] He set forth conflicting views of Lutero Rodrigues, Flávia Toni, and himself on some discrepancies in accounts of the incident. Conductor Rodrigues and Toni, director of the Institute of Brazilian Studies at the University of São Paulo, have studied Guarnieri's music extensively. The discrepancies revolved around when the sonata actually had been premiered. Silva's article contained a reproduction of a program for a 1933 concert at which the work was performed by Lavinia and violinist Edmundo Blois. He also questioned whether Guarnieri might have revised the 1933 work before Andrade saw it in 1934, and perhaps again before the 1940 Rio performance, which Guarnieri considered its premiere. Silva also noted the personal interactions which existed in the early 1930s between Guarnieri, his very articulate pianist wife Lavinia, Andrade, and serialism proponent Hans Joachim Koellreutter. Guarnieri was having periodic friendly correspondence with Koellreutter at this time regarding atonalism in music, which Lavinia was encouraging Guarnieri to pursue. Andrade, Guarnieri's respected mentor, was strongly urging him toward nationalism. It had become a four-way relationship that produced strain. After the 1940 performance and Andrade's praise, Guarnieri was very grateful to have reestablished a good relationship with his mentor. He also seemed to have resolved his musical direction by deciding to use what he could from atonalism within his own national direction. An *Open Letter* he would write in 1950 adds weight to this opinion. Guarnieri noted: "By 1934 I began to feel that my own personal sensibilities were not compatible with atonalism. I began to write works then that were free of a sense of tonality, non-tonal rather than atonal. They had an indecisive tonality, neither major nor minor, not in do nor in re."[19]

The years of the revolution, therefore, were helpful to the young composer in many ways. He went through his own personal musical revolution at this time, delving more deeply into his own creative resources. He was fortunate to have the guidance and friendship of fine teachers through whom he came into contact with Brazilian writers and poets. These were productive years, as can be seen from his catalog of works. Songs still tended to take precedence among his works, but more and more he moved into the purely instrumental forms as well.

PROFESSIONAL RECOGNITION

The year 1935 marked Guarnieri's official entrance onto the musical scene as a composer/conductor. São Paulo had continued to have its Week of Modern Art each year since 1922. In 1935 Andrade had been able to convince the mayor of São Paulo, Dr. Fábio Prado, of the necessity of having a Department of Culture that would include the support of an orchestra and a chorus. Andrade named the chorus the Coral Paulistano and asked Guarnieri to assume responsibility for its direction. Because there was virtually no choral literature yet written in Portuguese, the importance of this group becomes apparent with its responsibility to program choral works in Portuguese written by Brazilian composers. The Coral Paulistano thus became, under Guarnieri, an important vehicle for the development of Brazilian choral music.

There was another, more political aspect to his appointment as conductor of the Coral Paulistano. Guarnieri was now twenty-eight and still had not attained a degree or diploma in music to define him officially as a professional. Andrade was aware of this lack, as was the composer. Andrade was trying to help Guarnieri establish himself as a professional musician in the city for reasons relating to the 1931 artistic pension decree, as will be seen shortly. An appointed position seemed to be a way of giving him official status. It would be another six years before the Conservatory would award him an honorary degree in 1941.

It was on May 27, 1935, that Guarnieri presented himself formally for the first time in public as a composer. Held in connection with the Week of Modern Art, the program included his Cello Sonata no. 1 (1930) performed by Calixto Corazza, a group of songs including the *Quatro Trovas* (Four Songs, 1931) sung by Candido Arruda Botelho, a set of the *Ponteios* (preludes) for piano from the first volume which he was assembling between 1931 and 1935, and the 1932 String Quartet no. 1. The performers of the last piece were members of the Quartet of São Paulo: Zacharias Autuori, Luiz Oliani, Enzo Soli, and Bruno Kuntze. Before this concert Andrade had written in São Paulo's *O Jornal:* "Camargo Guarnieri, despite his age, is already in full maturity of spirit; he knows what he wants. His tonal thinking is fundamentally chromatic or actually atonal."[20] After the concert Andrade wrote:

> This concert has perfectly defined the notable position in which he has placed himself relative to our American composers. As a Brazilian, his works are fundamentally racial, but his nationalism is not the kind of research nationalism characteristic of Villa-Lobos and of other lesser composers of this generation. It is an enduring nationalism, I believe, which does not nurture itself directly on popular song, which is scarcely ever found in him. Camargo Guarnieri is not a popular composer in that sense. His work is, in its character, exclusively erudite art, not functional, but erudite.
>
> The artists who with their prestige and strength defend the works of this composer deserve our esteem. They know how to discover and understand a form which is already exceptionally defined, one of those few composers among us who has something to say. It is possible that the songs of Camargo Guarnieri still fall more on deaf than on listening ears, and this is good. Too much joy is the sign of impending sorrow, and to rise too quickly often destroys ambition. He is, in my view, more sincere and free because of this experience. Camargo Guarnieri has every right to his enormous ambitions.[21]

In July and August of this same year, Guarnieri presented two concerts in Rio de Janeiro, the first being essentially the same program that had been performed in São Paulo the preceding May. In the July 16, 1935, edition of *Diário Carioca,* Ayres de Andrade wrote the first of his many supportive reviews of Guarnieri's music:

> This is the first contact that I have had with the works of Camargo Guarnieri, and his material is classified definitely as a grand expression of contemporary Brazilian music. . . . One of the characteristic signs of his music is dissonance used as an expressive element. . . . Even just one hearing of his scores permits me to make a secure judgment on the qualities of this composer which are really noteworthy and which place him among the best composers of Brazil.[22]

Another critic, João Itiberê da Cunha, was also favorably impressed with his first hearing of the young composer. Artur Imbassai, however, was very critical, particularly of the harmonic materials used. He wrote in the *Jornal do Brasil* in 1935:

> We have composers, artists of undoubted talent, but sadly their talent is disoriented from the true paths and will be short-lived and confined to the members of their own circle who hear one another and exchange pleasantries. . . . Camargo Guarnieri is unhappily one of those initiated into the

new religion. The recent concert had two parts. I lacked the taste, patience, and courage to hear the second part, despite all of my good will and the sympathies which always arise within me for a genuine talent.

The cello sonata revealed in its first performance a cacophonic orgy of disconnected sounds, unrelated to all laws of aesthetics and melodic and harmonic sounds. Irreconcilable with the exigencies of the educated ear and good taste, it produced a cruel dismay, a pungent, infinite pain to realize the disappearance of the divine art of music which has been with us.

Some appeared pleased in view of the clapping which caused the song *Den-Baú* to be repeated. I must confess that I did not take part in the applause for this, nor for the composer of the pieces that I heard.[23]

Otávio Bevilacqua, critic for *O Globo,* wrote after this same program:

Camargo Guarnieri is a folkloric composer seized by the music in a popular vein where he seems to seek his inspiration. More than any other composer, his work has a national preoccupation. It seems that eventually Camargo Guarnieri will have the decency to abandon this early effort for a more characteristic and personal expression. His folklore in some cases is still not subordinated well enough nor filtered by his own temperament. The personal lyricism of the author nevertheless oozed out in some brisk, youthful passages.[24]

On August 7 of that same year, Guarnieri had some works included in a concert of chamber music presented in Rio's Instituto Nacional de Música. Andrade Muricy wrote:

Present were the elite—musicians and intellectuals. It had been some time since we had such a welcoming atmosphere as that with which we received the Paulistan composer. Camargo Guarnieri did not merely present a simple question; his work was heard and commented upon. I was immensely interested. All the questions which modern Brazilian music raises were strongly discussed, and few people were left indifferent.

Among our South American artists today, Guarnieri is a defined personality whose activities demand that he be watched with vigilance and high interest. . . . There is a persistent sense in all of this of a confidence in the artistic destiny of this young man.[25]

From these reviews, it is obvious that Guarnieri received his share of both praise and criticism, and both were helpful to him, as Andrade had noted. In fact, Guarnieri said that it was his critics who were most helpful to him through the years, beginning with his old teacher in Tietê, Virginio Dias. How he weathered the criticism is best illustrated in an article by Fernando Mendes de Almeida that appeared after Guarnieri's first successful conducting engagement on August 12, 1936:

Under the auspices of the Municipal Department of Culture, the composer Camargo Guarnieri for the first time had the chance last Sunday to direct the Central Municipal Orchestra. I said first time because he has had numerous such opportunities there to show his independence and musical propensities. Other times when he conducted, he sensed being restrained by the little grudges and bad will of others which prevented him from showing his full capacity in all its potential.

A national composer, he is attracted to the rugged ways of polytonality. Only now is Camargo Guarnieri beginning to be sought and comprehended by those who attend concerts.

An uncongenial figure to some, but understood by his friends, he would have been transformed into a weakling by the ostracism to which an unjust public condemned him if it were not for his persistence. But he has a geniality in his blood which is predestined. Because of this, he has begun to prevail. Those who once thought him terrible and crazy no longer hate his music.

Another thing which he has lacked is training in conducting. Still, in the face of his musicality, he showed numerous attributes which, until the day before yesterday, were unrecognized and unconfirmed.

As indicated above, he is a Brazilian in a land where sabotage in the matter of art is the rule for its citizens; he is a friend of polytonalism in a land where Puccini still lives! Yes, Puccini is still alive! Nationalist in his themes, he is a composer in a land where composers are few, in a land where victory depends upon tenacity.

Without trying to make him into a demagogue or historical hero, I feel my share of contentment to see that already he has begun to realize a prophecy which I made four years ago and which has since united us in a friendship which has grown firm.[26]

In 1936 another life-changing event for Guarnieri occurred. The French pianist Alfred Cortot was making a concert tour of South America. He met Lamberto Baldi in Montevideo and learned of Baldi's former student in Brazil. When Cortot arrived in São Paulo, he contacted the twenty-nine-year-old Guarnieri and was impressed with the music the latter shared during their visit. Cortot took it upon himself to write a letter to the governor of São Paulo. Armando Salles de Oliveira received the following:

Rio, July 11, 1936

My Dear Mr. Governor,

I hope you will permit a French musician to tell you of the great joy which I believe the composers of your country will experience in knowing of a compatriot of theirs—Camargo Guarnieri.

During my short stay in Brazil, I had the opportunity to become acquainted with all of Guarnieri's music. It has made such an impression upon me that I do not hesitate to say that his work represents one of the most per-

sonal musical expressions of our time and surely one of the most characteristic of the Brazilian genius.

I know that the government of the state of São Paulo has scholarships to
offer artists with special talents. I am certain that such a scholarship would
not be in better hands than those of Camargo Guarnieri, of whose success
on our old continent I have no doubt. His works would brilliantly represent
the specific tendencies of your still young school of Brazilian music.

I hope that my request will not seem inopportune to you but that you
will give it your attention. I have the honor, Mr. Governor, of sending you
my best regards.

Sincerely,
Alfred Cortot
President, Normal School of Music
Paris: Commander—Legion of Honor

Just as it had taken an outsider, Arthur Rubenstein, to "discover" Villa-
Lobos, so it took a French pianist to bring Guarnieri's talents to the attention of the Brazilian government.

The governor read the letter and passed it along to the Secretary of Education, who had taken the initiative to establish, on May 26, 1936, a new
artistic pension: Serviço de Fiscalização Artística do Brasil (Artistic Super-
vision Services of Brazil). Applications were open to all young musicians
but contained certain requirements that put Guarnieri in an uncomfortable
situation. If applicants held a music diploma, they could simply submit
their application. If not, they had to submit to a four-part exam in music
history, written counterpoint in four voices, an analysis of a sonata-allegro
movement, and a composition of a sonata-allegro movement. Guarnieri's
former Conservatory students were exempt from the examination, but he
had to take it. He did so on December 2, 1936, and subsequently was
awarded the stipend for study in Europe. Another scholarship requirement
restricted the recipients to those under thirty years of age, so it was imperative for him to go soon.

Before the stipend materialized, Guarnieri participated, as the official
representative of the São Paulo Department of Culture, in the first Afro-
Brazilian Conference in Bahia in 1937. It was his second trip outside of his
native São Paulo, the first being to Rio de Janeiro in 1935. Guarnieri stayed
in Bahia for fifteen additional days to collect examples of African and indigenous themes, some of which are now preserved in the São Paulo Museum of Folklore. He also took the opportunity to participate in an
African-Brazilian religious *condomblé* ceremony, which affected him deeply.

Another personal matter complicated his anticipated study abroad.
Though he and Lavinia had separated in 1932, the separation was not formalized until 1935. Flávio Silva indicated that this was upsetting to Guar-

nieri: "He did not have the minimum psychological condition to travel alone for a long period in Europe. A promise of a solution to these problems came from the Coral Paulistano itself in the form of a singer and pianist, Anita Queiroz de Almeida e Silva. He had begun a romantic relationship with her, and she could give him stability, including for the trip to Europe."[27] The decision was made to marry; this happened on the day before they left for Paris.

The stipend awarded for study was not enough, however, to sustain Guarnieri, his wife, and her mother, who went with them. Mário de Andrade again interceded for him and asked that he continue to be paid his salary as conductor of the Coral Paulistano during his absence. A project was also conceived whereby Guarnieri would study what was being done for mongoloid children in Europe, with the intention of establishing some kind of program when he returned to São Paulo. Shortly after this plan was approved by Mayor Fábio Prado, there was a change of administration, and a new mayor, Prestes Maia, was installed in São Paulo. He was not a man of culture, nor did he appreciate Guarnieri's music. The mayor's wife began an investigation of this additional stipend and managed to have it canceled, leaving him with only a meager monthly subsistence. This action presaged a difficult financial situation for the remainder of his experience abroad.

Guarnieri, Anita, and her mother, Dona Graça, left Brazil from the port of Santos on June 24, 1938, on the *Kosciuszko,* arriving in Paris on July 14, 1938, as the city was celebrating Bastille Day. According to letters Guarnieri sent home to his parents, his marriage to Anita was a good and healing choice for him. She was a supportive, loving presence in his life for sixteen years. Guarnieri wrote in an April 11, 1987, letter to Maria Abreu, "She did everything she could to help me, even during the time we lived in Paris and in subsequent years until 1954."[28] Abreu also observed that, possibly because they had no children, Anita's care for her husband was almost maternal. When I met Anita in London, Ontario, at an International Society for Music Education conference in the early 1980s, she still spoke with great respect for Guarnieri.

Guarnieri found simple living quarters in Paris and began contacting possible teachers. He entered the harmony class of Charles Koechlin and the conducting class of François Ruhlmann, who conducted the Paris Opera Orchestra. Guarnieri had not at first indicated to Koechlin that he was a composer. Near Christmas of that semester, however, he gave several of his songs to Madame Andree Antemar, a vocal teacher, who immediately contacted Koechlin and expressed her admiration for the music. Koechlin began to take an interest in Guarnieri, and they became great friends. When Guarnieri asked him one day how he could so easily treat a student almost as an equal, Koechlin replied in his picturesque way, "It is as if a little saint humbly arrived from the Redeemer and said, 'I also work miracles.'"[29]

Guarnieri's stay in Paris was helpful to him in many ways. He came into contact with Nadia Boulanger, Darius Milhaud, the philosopher Gabriel Marcel, and a host of other world-famous musicians. He had several opportunities to present groups of his songs in recital in Paris and to conduct ensembles. Cortot performed his *Dança Brasileira* and *Toada* in Paris to a most receptive audience. One letter that was published in the *O Estado de São Paulo* gave an indication of his progress, which was watched closely back in São Paulo. It read in part:

> I gave two concerts with the Paris Symphony [Orchestra] and took part in interpreting my compositions with Christina Maristany who is, without doubt, one of the most applauded singers in the world. Also in Paris, I met so many French musicians, and many of them showed a great interest in my work, offering praise, which touched me deeply.
>
> I worked in conducting the orchestras and choruses under the chief of the Paris Opera Orchestra, Francois Ruhlmann, and I was taught composition by Charles Koechlin, a musician with an international reputation.[30]

A shortage of funds continued to be a problem. To complicate matters even more, the impending Second World War caused sufficient tension in Paris toward the end of 1939 to make it imperative that Guarnieri should leave. He sought help from the Brazilian ambassador, who finally secured a third-class passage back to Brazil for his wife, mother-in-law, and Guarnieri. They landed in Bahia on November 25, 1939, after eighteen months in Europe.

When Guarnieri arrived in São Paulo, he found himself in an awkward position. Someone else was flourishing as director of the Coral Paulistano, which he had founded four years earlier, and he had neither students nor his Conservatory job. He used his time preparing some new works, and within the next few months presented a number of concerts in both São Paulo and Rio de Janeiro.

The first program given in January in São Paulo received mixed criticism. At this time he presented the *Toada Triste* (Sad *Toada*) and *Três Poemas* (Three Poems), which had been written in Paris. Guarnieri still had the ever-present critics, but both Fernando de Almeida and Mário de Andrade rose to his defense. Almeida directly attacked the position of some critics and praised Guarnieri's ability to withstand their onslaughts. Andrade focused more on the composer's growth during his stay in Europe:

> It is important to verify that the new works [*Três Poemas*], composed in the dazzle of his Parisian stay, demonstrate that the Paulistan composer resisted

the cosmopolitan invitation of the great international city of Paris. His daily contact with French professors, known to be very intelligent, and even the daily hearing of music of the world did not rob him of his very intimate Brazilian musicality nor of his great originality.[31]

In another publication, Andrade carried these thoughts further:

Camargo Guarnieri went to Europe, not as a boy of our hopes, but in his thirties, and the full development of his manhood. He was already a formed artist with some works clearly defined when he left. He returned neither new nor different. He had deepened his personal qualities, enriched his music despite the elements and experience which did not distort but rather refined it.[32]

On May 27, 1940, another concert at the Escola Nacional de Música in Rio was devoted to Guarnieri's music. He programmed the songs *Porque* (Why), *Tristeza* (Sorrow), and *Quebra o Coco* (Break the Coconut, Girl), *Menina,* his First Violin Sonata, two other pieces for violin, the *Peças Infantis* (Children's Pieces), *Toada Triste,* and First Piano Sonatina, and the *Flor de Tremembé* (Flower of Tremembé) for fifteen solo instruments. This program was generally very well received.

In April 1941 the Escola Nacional de Música presented another concert of Guarnieri's music which included the Piano Sonatinas nos. 2 and 3, the *Toada Triste* and *Tocata* for piano, nine songs dating from 1936–41, and the Violin Sonata no. 2. Though written eight years previously, the Second Piano Sonatina was probably the most difficult to listen to and was undoubtedly the work which caused João Itiberê da Cunha to write after the program: "Atonalism is witchcraft! Innocuous magic, but absolute nonsense. . . . If Camargo Guarnieri would follow our advice, he will not go wrong and posterity will be grateful to him."[33] Bevilacqua gave the composer a good review in *O Globo,* as did Andrade Muricy, who brought to his article a longer-range view of the young composer:

Only culture permits one to understand the consequence and importance of certain occasions. How many persons would have been aware of what happened on April 24 in the Salão Leopoldo Miguez where we heard a series of first performances of the works of Camargo Guarnieri?

Only posterity can say if some of these works endured, and remained new and vital. Contemporaries frequently are deceived regarding the value of recent artistic and intellectual works. Fashion often influences their judgments, a thousand circumstances of time and place that later disappear. It is always difficult to explain the motives for the applause or condemnations of past generations. These judgments are so often reversed while others are confirmed.

Brazil can count on its fingers its truly significant composers. I will not enumerate them here, but I do hold that Camargo Guarnieri is surely one of them and is a person of greatest value. Camargo Guarnieri was born to sing. He is inebriated ancestrally with a Latin song in his soul. His lyricism is ardently original, leaving nothing to be insinuated.[34]

INTERNATIONAL RECOGNITION

Guarnieri continued to spend his time on new compositions and gradually to build again his own class of students, in both piano and composition. He submitted his Violin Concerto no. 1 of 1940 to an international competition sponsored by the Fleischer Collection of the Philadelphia Free Library, and in 1942 was notified that he had won the first prize provided by Samuel S. Fels.

In April of this same year, he received an invitation from Alfredo de Saint-Melo, director of the Panama Conservatory of Drama and Music, to come for a period of two years to teach composition. This invitation started a storm of controversy in the Brazilian press that actually served a helpful function in bringing Guarnieri's situation to the attention of the public. It was a difficult choice for him to make because of the prestige and money that it would have offered. D'Or (Ondina Dantes) wrote in the *Diário de Notícias:*

> The notice (of an invitation) was confirmed by the Paulistan maestro who declared: "It was a surprise to me. It is difficult to explain the satisfaction it gave me. I confess that if I accept it, I will be doing something personally very difficult. Understand that it is very hard to abandon people, perhaps forever, the land in which I was born, where I have lived the greater part of my life, where I do my work." But it is also Guarnieri who said: "When I live as I do, burdened with economic troubles, such a proposal as this seems like a gift from heaven."[35]

João Itiberê da Cunha, who at times had given Guarnieri some rather harsh criticism, now came to his rescue. In an April 16, 1942, article he wrote:

> Camargo Guarnieri is a cherished glory to the state in which he was born and to the country where he belongs. He deserves precious treatment. He must at least be guaranteed a subsistence in the land of his birth. This he does not have! His life is one of chance. . . . The leaders in São Paulo and the country do absolutely nothing for this illustrious national artist—he deserves the protection of both—and they take satisfaction in letting him take to Panama the experience of his insights, all the subtlety of his professional

wisdom, and his giftedness. What we will lose by the improvidence and lack of patriotism the Panamanians will gain at our expense.[36]

The São Paulo paper *Folha de Noite* also carried a supportive editorial on April 10, 1942:

How can São Paulo release for two years such an artistic power? The America in the other hemisphere is smuggling our artists away from us! The great pianist Guiomar Novaes Pinto is seldom here, even though she has her enthusiastic public who acclaim her two or three times a year. Francisco Mignone, talented composer of the *Maracatu do Chico Rei* [Maracatu of King Chico], has also been discovered there and has been offered a year's contract. Dinorah de Carvalho has also received an invitation to visit the country of Uncle Sam. This should happen to Brazil??? Our great Brazilian music will move to the northern continent. . . . What the devil! Men cannot live by bread alone. A day will come in which Brazil will do justice to her own illustrious artists![37]

In the midst of this heated controversy over his invitation to Panama, Guarnieri, along with several other Brazilians, received an invitation from the Pan American Union to be a guest of the United States Department of State for a period of six months. This opportunity relieved Guarnieri of the pressure involved in the invitation to go to Panama, and it gave him a chance, not only to study the musical scene in the United States, but also to become known among an entirely new group of musicians. He left São Paulo on October 29, 1942, and did not return to Brazil until May 1943.

Acceptance of the invitation from the Pan American Union presupposed that Guarnieri had some money for the trip—which he did not! He was able eventually to secure enough money through the help of the São Paulo Society for Artistic Culture. Guarnieri called the director of this group, Senhora Esther Mesquita, who belonged to a Paulistan family that had for generations published the principal newspaper in São Paulo. He asked if the Society would be willing to sponsor a concert of his music to raise money for his trip. She told him to call back the next day and that she would see what she could do. When Guarnieri called her again, Senhora Mesquita told him that the group had agreed to commission an orchestral work from him. Guarnieri willingly accepted the offer and composed the *Abertura Concertante* (Concert Overture), which was premiered by the orchestra of the Society on June 2, 1942. It was subsequently performed several times on his American tour.

The months spent in the United States were rich ones for Guarnieri, who celebrated his thirty-sixth birthday there. On December 1, in a ceremony held in the Pan American Union in Washington, D.C., Guarnieri received in person the cash award for his violin concerto, which had been the winning piece in the Fleischer Music Collection competition. Serge Koussevitzsky and Howard Hanson, who were two of the jurors in the competition, became close friends of the young Brazilian.

The Columbia Broadcasting System sponsored two concerts of Latin American music and included works of Guarnieri. The first program on February 3, 1943, included the first, third, and fifth movements of his *Suite Infantil,* which was his first piece for orchestra, dating from 1929. The second concert on March 18 included the two *Cantigas* (Songs) and the *Encantamento* (Enchantment) for violin, and a number of his songs sung by the Brazilian soprano Olga Praeger Coelho with Guarnieri at the piano. Remo Bolignini was the violinist for this program.

On March 7 a special program was presented by the American League of Composers at the Museum of Modern Art in New York City. Pianist Arnaldo Estrela was on hand to play, and Jennie Tourel sang a number of Guarnieri's songs. Included were his string trio, the First Cello Sonata, the Third Piano Sonatina, *Toada Triste* and *Tocata* for piano, and the Second Violin Sonata. Guarnieri drew complimentary reviews from many critics for this program. For example, the *New York World Telegram* carried the following remarks the morning after the March 7 concert: "To judge by what was heard last night, Mr. Guarnieri possesses gifts of no mean order. He writes with a directness, his aim apparently being to tell his story in as unaffected manner as possible."[38]

The composer-critic Virgil Thompson also wrote of the "excellence from Brazil." Though what Thompson heard was only some of Guarnieri's chamber music, he sensed that the composer had a much broader talent that could not be completely expressed through these few works. He noted the authentic Latin flavor of the music as well as its architectural soundness. He closed by saying, "All in all, his work is marked by an authority and amplitude, an ease also that are rare in any hemisphere, particularly in this one. He is obviously a musical author with weight and a cutting edge."[39]

Boston was the setting for several programs of Guarnieri's music. Nicolas Slonimsky arranged one chamber music program there in March that featured the music of both Guarnieri and Villa-Lobos. Through his contact with Koussevitzky at the Pan American Union, he was invited to conduct the Boston Symphony Orchestra in two performances of his *Abertura Concertante,* the first on March 26 and the second a few days later. This was obviously a great thrill for Guarnieri, and his pleasure was matched by the enthusiastic reception of his work.

Another highlight of the American tour was his visit to the Eastman School of Music at the University of Rochester in upstate New York. Guarnieri was struck by the high caliber of the student orchestra, which he conducted in his *Encantamento* and *Dança Brasileira.* The insistent clamor to repeat the latter piece established the tradition of performing it twice in succession. The quality of music education in the United States made a great impression on him, and he nurtured hopes of inaugurating similar programs in Brazil.

The entire group of Latin American composers who were being entertained by the State Department also participated in the Music Educators National Conference, which was held in Milwaukee, Wisconsin, in 1942. This was the first of several trips by Guarnieri to this city.

RETURN TO BRAZIL

Life could not have been the same for Guarnieri when he returned home this time. Behind were his first international award for a composition, familiarity with the most prominent musicians in both Europe and the United States, and an increase of confidence in himself and in his own sense of musical direction. The *São Paulo Gazette* held an official welcome home reception for him on May 16, 1943, after which he settled down into his confirmed role of composer-teacher-conductor.

Guarnieri had already received two prizes from the São Paulo Department of Culture in 1937 for his *Coisas Deste no Brasil* (Things from Brazil) for chorus and the *Flor de Tremembé* for instruments, in addition to the commission for the *Abertura Concertante.* The works that he wrote in the years immediately following his return from the United States continued to add to his growing renown as a Brazilian composer.

He next submitted his First Symphony under the pseudonym of "A Paulistan from Curuçá" in a contest sponsored by the Council of Artistic Orientation of the State of São Paulo. "Curuçá" was a reference to his home town of Tietê. The jury consisted of Francisco Mignone, Arthur Pereira, Mozart Tavares, and Corrêa Junior. The prize was 10,000 cruzeiros to be given for a work "of Brazilian and modern expression, a theme of free invention by the composer, without using themes taken directly from folklore." Guarnieri won the first prize, entitled the "Luiz Alberto Penteado de Rezende," and he accepted his award on July 6, 1944, in the Municipal Theater of São Paulo from the hand of his good friend Caldeira Filho.

On November 18 of that same year, Guarnieri was notified by telegram that his String Quartet no. 2 had been awarded the first prize of $1,000 in the first Quartet Contest sponsored jointly by the Chamber Music Guild of Washington, D.C., and the RCA Victor Recording Company. There had been over three hundred entries in this contest with twenty from Brazil and 116 from the other Latin American countries. Another Brazilian, Claudio Santoro, received an honorable mention in this contest. The jury included

Claudio Arrau, Jascha Heifetz, William Primrose, Edgard Varèse, Germaine Tailleferre, Charles Seeger, and Wanda Landowska. Needless to say, winning this prize solidified Guarnieri's enviable reputation on the North American continent and did not exactly lower it in his own country. The prize-winning check was sent to the Itamaraty Palace by the Brazilian ambassador, Carlos Martins, and it was presented to Guarnieri in Rio de Janeiro in a formal ceremony on January 17, 1945. The quartet was performed in Town Hall in New York City on January 26 and in Washington, D.C., the following day. Both performances were received favorably.

The First Symphony had barely been completed when Guarnieri began his Second Symphony, which he completed in 1945. In 1947 he submitted the latter work in an international competition for a Symphony of the Americas, offered by a group based in Detroit. It won the second-place "Reichold Prize" of $5,000 from among over eight hundred entries. This again bolstered the composer's status in the community of American composers.

Guarnieri had also assumed the responsibility of supervising conductor of the São Paulo Municipal Orchestra, and he gave a good deal of time to its activities. He was asked to prepare a special program of his works for a concert honoring the First Medical Congress of Brazil. This program on March 9, 1945, included his *Abertura Concertante,* the *Toada à Moda Paulista,* the First Piano Concerto, and the Brazilian premiere of his First Symphony. Later that year he undertook a tour throughout Uruguay, Argentina, and Chile, conducting these same works with orchestras in each city.

In 1946 Guarnieri completed his Second Piano Concerto and entered it in a competition sponsored by the São Paulo Department of Culture. The piece won the Alexander Levy First Prize. It was performed the following year over the CBS radio network in the United States with Lidia Simões as soloist. The same year another program totally devoted to Guarnieri's music was given in the São Paulo Municipal Theater, which included the String Trio, several pieces for piano, the *Treze Canções de Amor* (13 Love Songs), and the Second String Quartet.

Guarnieri's second trip to the United States was made in 1947, and again there were several concerts featuring his music. Koussevitzsky invited him to Boston, where the composer conducted the Boston Symphony Orchestra in his First Symphony. The League of Composers sponsored a concert of music by Guarnieri and the Argentinean composer Alberto Ginastera. Guarnieri's Flute Sonatina received its American premiere at the Fourth American Festival of Music in Washington, D.C. The National Chamber Orchestra under Leon Barzin performed the First Piano Concerto, and Guarnieri's Second Piano Concerto was played by Lidia Simões with the CBS Orchestra. The Second Quartet and the Second Piano Concerto, recorded in 1946, gave Guarnieri additional exposure back in his own country.

If one examines the large number of national and international prizes Guarnieri received in the five-year period following his first trip to the United States in 1942–43, one might get the mistaken impression that he was composing only major, prize-winning works. On the contrary, he continued to produce the small pieces for piano and the songs which constitute such a large part of his contribution to Brazilian music. He was also working as conductor of the São Paulo Municipal Symphony Orchestra, and he continued teaching in his own studio, at the Conservatory of Drama and Music, and at various schools and conservatories throughout the state of São Paulo.

The local papers in São Paulo frequently interviewed him to ascertain his position on various cultural issues. By accepting positions within his own civic community, he continued to influence developments there. Gradually medals and plaques of honor—*paraninfos*—began to come his way from schools where he taught, from other cities in the hemisphere where he conducted, and from organizations of various kinds. He was requested to serve on juries of music, both in Brazil and in other countries.

Guarnieri felt the responsibility of his position as a musical leader in Brazil, and he did not hesitate to express his views. In 1950 he publicly spoke out against the serial method of composing as practiced by Hans Joachim Koellreutter in Salvador, Bahia. His *Open Letter* and its effects will be discussed in Chapter 3. This letter and the controversy it created still mark Guarnieri's reputation in Brazil. It placed him in the forefront of those composers who continue to use traditional forms, and to use instruments in traditional ways.

The decade of the fifties found Guarnieri busy with composing, teaching, and conducting, which kept him on a regular schedule of intense, profitable activity. Service on musical juries and receiving of awards continued. In 1953 he was invited to serve on a jury in Belgium with Gian Francesco Malipiero, Bohuslav Martinů, and Frank Martin at the request of Queen Elisabeth of Belgium. Here he had the opportunity to review 439 manuscripts entered by composers from all over the world. In 1954 he received the Honor of Merit medal from his native city of Tietê. This same year, the 400th anniversary of the founding of São Paulo, his Third Symphony was written to commemorate this event, and it took first prize in a competition sponsored by the São Paulo Municipal Department of Culture. He also received a commission from the Louisville Symphony Orchestra in the United States; for this he wrote the *Suite IV Centenário,* again in commemoration of São Paulo.

Guarnieri had also developed a substantial class of composition students, whom he taught in his studio on Rua Pamplona. Most of the principal composers of the latter half of the twentieth century found him there. Guarnieri claims to have had the only "school of composition" in Brazil, and his legacy of successful students surely testifies to this claim. Sergio Vasconcellos Correa wrote of his importance as a teacher:

> The courses in composition taught in the conservatories and music schools of the country during the first half of the 20th century never made possible the flowering of real talent. Not only was their structure rigid and academic, but they were generally directed by poor teachers and worse composers.
>
> This was the state of things until the emergence of Camargo Guarnieri, whose musical and aesthetic education he owes to Mário de Andrade, Lamberto Baldi, and Sá Pereira (in Brazil) and to Charles Koechlin (in France). Motivated by the propagation among us of the twelve-tone theory, together with philosophical concepts that were incompatible with his aesthetic ideas, he published his famous *Open Letter to Musicians and Critics in Brazil,* dated November 7, 1950.
>
> With these premises as a foundation, and taking the *Essay on Brazilian Music* (1928) by Mário de Andrade as his point of reference, Camargo Guarnieri not only proceeded in his triumphant career as composer, but also undertook the responsibility of guiding young composers. Thus the first school of composition with absolutely national characteristics came into being, emerging in the artistic realm of the nation.[40]

In November 1953 he publicly presented a group of these young composers featuring their own works. The *São Paulo Gazette* on October 28 announced the event: "The fact is absolutely exceptional! It is the first time that an event of this kind is announced in the country, or perhaps, it is actually the first presentation of a group of young composers in their own works."[41]

The concert took place in one of the city's principal halls on the Praça de Republica in São Paulo. The students included Arlete Marcondes Machado, Ascendino Teodoro Nogueira, George Olivier Toni, Osvaldo Lacerda, and Silvio Luciano de Campos. Remembering that this was three years after his *Carta Aberta,* Guarnieri used the opportunity to write, in the program notes, of the importance of the event to Brazil:

> Today are presented to the public of São Paulo five young composers whom I have had the satisfaction of helping develop, guiding their sensitivity and creative talent toward the great world of Brazilian music.
>
> If they have experienced such joy in giving our people the fruit of their successful work, still greater is my joy in seeing yet another rich gem of the

inexhaustible treasure of national Brazilian music shine forth under my direction.

It would be more than false modesty not to declare here that this is a really important day for Brazilian music. This is the first time that a Brazilian composer, with a deliberate national orientation, brings together in a presentation like this, in organized form, some young countrymen, and to constitute with them a nucleus of a national school of composition.

This fruit that today is gathered is not the product of chance: On November 7, 1950, exactly three years ago, I directed an *Open Letter to Musicians and Critics of Brazil,* calling them to the defense of Brazilian music. At the same time I invited them to a broader and more profound debate regarding the future of the arts in our country. Many heard and responded to my call. . . .

These five musicians who have taken seriously the path of a national music, which is the patrimony of the Brazilian people, represent the best fruit of the *Open Letter* which I had the honor of writing. They have begun a beautiful but difficult journey in the world of music, but I believe they will succeed.

My deepest hope is that these works will be loved and understood by people, will represent a stimulus for new energies and serve as an instrument for a new and more perfect understanding among all people.

One day in the not too distant future, these names will cross our frontiers to bring to others the fraternal message of a Brazilian music, happy and hopeful, which will contribute to the joy of all.[42]

In 1962 Guarnieri again presented seven students in a similar program of their works. This time it was in the Municipal Theater with works by José Antônio de Almeida Prado, Lina Pires de Campos, Marisa Tupinambá, Nilson Lombardi, Osvaldo Lacerda, Pérsio Moreira da Rocha, and Sérgio Vasconcellos Corrêa. This concert was again received very positively.

Osvaldo Costa de Lacerda remembers Guarnieri as being very strict in the first lessons he had with him. Guarnieri started students working on a theme with variations, gradually moving into counterpoint through the musical invention form. Osvaldo wrote:

> Guarnieri spoke little but listened and observed much. His teaching was very gradual, geared to the strength of the student. At first, Guarnieri would be very firm with a student. He did not accept suggestions; he determined what must be done. As time went on, however, one learned through practice, and Guarnieri became freer little by little, until the last classes were transformed into a pleasant conversation in which the teacher suggested and guided rather than corrected.
>
> Guarnieri's mere presence was sufficient to inspire in his students strong feelings of confidence and an intense desire to excel in the art, so great were the force of his mental and spiritual qualities.[43]

Walking down Rua Pamplona to his studio in São Paulo (1969).
Photo by M. Verhaalen.

Having experienced the generosity of his first teachers in São Paulo, who refused to accept payment for his lessons, Guarnieri often returned the favor to many of his own students. In fact, he found it very difficult to ask for payment from them. His wife Vera Silvia related this charming story of how he would explain this unwillingness: "This student is so talented. It is a gift of God, and I can't accept any payment for that." Or he would say, "This student can't afford lessons," or "This student isn't really working very hard. I can't take credit for being his teacher." Teaching was a labor of love for him.

Kilza Setti observed, "It is hard to say what Guarnieri's most important contribution was. On the one hand he had this vast and expressive musical output. On the other, there was his continued concern with forming new composers."[44] This preoccupation was lifelong, and he was always there when students sought his assistance in his penthouse studio on Rua Pamplona. Osvaldo Lacerda remembered that he was never late for a class.

In his studio
Photo by M. Verhaalen.

From 1955 to 1960 Guarnieri served under Clovis Salgado in the National Ministry of Education and Culture in the capacity of Technical Assessor in Musical Matters. The composer's six-month stay in the United States in 1942 as a guest of the Pan American Union had enabled him to visit various music schools in that country. His brief stay in Paris had also exposed him to the French models of conservatory education. These experiences had born in him the hope that Brazilian conservatories could develop similar programs. In his position of Assessor, Guarnieri developed a plan for the teaching of music to Brazil's talented students. He described it thus:

> Unhappily, here in Brazil students are only able to get a federal diploma after they complete the high school level, since the conservatories do not have humanities in their courses of studies. Therefore a student is obliged to finish high school and then enter the conservatory, and this takes many years. I proposed in the project that students do as is customary in the

United States, Europe, and Russia: attend a school from seven in the morning until six in the evening and study all subjects right in the conservatories, both music and humanities. I gave the plan to Clovis Salgado. He read it and found it very interesting and wanted to take it to the Congress. I asked him instead to appoint a commission in Rio de Janeiro of musicians who could study it with me so that not only my name would appear on it. With me then were Andrade Muricy, Otávio Bevilacqua, and Moacir Licera. We all studied it and gave our suggestions.

When the project had been perfected, we took it to Minister Salgado and he said, "Now we can publish it!" I noted that Brazilians like to criticize things, and I thought it would be better if we could duplicate it and send it to all the music schools in Brazil and ask for suggestions, so we sent out four hundred copies all over the country. The results were very disheartening: only two schools responded, and those responses were negative! One answer came from Joanidia Sodre, Directress of the Escola Nacional in Rio, and the other was from a school in Porto Alegre where the director submitted a completely different plan.[45]

His plan for the revision of conservatories did not materialize at that time. However, by the late 1960s a renewal of interest in curricular renovation in conservatories was very evident throughout the country. It was a period in which research into various aspects of Brazilian music was beginning to take hold. Gifted young Brazilian musicians were being sent abroad for higher degrees. It was the "jump start" time for music in higher education, with universities gradually introducing master's and doctoral-level programs. New original teaching materials written by Brazilian authors began to appear. Perhaps Guarnieri's efforts a decade earlier were not in vain.

He was not alone in trying to renovate the educational system in Brazil. Twenty-five years earlier Villa-Lobos had also worked for the São Paulo Ministry of Education; in 1930 he had presented a plan whereby music performances would be held in schools throughout Brazil. His efforts bore many fruits in the next fourteen years, including the introduction into the schools of choral music which drew upon Brazilian folk music. Following the lead of Zoltan Kodály, Villa-Lobos introduced the practice of teaching singing through the use of solfège hand signals. He also prepared printed materials, which gave a certain longevity to his efforts. Twenty years Guarnieri's senior and residing in Rio de Janeiro, the two men met on occasion as friends but lived separate lives. Both made their contribution to Brazilian music education: Villa-Lobos to the elementary school level, and Guarnieri, less successfully, to the conservatories of the country.

After the death of Villa-Lobos in 1959, Guarnieri became Honorary President of the Brazilian Academy of Music, an organization in which he had held the fifty-seventh chair entitled "Leopoldo Miguez." In 1957 he received both the Ricordi Medal and a Diploma of Honor from the city of Caracas, Venezuela. In 1958 he served on the famous piano jury in Moscow that awarded Van Cliburn the Tchaikovsky Prize, and in 1959 he received from his own state of São Paulo the Medal of Civic Valor.

Guarnieri's involvement in both teaching and serving on musical juries increased even more. At a November 23, 1958, faculty meeting of the São Paulo Conservatory of Drama and Music, he was unanimously elected Director of the Conservatory, a position from which he resigned the following October, realizing that the reorganization of the Conservatory that he favored would take more time and energy than he cared to expend on it. He was unwilling to deal with the politics of running the institution. The strong emphasis on piano study had been ingrained in the school since the turn of the century when Luigi Chiafarelli built up the piano department. This situation Guarnieri referred to as "pianomania," and he would have preferred to replace it with a more balanced curriculum which would prepare performers of all instruments, as well as composers. His general discouragement with the failed national plan for renovation of conservatories undoubtedly added to his impatience with the school he was trying to lead. In 1960, however, he took upon himself additional teaching at the school in piano, orchestration, and composition.

That same year Guarnieri traveled to Europe and made a nostalgic visit to the town from which his father had come. Over two hundred of the most prominent citizens of Caltanisetta, Sicily, were present when he was awarded a gold medal.

Guarnieri's marriage to Anita ended in 1954. On May 20, 1961, Guarnieri married again, this third time to the pianist Vera Silvia Ferreira, daughter of a close friend. This marriage was blessed with three children: Tânia born on January 14, 1963, Miriam on June 5, 1965, and Daniel Paulo on June 8, 1971. The two girls, Tânia and Miriam, studied violin and cello, respectively. Tânia has continued to perform and record her father's music for violin. Vera Silvia chose to give up her study of piano to raise the children. She was a strong, faithful support to Guarnieri through their thirty-two years of marriage. Since she was also fluent in several languages, she was of great assistance to him as they traveled or hosted guests from other countries. He was also fluent in Italian and French, but he never learned to speak English.

The year 1961 provided the opportunity for another visit to the United States on an exchange program. It was also the year in which he wrote his second opera, *O Homen Só,* which was given its premiere in 1962. The next year he was back in the United States, again to serve on the jury of the Dimitri Mitropoulos International Conducting Competition in New York.

With his three children: Miriam, Daniel Paulo, and Tânia (1987).
Photo by M. Verhaalen.

By chance he discovered some forgotten sketches he had made in 1958 for a symphony; these he developed into what became his Fourth Symphony, subtitled *Brasilia*. This work, dedicated to Leonard Bernstein, received its first performance in Tivoli, Portugal, in 1964 and its Brazilian premiere in Rio in 1965. It had its American premiere in Maine by the Portland Symphony Orchestra under Paul Vermel in 1967 in Guarnieri's presence, and was performed by the Milwaukee Symphony Orchestra in 1971. In 1964 his Third String Quartet was premiered in Washington, D.C., but he was not present. The year 1967 saw his third trip to the United States in seven years and his fifth since the initial visit in 1942–43.

In 1967 Guarnieri began to make monthly trips inland to the University of Uberlândia and to the Conservatory of Goiânia of the Federal University of Goiâs. For many years he spent a total of one week each month on these trips, dividing his time between the two schools in an effort to raise the standards of music education in places other than the few large cities of Brazil. He expressed great pleasure at finding a great amount of real talent there, and, although it was at a cost of great personal energy, he was willing to do that. The late 1960s and 1970s were a period of exponential growth in both the number and quality of Brazilian conservatories, and Guarnieri played his part in assisting that development.

In 1969 the State of Guanabara initiated an International Composition Contest under director Edino Krieger. Guarnieri entered a cantata, *O*

Vera Silvia and Guarnieri at Alverno College, Milwaukee, December 1970.
Photo courtesy of the Milwaukee Journal.

Guaná-bará, in the competition, not realizing that it was directed principally at the younger generation of composers. Along with Francisco Mignone and Radames Gnatalli who had also entered works, Guarnieri's music
was literally jeered and booed by the young audience. Ironically enough, six
of Guarnieri's students were among the winners, and one of them, José Antônio de Almeida Prado, won the first prize, while second place was given to
another of his students, Marlos Nobre. Publicity had not made the focus
clear enough, but the episode did point out the musical generation gap that
existed.

The Second Guanabara Composition Contest held in May 1970 managed to rectify procedures in a way that the generations were able to meet
and to participate with more equitable understanding and respect. Edino
Krieger secured commissions for works from the older composers of South
America. These pieces were performed on the same programs as those
pieces which were included in the classified portion of the competition. It
was for this second contest that Guarnieri wrote his Fifth Piano Concerto,
commissioned by the *Jornal do Brasil.* It was premiered in Rio on May 16,
1970, with Lais de Souza Brasil as pianist.

Guarnieri made several more trips to the United States in the 1970s. He
and his wife Vera Silvia were guests at a four-day Festival of Brazilian Music
held at Alverno College in Milwaukee, Wisconsin, in 1970. Visits to the

**Camargo Guarnieri,
Milwaukee, 1970.**
Photo courtesy of the
Milwaukee Journal.

University of Wisconsin campuses in both Madison and Milwaukee were arranged for him, and the Milwaukee Symphony Orchestra acknowledged his presence at their concert by performing his *Dança Brasileira*. It was this introduction to Milwaukee that caused Guarnieri to want his young daughter Tânia to study at the String Institute at the University of Wisconsin–Milwaukee, which she did between 1983 and 1985.

Guarnieri's Fourth Piano Concerto was premiered in Porto Alegre by Roberto Szidon in 1972. The Federal University of Porto Alegre had been a very receptive, helpful institution to the composer over the years, supporting him and his music in various ways. He had many friends there, in particular Zuleika and Paulo Guedes and Maria Abreu, a music critic who wrote many reviews of his music.

In 1973 Guarnieri returned to the United States to conduct the Chicago Symphony Orchestra in his Fifth Piano Concerto. Lais de Souza Brasil was the pianist for this performance. She has had a great respect for Guarnieri's music and has performed most of what he has written for piano. She has also recorded many of his major piano works. In this same year, Guarnieri received the "Notário Saber" title from Brazil's National Education Council. This is an honorary distinction in an area of achievement for a person without a formal degree.

Lais de Souza Brasil gave the Fourth Piano Concerto its São Paulo premiere on July 22, 1975. That same year marked the thirtieth anniversary of the death of Mário de Andrade. Guarnieri conducted a memorial concert with the Orquestra Sinfônica Municipal with music based on Andrade's texts. The program included the four poems of Macunaima and the opera *Pedro Malazarte,* among other selections.

The year 1975 also marked an important event both for Guarnieri and for the city of São Paulo. On November 28 the University of São Paulo inaugurated its Orquestra Sinfônica, which had been created specifically for Guarnieri and a group of professional musicians. He was delighted to have his own ensemble. The orchestra was first organized with only string instruments with the intention of eventually adding winds. Guarnieri said of this group, "With the creation of the Symphony Orchestra of the University of São Paulo has come the realization of an old dream: to have my own orchestra and to work, not as with inferiors, but with friends as one would in a family. An orchestra is like the human body: only if it has good interaction will it work harmoniously."[46] The USP Orchestra gave its first concert on February 21, 1976. His Concerto for Strings and Percussion was premiered that year by the group, and Guarnieri received from Brazilian President Ernesto Geisel a commendation for his contributions.

Guarnieri's seventieth birthday on February 1, 1977, began a series of important celebrations. His birthplace, Tietê, honored him with the title "Distinguished Citizen of Tietê." His seventieth birthday coincided with the city's 135th anniversary, and Tietê made use of the occasion. On March 8 Guarnieri brought his USP Orchestra to Tietê for a concert. At 8 in the morning, a plaque of his father, Miguel, was placed in the Museu Cornelio Pires, and at 10 o'clock the entire family was honored with a reception at the Museum. The local band played an arrangement of the piece that Guarnieri had written there as a child, his *Sonho de Artista.* In November Tietê held a "Camargo Guarnieri Week" with various musical events.

As part of the commemoration of his birthday, his Concertino for Piano was recorded on an LP Phonodisc with Lais de Souza Brasil as soloist. Claver Filho ran a series of three articles on "Guarnieri e o Dodecafonismo" in the *Correio Brasiliense* on March 9, 11, and 13, 1977. Guarnieri was still convinced that it was impossible to write Brazilian music using dodeca-phonic techniques or serialism. There were numerous other articles and in-terviews commemorating his anniversary. On July 30, 1977, his Symphony no. 5 was premiered at Campo do Jordão. It was performed again in São Paulo on August 8 under Eleazar de Carvalho.

In November of that year Venezuela awarded Guarnieri another honor. Venezuelan president Carlos Andres Perez presented him with the "Order of Andres Bello" insignia for his great cultural contributions to his country. At the end of the month the Federal University of Porto Alegre conducted its first Camargo Guarnieri National Piano Competition. In São Paulo there was also a "Camargo Guarnieri Festival" of three concerts. On No-vember 24 Lais de Souza Brasil performed selected *Valsas, Ponteios,* and *Es-tudos,* and his Piano Sonata. On November 25 a string quartet was in-cluded on a program, and two days later his *Missa Diligite, Improviso* no. 3, a string arrangement of the *Toada Triste,* and the Concerto for Strings and Percussion were performed. In December the Brazilian Ministry of Exte-rior Relations published *Catálogo de Obras,* a catalog of his works. One gets the sense from all of this that Guarnieri received a great outpouring of ap-preciation and honor from his own country, and he did. His comments in interviews throughout these years, however, indicate that, financially, life continued to be a struggle.

On May 2, 1978, Tânia, his violinist daughter, premiered at the Museu de Arte de São Paulo the violin sonatina which he had written for her. In October of that year Guarnieri received the "Roquette Pinto" award for his contributions to erudite music. He also gave an extensive interview on his life and beliefs to Silveira Peixoto. When asked why he composed, Guarni-eri responded, "I compose as I breathe. For me, to compose is a vital func-tion."[47]

In July 1979 Lais de Souza Brasil recorded a live performance of the en-tire series of *Ponteios* for piano. These had been recorded by Isabel Mourão in 1962, but as with other major contributions to literature, they deserve, and now have, more than one interpretation. In November Tietê had its third "Camargo Guarnieri Week" with musical festivities in his honor. The next two years did not see the production of many compositions, only a cantata, *Canto de Amor aos Meus Irmãos do Mundo* (Song of Love to My Brothers of the World), in 1979 and one song in 1980.

The decade of the 1980s found Guarnieri busy with his daily orchestral rehearsals that would normally leave a younger man little energy for com-posing. Guarnieri accepted an invitation to conduct the Orquestra Sin-fônica de Belo Horizonte, in Minas Geiras in central Brazil, in June 1980 in a program of his own music. Included were songs with orchestra, sung by

Lia Salgado, the *Choro* for Violin and Orchestra with his daughter Tânia as soloist, and the Fourth Symphony.

The year 1981 saw the completion of a few songs, a piano piece, and his Symphony no. 6, which was commissioned by the São Paulo Municipal Secretary of Culture. He wrote this work in a very short span of time between January 31 and March 1. In August 1981 Guarnieri headed the jury of the Robert Casadesus Piano Competition at the Cleveland Institute of Music. He was honored there one evening with a dinner and a concert which included his Concerto for Strings and Percussion. This was his eighth trip to the United States.

It could be expected that in the year of his seventy-fifth birthday, 1982, there would again be articles on Camargo Guarnieri. Maurício Ielo in the *O Estado de São Paulo* wrote that Guarnieri is "first of all, a man of polemics."[48] He noted in the article that Guarnieri had both defenders and opposition in extreme camps of opinion. Criticism did not stop the flow of compositions, however. There was the Sonatina no. 8 and six shorter pieces for piano, two songs, and a choral setting of Psalm 23, a cantilena for cello and piano, and two guitar studies.

He wrote only one song in 1983, but his conducting and other activities continued. On June 16 a recording of his USP Orchestra was launched. It included his own Concerto for Strings and Percussion and other contemporary Brazilian works. The recording commemorated the fiftieth anniversary of the University. His Sonatina no. 8, a series of *Improvisos,* and a new *Toada Sentimental,* all for piano, were premiered on November 1 by Cynthia Priolli.

The following year saw the appearance of another recording, this one of piano music performed by Belkiss Carneiro de Mendonça of Goiânia. It included Guarnieri's first sonata for piano. Belkiss played a recital in São Paulo in October, including Guarnieri's *Valsas,* which she had also just recorded. In June he received the "Shell Prize" for his symphonic music, and he completed a commissioned cantata for the fiftieth anniversary celebration of the University of São Paulo, using a text by his brother Rossine. This work was awarded a prize in 1985 as "best choral work" from the São Paulo Association of Theater Critics.

With all of his previous activities continuing, Guarnieri wrote his Symphony no. 7 between December 10 and 22, 1985. It was commissioned by his friends Max and Betty Feffer for the sixtieth wedding anniversary of Max's parents. Two *Ave Maria*'s and several piano pieces were also added to his catalog. He conducted the Municipal Symphony Orchestra on September 27 and 28 for the opening of the new São Paulo city auditorium, the Salon of the City of São Paulo. On this program he included his *Suite Brasiliana,* the *Choro* for Piano and Orchestra, and the Symphony no. 6.

With his brother,
Rossine (1969).
Photo by M. Verhaalen.

The year 1986 saw the creation of several smaller pieces: three *Momentos* for piano, part of a series of ten such pieces, an *Ave Maria* for solo voice and organ, a second *Valsa* for guitar, and the beginning of his seventeenth concerto, *Sarati* for Piano and Orchestra, named after the building in which he had his studio. This author was present when he was completing this work on the morning of his eightieth birthday, February 1, 1987. It was a joyous day for Guarnieri. Early that morning he sat in the large overstuffed chair in his studio, receiving calls from friends. The principal event of this birthday was a Mass in the Church of St. Terezinha in the afternoon, during which a special chorus sang his *Missa Diligite* (Love One Another Mass) as part of the service. It was a warm and heartfelt tribute to a great man who had given so much to his country and to the world of music and culture.

Thus at age eighty, Camargo Guarnieri in some ways was still at the prime of his career, still composing and still conducting the String Orchestra of the University of São Paulo with its daily rehearsals. His life had been given to composing and to teaching, and at eighty his music truly reflected the great intensity of his life. Vasco Mariz noted on this occasion:

> Truly, to affirm that Guarnieri is the greatest Brazilian composer would be to diminish the ever present image of Villa-Lobos, still unsurpassable until this day. Nevertheless I must say that this Paulistan composer, along with his works, with their perfection and purity of artistic design, by his sensitivity

Receiving phone calls on eightieth birthday (1987). *Photo by M. Verhaalen.*

and the way in which he communicates the sound of Brazil, is the greatest
of all contemporary composers in this country."[49]

A family tragedy struck in February 1990 and deeply impacted Guarnieri. His eighteen-year-old son, Daniel Paulo, was in a car accident which
left him comatose for months. The long period of minimal recuperation
created an additional challenge for the family. Friends and the local government assisted by providing conducting opportunities for Guarnieri, whose
own declining health made this a very difficult situation. A portrait of the
composer that had been painted by Cândido Portinari many years earlier
was sold to help pay the expenses for Daniel Paulo's care. Then a malignant
tumor in Guarnieri's jaw made his taking part in public performances more
than he could manage, but he felt compelled to continue his efforts. These
were difficult times, especially for his faithful wife Vera Silvia, who continued to care for both Guarnieri and Daniel Paulo.

His last trip outside the country was in January 1992 to receive from
the hands of the President of Portugal the honor "Ordem de Santiágo da
Espada" with the degree of commander. By the middle of 1992, his health
had deteriorated greatly, but in December he had another joy by being honored with the Gabriela Mistral Prize from the Organization of American
States in Washington, D.C., as "the greatest musician of the Three Americas," truly a crowning glory of his creative life.

With the author in São Paulo (1990). *Photo by M. Verhaalen.*

On Christmas 1992 I telephoned from Milwaukee to wish the Guar-
nieris a Merry Christmas. Vera Silvia said she couldn't talk because Guarnieri had just collapsed and the ambulance was arriving. A close friendship of
twenty-four years with the composer caused an intuitive urge to communicate at that moment when his life was taking a major turn. On Christmas night, a crisis necessitated surgery from which he did not recover. He
passed away in the evening of January 13, at 8 o'clock, at the University of
São Paulo Hospital. The family had hoped to have his final service in the
University auditorium where he had worked for seventeen years, but because it was undergoing renovation, his body lay in state in the Municipal
Theater in downtown São Paulo. This was fitting since this magnificent
theater, renovated in 1985, had also been his "professional home" for thirty-
five years.

At 11 the next morning, January 14, 1993, a long funeral cortege accompanied his body to the Gethsemani Cemetery in the Morumbi area, in
the south zone of São Paulo, a section of the city that Guarnieri had loved
for its natural beauty. He was interred there shortly after noon. Thus closed
an important chapter, not only in the life of one grand man, but in the musical history of a great country.

After his death an incomplete concertino for violin, dedicated to his
daughter Tânia, was found on his piano. Guarnieri has left us a musical

legacy of some of the most beautiful, sensitive, and extremely well-written works created in the twentieth century. Some have been recorded, many were published, but without doubt his total catalog merits being made available. That is happening in a project to reedit or create new compact discs of all of his music.

When he was young, many often judged Guarnieri to be in the vanguard; some younger composers in his later years thought he was too attached to the past. The final judgment will be based on his talent and what he produced—his music. It is the quality of the writing that will speak of greatness. Time will judge his entire contribution to Brazilian music. There is ample evidence that he will stand this test of time.

TWO

Evolving a National Music

ETHNIC SOURCES

The history of music in Brazil is long, rich, and complex. As with the United States, Brazilian music has been fed by three principal sources: the indigenous people, African slaves, and European settlers—the Portuguese in the case of Brazil. Precisely what each of these groups has contributed is difficult to determine because none of them remained a pure source for very long, and the rapid amalgamation of other influences in the new setting continued to blur the distinctions even more. Furthermore, both the Indians and the Blacks represented a complex of smaller tribes and groups, each with their own language and customs, and therefore neither was a simple, unified cultural entity.

The Jesuits, who landed on the northeast coast in 1500 with Cabral, began catechizing the Indians and capitalized on the musical abilities of their converts. The use of Gregorian chant with its limited range, free rhythm, and syllabic style was an easy bridge to the Indian chants, which possessed similar qualities. The Jesuits created *autos,* religious dramas, which taught aspects of the Catholic faith. The instrumental contribution of the Indians was minimal, although they had a fairly large number of percussion instruments. They had used the flute in ceremonial music, and the Jesuits gradually introduced them to other instruments.

In addition to the limited melodic and rhythmic contributions, Mário de Andrade credited the nasal quality still present in the singing voices of many Brazilians to the Guarani Indian influence.[1] In the overall picture of Brazilian music, however, the Indian influence was restricted, since they did not blend culturally with the Portuguese as readily as did the Blacks. The restrained temperament and contrasting lifestyle of the Indians caused them to retreat into the backlands, rather than mix with the Portuguese. Fernando de Azevedo noted that the Indians were basically hunters and planters, and this also impeded them from mixing easily with the Portuguese.[2]

There appears to be Indian influence remaining in the São Paulo area, where Indian names abound for streets, villas, rivers, and surrounding towns. Indian influence is seen in the music of Guarnieri, in short melodic motifs, such as in his early concertos, rather than in long, extended lines. Eurico Nogueira França maintains that, although the Indian elements in Brazilian music are difficult to pinpoint and analyze, "There are revealed numerous Indian expressions in Brazilian popular music, and the Indian's psychological profile is detailed in the emotional substratum of the music of our people."[3] What today is referred to as the "Mode of the Northeast," with its raised fourth and lowered seventh degrees, developed from a blend of Indian tunes and the modal melodies of their Jesuit catechists. It is found frequently in Guarnieri's music.

Brazil engaged in an importation of slaves from Africa, beginning in 1538, which surpassed that of the United States. By the end of the 1800s, Blacks constituted one-third of the Brazilian population. For the Portuguese settlers, the dark-skinned Moorish women back on the Iberian peninsula had been ideals of beauty, so the Black women on their *fazendas* proved equally attractive to male settlers. Oneyda Alvarenga traced the origins of these Blacks primarily to Nigeria, Dahomey, the Gold Coast, the Portuguese colonies of Angola and Mozambique, and the Sudan.[4] Each of these groups brought with them a vital culture, political organizational principles, family structure, and an agricultural orientation more closely attuned to the lifestyle of the Portuguese than was that of the Indians. Because of their subservient position, the Blacks were forced into closer contact with their Portuguese masters and served as a leaven in the developing new mixture of races. They gradually became a dominating force in the formation of the Brazilian culture.

On September 4, 1850, Pedro II, resident Portuguese ruling monarch of Brazil, signed a law that forbade the importation of slaves. The powerful *fazendeiros* (landowners), however, who needed slave labor, made it difficult to enforce. In 1871 the *Ventre Livre* (Free from the Womb) law directed that all children born of slaves would be free, but it was not until May 13, 1888, that slavery was finally abolished by the signature of Princess Isabel, daughter of Pedro II, while her father was away.

Among the contributions of the Blacks to Brazilian music are the vigorous dances which gradually reached the urban salons in somewhat modified form, and the highly complex rhythms enunciated on a whole battery of rhythm instruments transported from Africa. Their songs, like those of the Indians, were rather restricted in melodic range and were word oriented. The texts were modified to fit their experiences in a new land. They also brought music from their religious and cultural celebrations in Africa.

Fernando de Azevedo noted that the mixing of the Indians and Blacks with the Portuguese took place principally during the first two centuries of European settlement, that is, the sixteenth and seventeenth centuries.[5] This intermingling has produced a fusion and blending of the races in Brazil that is unique. It has given a seemingly endless font of inspiration and resources to the development of the country's music.

If the Indian and Black influences do not represent completely unified sources, neither does the Portuguese. Portugal itself had endured Moorish invasions between the ninth and eleventh centuries, was bound by its powerful neighbor Spain, and was dominated at various times by the French. The contributions of the Portuguese to the Brazilian musical culture were their poetic and four-strophe song forms with their distinctly nostalgic character, the system of harmonic tonality, some dance forms, and a more varied array of musical instruments. Andrade submitted the proposition that it was actually the Portuguese, not the Africans, who contributed syncopation to Brazilian music.[6] It seems that, with this idea, Andrade was distinguishing the complex amalgamation of many accompanimental patterns common to the Blacks from the supple, subtle melodic lines of the Portuguese song forms.

Luiz Heitor Correa de Azevedo, Brazilian ethnomusicologist, reinforced some of Andrade's ideas and findings in his own book, *Música e Músicos do Brasil* (Music and Musicians of Brazil):

> In place of the African songs, which the Brazilian Negro could not preserve, there arose another music created and adapted by him throughout the country. It is impossible to establish a real musical relationship between this new music and what we know of Africa. It is purely Brazilian music, Negro-Brazilian music more precisely, which, in its origin and strength constitutes a musical folklore for vast segments of our people and which has an influence upon almost all other adjacent segments of our musical manifestation.
>
> What the musical folklore of the Brazilian Negro has adopted is a melodic form in which there are evidences of European accentuation from Portuguese songs, and this can be seen without difficulty.[7]

There were so many other Europeans who emigrated to Brazil, even during the early years, that distinctions between Portuguese, Spanish, and German influences became less clear. The Spanish guitar, tango, and habanera; the polka, Schottische, waltz, and mazurka of northern Europe— all were transported and transformed into their quasi-Brazilian counterparts. Having been driven out of Spain in the early 1500s, many Jews also emigrated to Brazil and brought their Hasidic musical culture. Andrade wrote very forcefully of the necessity of having a broad concept of Brazilian music which acknowledges all of its European sources:

Brazil without Europe is not Brazil. It is a mirage without national entity, without ethnic psychology, without any reason for being. The Brazilian individual who writes music exclusively from Amerindian elements will only make exotic music for Brazil. Brazilian music is actually a deformation of the European, Amerindian, and African elements.[8]

There are two points to be kept in mind when speaking of the process of assimilation of Brazilian folk elements. The first is that large numbers of foreigners have continued to emigrate to Brazil, even within the last one hundred years. There is a tendency to look upon these newer influences as distinct, rather than to accept them as part of the ongoing process. Santa Catarina and Porto Alegre still have their German settlements, and São Paulo is home to clusters of Japanese and Chinese as well as Italians. Curitiba's St. Stanislaus Catholic Church was still celebrating mass in Polish in the 1980s. The popular music of Paraiba in the Northeast bears a strong resemblance to polkas, Schottisches, and the foxtrot, and the carnival songs of the 1930s sound vaguely like the American cakewalk. Thus, wherever emigrants settle in Brazil, it would seem that they should be recognized as Brazilian, and the music which flows from their new experiences should also be considered Brazilian, as Andrade urged.

The second point refers to the vastness of Brazil and the distinctiveness of the folklore of various regions of the country. In 1969 an issue of *Vozes: Revista de Cultura* was devoted to the folklore of the country. One author wrote:

> The great number of human types we have range from the Tapuio of the Amazon to the Cearense Jangadeiro, from the northeast Vaqueiro to the Baiano of Salvador, from the Garimpeiro of Minas Gerais to the Gaúcho of Rio Grande do Sul, from the São Paulo Caipira to the Candango of Brasilia, from the Canoeiro of São Francisco to the Teuton of Santa Catarina, and these all also vary in their folkloric manifestations in these diverse regions.[9]

The musical language and contributions of each of these groups are at the disposal of contemporary composers. Guarnieri has also drawn upon many of them, in addition to that of his own São Paulo.

American Blacks had their spirituals, and many folk songs from the British isles were added to the singing tradition of the Appalachian peoples. Because of its Puritan origins, however, for its first three centuries the United States did not accept the miscegenation of races that Brazil experienced, nor the celebration of this mixture of musical cultures. Americans' most obvious acceptance of their innate musical richness is jazz, an art form that flowered in the first half of the twentieth century and influenced many different musical styles in the second half.

BEGINNINGS OF ERUDITE MUSIC

Brazil was in the throes of settlement in the seventeenth and most of the eighteenth centuries. Music-making was an informal, but important, element on the *fazendas* (plantations). Early formal music education was mainly a result of Jesuit activity, and it was Padre Manuel de Nobrega who established the first school in which music was taught, in Bahia in 1594. The Jesuits educated the native Indian populations in their encampments called *reductions* until they were expelled in 1761.

The discovery of gold and precious gems in the middle of the country began to influence the culture, particularly that of Minas Gerais. Hundreds of ornate churches were built in Ouro Preto and São João del Rey in particular. Musical instruments were built, and European teachers were imported to nurture the growing musical culture. Organs were constructed as early as the sixteenth century. All of this laid a firm foundation for a rich flowering of erudite music in the late eighteenth century.

Francisco Curt Lange, an Argentine musicologist, discovered hundreds of manuscripts in Ouro Preto in the 1940s, evidence of a rich and active music culture dating back two hundred years to the mid- and late 1700s. Brotherhoods of musicians were supported in the eighteenth century to write large choral and instrumental works for church services, a phenomenon called the "Mineiro Baroque." Lange reconstructed many of these fragmentary manuscripts. Recordings of them bear stunning witness to Brazil's early musical heritage from the later 1700s. Hearing these pieces, one might suspect that they had come from the hand of Haydn or Mozart. They transport a listener to the colonial world of harpsichords and small chamber ensembles as well as dramatic orchestral overtures and operatic forms. Liturgical compositions were written in Church Latin, but other art songs and *modinhas* (a Portuguese art song form) used Italian.

One might expect that European influences would be found among composers living in Rio de Janeiro or other coastal cities, but to find such a rich heritage of classical-sounding music in the isolated interior of the country is nothing short of astounding. By contrast, in the United States at this same period, the early 1700s, Blue Laws and more Puritan attitudes strictly regulated music and dance, as they would for over two hundred years. Whereas Brazil had dozens of composers writing both religious and secular instrumental and vocal music, original music in the United States was limited to hymns and psalm settings. Music societies tried to import oratorios and adapted operas, but America had only a few amateur native composers of religious music: William Billings (b. 1770), Benjamin Carr (b. 1768), and Raynor Taylor (b. 1747). This is important to remember as we consider the flourishing musical life of America's "Third World" neighbor to the south.

THE NINETEENTH CENTURY

Brazil's continuing relationship with Portugal influenced the culture in the new land. The reigning regent in Portugal, Dom João, was drawn unwillingly into the struggles between England and Napoleon. He chose to leave Portugal with his family, the Braganzas, for Portugal's thriving colony Brazil. He landed in 1808 and took up residence in Rio, from which he continued to reign over Portugal. Dom João brought all the riches of court life with him and did much to establish the arts. In 1816 he invited a "French mission" to share European artistic developments. He returned to Portugal in 1821, leaving his young son, Pedro I, a musician and composer, to rule from 1822 until his abdication in 1831. The latter's son Pedro II ruled for forty-nine years until the establishment of Brazil as a republic in 1889.

This Brazilian colonial period, which lasted until Pedro II's accession in 1832, was by no means without its composers of serious music or a cultural life. Among them were José Joaquin Lôbo de Mesquita, Marcos Coelho Netto, Francisco Gomes da Rocha, Joaquim Manuel, and perhaps the most influential, José Maurício Nunes Garcia. Maurício, a mulatto, was ordained to the priesthood in 1792 and became director of the Royal Chapel in Rio. His music reflects the European style which he heard from visiting guest musicians. He left a large musical heritage when he died.

Gerrit de Jong, author of an article in 1962 which was the first, brief history of Brazilian music in the English language, traced its development to the present from an early dominance by religious music through the gradual secularization brought about by the widespread importation of Italian opera in the mid–nineteenth century.[10] While other European countries were searching for their own aesthetics of nationalism in the nineteenth century, Brazil was glorying in an almost completely Italianized music culture within its concert halls. This dominance lasted well into the twentieth century. Nicolas Slonimsky quoted Luigi Chiaffarelli (1856–1923), Italian director of the piano department in the São Paulo Conservatory, as stating in 1906, "I regard Brazil as a musical province of Italy."[11] Many of the Italian opera performers who came to the Brazilian stages decided to stay, and Brazil's ornate opera houses stem from this period. The huge wave of Italian immigrants at the end of the century which deposited great numbers of people in New York, Buenos Aires, and São Paulo included the father of Camargo Guarnieri.

Some efforts at establishing a national music had been made in the mid–nineteenth century. De Jong noted that a Spaniard, Jose Amat, founded the Imperial Academy of Music and the National Opera in 1857 in Rio for the purpose of developing opera in the Portuguese language, "the first organized attempt in Brazil at creating a truly national music."[12] This school was closed in 1865, but not before Carlos Gomes directed what is considered to be the first Brazilian opera, *A Noite de São João* (A Night of Saint John) by Elias Alves Lobo. Gomes's own opera of 1870, *O Guarani,* has remained in the Brazilian repertoire as one of the most powerful expressions of nineteenth-century Brazilian music. Though it dealt with an indigenous theme, the meeting of the Indians and the Portuguese, it was Italian in both its style and musical language.

Others also entertained ideas of a more national expression. Brasilio Itiberê da Cunha (1846–1913) wrote an opera, *Sertaneja* (Backlands), but its musical language was European. Alexander Levy was born in 1864 but did not quite live into the twentieth century. He died at the age of twenty-eight, leaving only a vague promise of possible nationalistic or folkloric compositions. Leopoldo Miguez (1850–1902) expended much of his energy in founding the Instituto Nacional de Música in Rio de Janeiro, but his few compositions sound more Wagnerian than Brazilian. Henrique Oswald (1852–1931) was a fluent composer, but his works too were European in sound. Alberto Nepomuceno (1864–1920) as França recalled, had a "nationalistic preoccupation,"[13] and he was the first to write Brazilian art songs in the Portuguese language and the Mixolydian mode. Until that time Italian was used in all erudite music, although popular and folk songs used Portuguese.

Thus, by the end of he nineteenth century, a worthy group of Brazilian composers had mastered European techniques and styles. Most had studied in Europe, as many early American composers had to do if they wanted advanced study. A few had begun to listen to their own national songs and were forming a collective consciousness. Ernesto Nazareth (1863–1934) was one who began playing keyboard versions of folk material in the salons of Rio. Directions were still not completely clear, but at least the movement had begun toward achieving an independent Brazilian musical statement.

Meanwhile the subterranean stream of the people's music had grown very strong in the course of the nineteenth century, almost in direct proportion to the inaccessibility of the erudite music of the same period. What is interesting is that music which had originated within certain social classes began to break across class barriers. The white population was suddenly intrigued with some of the stimulating dances of the Blacks. The more sensual dances began to appear, inconspicuously in certain urban clubs. The Carnival celebrations began to change character and to stir more interest and support, growing from local group exhibitions into a national phenomenon, a civic celebration in every hamlet. They were a blending of folk and popular music, a fusion of more formal technique with the reality of human experience and expression. What began gradually in the late nineteenth century was to flower in the twentieth.

THE TWENTIETH CENTURY

The majority of composers mentioned above came from, or were associated with, Rio de Janeiro. A curious shift in the center of composers' activity took place in the early twentieth century—from Rio to São Paulo. Luigi Chiaffarelli established and directed a piano department in the São Paulo Conservatory of Music and Drama which flourished for nearly forty years. Under his influence and that of the other teachers whom the Conservatory imported from Italy, the school produced Guiomar Novaes, Antonietta Rudge, and João de Souza Lima, among others. Andrade described the situation of that period in which *pianolatria* flourished at the Conservatory:

> A large international publisher [Ricordi], supported with Italian funds, was located in São Paulo, certain of many sales of its editions in the midst of the thoroughly Italianized Conservatory. It published in Portuguese the great Italian and other works. One of the Conservatory's most characteristic and best products was a pianist who did not seek virtuosity but actually abandoned the piano for composition: this was the great composer and conductor Francisco Mignone. And what is more interesting is that even musicological works were written outside the walls of the Conservatory and were aimed directly at the pedagogical establishment, as was the case with such important books as those of Furio Franceschini and Sá Pereira. Furthermore, the Conservatory became an important nucleus for national composition for Camargo Guarnieri, Arthur Pereira, and the Mineiro, Frutuoso Viana, who came to São Paulo. . . . The Conservatory was forced by social conditions to become a center of both musicology and composition.[14]

Undoubtedly the greatest force and spokesman for the "social conditions" was the author of the above quotation. In Andrade, Brazil found a powerful exponent of the national music, and a theoretician as well. Son of the secretary-treasurer of the Conservatory and a man of many interests, Andrade's actual position on the Conservatory staff was that of professor of music history and aesthetics, although his own complete published works reflect his broad interests, as noted earlier. His influence was pivotal in Guarnieri's development. França has written of Andrade:

> A writer, poet, musician, he brought to music his most legitimate concerns. The breadth of the vision of this great writer gave impetus to the Week of Modern Art in 1922. He it was who opened our eyes to the socializing force

of music found in the collective phenomenon, in the folkloric aspect, and he recognized that musical works, already on a plane of high musical artistry, must have an opportunity to resound and penetrate the hearts of the people. Any musician who discovered Mário de Andrade saw irresistibly the life of responsibility of this writer to whom Brazil owes the greater part of its revolutionary artistic movement. Himself adept at pure music which was free from extra musical allusions and elements, Mário still saw in the folkloric substratum of compositions, in the interested art of the people, the necessary principle of universality.[15]

The Week of Modern Art, held in São Paulo in 1922, created a shift in Brazil's musical paradigm. Guarnieri was just fifteen at the time, the year his family moved to São Paulo, Mignone was twenty-five and studying in Europe, and Villa-Lobos was thirty-five. Of this creative trio, only Villa-Lobos participated personally in this momentous event. Lectures, exhibitions, and concerts all focused on the need to create a Brazilian artistic environment through use of national cultural forms rather than European models. Another Congress in 1937 placed emphasis on using Portuguese as the national sung language, rather than Italian, which had been used for several hundred years. Thus, the national movement in music which had taken place in Europe in the middle of the preceding century was finally late-born in Brazil. Villa-Lobos, Mignone, Guarnieri, and a few other composers became its principal proponents and exemplars.

As mentioned above, Andrade's first written statement on Brazilian music was the *Ensaio Sôbre a Música Brasileira* (Essay on Brazilian Music) of 1928. His regular articles in the various newspapers of São Paulo frequently touched upon the subject of a national music, and many of them also appeared in book form in 1933 under the title *Música, Doce Música* (Music, Sweet Music). In 1939 his *Evolução Social de Música no Brasil* (Social Evolution of Music in Brazil) focused still more clearly on the social sources and aspects of a national music. The *Pequena História de Música* (Brief History of Music) has been reprinted in six editions and deals more chronologically with the development of music, particularly in Brazil. It was in the *Essay* of 1928, however, written the year in which Guarnieri met him, that Andrade laid the basis of a national music. He wrote:

> A national art is not created by the undiscriminating and wavering choice of elements; a national art already exists in the consciousness of the people. The artist has only to give those existing elements a more erudite transposition which makes popular music into artistic music, that is, gives it an immediate disinterestedness.[16]

Throughout his writings Andrade's emphasis was on the source of the elements which constitute national music. He believed that if music became excessively individualistic and strayed from its sources, it was destructive of the national utterance, an idea which was also present in Guarnieri's letter of 1950 to musicians and critics in Brazil. For Andrade, the ultimate criterion of music was social, not philosophical. He held that no composer could be universally revered if he did not have strong national roots. Thereby, he was not advocating the creation of folkloric or exotic music. What he was saying was that unless a composer's entire subconscious is penetrated by his own culture, he is incapable of composing authentic, meaningful music. These national roots for Brazilians lie in the people's music, in popular music, particularly in the folk forms such as the *cocos, desafios, martelos, rodas, toadas, frevos, maxixes,* and *sambas.*

Andrade also urged the acceptance of the variety of ethnic sources within Brazil: "Brazilian music must signify all national music, whether or not it intends to have an ethnic character." Furthermore, he maintained that "The real historical criterion of Brazilian music is that musical manifestation, whether created by a Brazilian or a nationalized person, which reflects the musical characteristics of our race."[17]

Another important section of the *Essay* was devoted to the precise qualities which might determine the Brazilianism of music. Andrade reasoned that neither orchestration nor harmony could possibly have any national characteristics. His final analysis was that the national song and dance forms contained those elements which could be transformed into erudite music, that is, the rhythmic and melodic formulae, both of which are influenced by the oratorical rhythms which stem from the language itself.

In his 1939 essay *Social Evolution of Music in Brazil,* Andrade categorized the development of music in three stages, all of them social: music for God, for love, and then for country. He stressed the point that religious music is essentially social and that the early Jesuits had served the process of colonization more than they served the Church with their catechesis, processions, Holy Week pageants, and music. He then delineated the principal stages in the development of a national music. He wrote, "Carlos Gomes is the profane synthesis of the whole first phase of our art music, a phase which I call 'international.'"[18] What followed this "international" or actually European phase was a period of "national consciousness" and then the "national phase," which began with Villa-Lobos and which was to include Francisco Mignone, Guarnieri, Frutuoso Viana, Oscar Lorenzo Fernandes, and Radames Gnatalli.

From a vantage point enriched by several more decades than Andrade had at his disposal, we might now subdivide the development of national music into the following five stages:

1. International—The traditional musical techniques of Europe were used

2. Incipient National—A Brazilian awareness in topics was evident but conventional harmonies and forms were used to express them (Carlos Gomes)

3. Nationalistic—Brazilian topics and musical language drawn from ethnic and folkloric sources predominated (Villa-Lobos); Andrade noted the danger of falling into exoticism, an early preoccupation for Villa-Lobos

4. National—There was a subconscious absorption of folkloric elements; the music breathed their spirit but did not actually quote them directly (early Guarnieri)

5. Universal—There is a return to a more international preoccupation which uses whatever avant-garde or more modern musical materials are in vogue (later Guarnieri).

Villa-Lobos wrote most of his music within the second, third, and fourth stages. Though Guarnieri's first few pieces are considered by some to be a nationalistic expression, he most likely could be said to have begun in the fourth phase and made regular excursions into the fifth stage in most of his later works.

With regard to national awareness, the Brazilian musical situation at the turn of the twenty-first century is wide open. The vast new generation of younger composers are writing in all conceivable styles, including electronic music. Electronic studios exist in most of the large universities, and many now offer doctoral degrees in music. Brazilian musicians are resident also in other parts of the world. Semiotics is the current analytic mode for an entire group of Brazilians centered at the Catholic Pontifical University (PUC) in São Paulo. Musical research into every possible related topic has exploded from virtually nothing thirty years ago. AANPOM is the acronym for the country's principal research organization, which holds regular meetings to report hundreds of research projects by Brazilian scholars. Interestingly, titles of compositions by many young composers reveal a revived interest in Brazilian folklore, something that was not acceptable a few decades ago. In 2003 groups of Brazilian musicians were petitioning the Brazilian government to support both more research into ethnic musical sources and the creation of multimedia works involving the arts.

This land that fairly vibrated for centuries with the pulse and sound of folk and ethnic music has finally taken its place among the leading erudite musical cultures of the world. Nothing could be said about contemporary compositional trends that would remain current for very long. What seems to be remaining constant, however, is the tremendous vitality of the Brazilian creative spirit. It suggests the image of a "musical giant" who can sing, dance, and play.

THREE

Compositional Style

The particular style of Guarnieri's music has been one of the most important aspects dealt with in every review or critique of his music over the years. Although it is important to consider each of his works, some general considerations apply to everything he has written. An overview of his catalog provides a sense of the span of his ability to deal with an array of musical instruments. Another obvious element in his works is his dedication to creating a national music. Beyond that, however, there are personal elements in his life that shaped who he was, and therefore, how and what he wrote.

CATALOG

In perusing Guarnieri's catalog, one sees that he created a great deal of music in virtually every medium throughout the greater part of the twentieth century. Having lived through all but seven years at each end of that century, he was heir to an explosion of ideas, recording and printing developments, and a musical dialogue that saw a tremendous development in how music was viewed and written. He was, however, no silent or passive heir, but rather a central figure in the development of music in his country, especially in the creation of a distinctly Brazilian music.

Guarnieri liked to write in groups of ten, especially his music for piano. For example, there are ten *Valsas,* fifty *Ponteios,* ten *Improvisos,* ten *Momentos,* twenty *Estudos*—all for solo piano. That he made this a goal is revealed in the fact that, as his health was waning and he had not yet finished the set of twenty *Estudos,* he incorporated two previously written separate pieces to complete the set. He wrote seven sonatinas for piano before he finally produced his Sonata of 1972. The Eighth Sonatina closed this series in 1982. There are also ten pieces for piano and orchestra. Almost all of his solo piano music is published, which has enabled frequent performances and recordings.

When asked which was his favorite medium, Guarnieri replied that he didn't have a preference. One could assume from this that the piano was his favorite instrument. He was a fine pianist, but songs were also a medium close to his heart. They were able to carry the deep emotional content that Guarnieri projected so profoundly. There were very few months of his life in which he did not write a song. Most were written for solo voice, though he has a number of choral works for mixed voices and several pieces for children's voices. The solo songs show a preference for short texts of love and affection, drawn from the writings of great Brazilian writers, including his sister Alice and his brother Rossine. His contrapuntal gifts always ensured that accompaniments were supportive but complementary to the vocal line.

Toward the end of his life, he wrote several *Ave Maria's* and a *Missa Diligite,* all in a simpler, modal polyphonic style with less rhythmic syncopation. In addition to the mass, Guarnieri composed two one-act operas, seven cantatas, and a psalm. Four of these works were written during his last active decade as a composer.

Guarnieri also found strings to be a very comfortable medium of expression. Many of these works are among his earliest. There are seven sonatas and one sonatina for violin and piano, one sonata for viola and piano, and three sonatas for cello and piano. There are also several individual pieces and two violin concertos, three *choros* with orchestra, one each for violin, viola, and cello. He frequently transcribed his piano pieces for a solo string instrument with piano.

There are relatively fewer pieces for wind instruments in his catalog. His familiarity with the flute resulted in three *improvisos,* a charming sonatina, a flute duo, an *improviso* for flute and string orchestra, and a *choro* with orchestra. There are three French horn studies, a *choro* for clarinet and orchestra, and another for bassoon and orchestra.

The orchestral compositions of Camargo Guarnieri add an entirely new dimension to the understanding of his style. Their contrapuntal conception, the fragmentation and litany-like treatment of thematic material, the ostinatos and the rhythmic vitality—all are given new possibilities when the sheer number of possible instrumental combinations and unlimited timbre options are added as leaven to his textures. The orchestra was a medium in which he was completely at home. In this category he has a number of individual pieces, several suites, chamber music works, overtures, and some transcriptions. Finally, his seven symphonies span much of his creative career from the Symphony no. 1 in 1944 to the Seventh in 1985. There are also twenty-five pieces for a solo instrument with orchestra.

GUARNIERI'S NATIONALISM

The qualities which Renato de Almeida attributed to all nationalistic Brazilian music apply especially to the music of Guarnieri:

> Almost all of our popular musical creations are strongly rhythmic, and it would be difficult to be a composer and not use in one's works the rhythmic elements of our race. Conceived polyphonically, Brazilian music can avoid the violence of its rhythms through the use of elastic and interlacing melodic lines, yet not lose that rhythmic basis, which is such a font of dynamic creation.[1]

Guarnieri himself also attributed his nationalism to a digestion of popular music. In a 1991 interview he said, "I traveled much in the interior; I was in the North and Northeast. Popular music entered me, was filtered and came out in what I call national music."[2] "Popular" in this sense also includes the various ethnic and folk musics.

In his book *Composer and Nation* (1960), Sidney Finklestein raises a number of interesting questions regarding the relationship of folk elements to the national character of music, questions which can give some insight into Guarnieri's place as a national composer. Finklestein wrote:

> Is the use of folk music in composition a superficial affectation, or does it infuse music with a national character down to its very roots? If so, is this desirable? Is "national" music of any kind a provincialism opposed to a truly great "universal" music? Is the use of folk music simply a matter of quoting an actual folk song, or is there a deeper approach, more creative, involving the living core of folk music as a germ cell in musical growth? Can the folk music of a nation be married to traditional, existing forms, or should its use inspire new musical forms?[3]

Finklestein noted that the great composers all had strong ties to their own culture, and he cited Mozart, Beethoven, Bach, and Chopin as examples. He would undoubtedly concur with Mário de Andrade that they also felt strongly about the social movements and political situations of their own day.

In analyzing Guarnieri's music in terms of Finklestein's questions, one first of all must recognize that Guarnieri underwent a process of growth as a composer. His use of materials, whatever they may have been, was continually refined over the course of his seventy-five years of composing. From the almost unconcealed folklike quality of his First Piano Sonatina, for example, he moved through deepening stages of assimilation of his own culture. It was almost inconceivable that he write anything that did not breathe the rhythms, melodic qualities, and moods of Brazilian music, the soil and soul of the country itself. Therefore in answer to Finklestein's first question, yes, Guarnieri's music is indeed infused with a national character down to its very roots. More will be said on this in connection with the third question.

Finklestein seems to answer his own second question with regard to national music being either provincial or universal when he acknowledges the national current in great composers of previous centuries. It would seem to be a question, not of what materials are used by a composer, but how they are used and the degree of mastery that a given composer brings to his or her craft.

More to the point are Finklestein's third and fourth questions regarding the use of folk elements and their relation to existing, traditional forms. Guarnieri's nationalism does not reside in the reiteration of folk tunes or in the unaltered use of folk elements. There are very few examples among his works of direct use of folk music, and these are fairly obvious, such as the *Variations on a Theme of the Northeast* for Piano and Orchestra, or the "O Teiru" theme of the Symphony no. 3, the second theme of the first movement of the Sonatina no. 3 for piano, and the Mineiro folk melody used in the fifth movement of the *Suite Vila Rica* for orchestra.

Within the rich heritage of Brazilian folk music, there are many small forms among the songs and dances which are not design types as much as they are moods, qualities, or styles. Among the melodic types, for example, are the *rodas, toadas,* and *modinhas,* which are each distinctive in style and mood, though they do not necessarily have any unique structural design. Likewise among the dances there is a common source of rhythmic figures which is used interchangeably in the numerous dances; what is distinctive is the choreography and perhaps the tempo. These melodic and rhythmic motifs permeate the music of Guarnieri and often dictate his style, texture, and, in a lesser degree, the structures themselves. His works exemplify to some extent what Andrade had believed: each country will eventually develop its own forms.

Guarnieri was perhaps more consistent in the use of the traditional forms than either Francisco Mignone or Heitor Villa-Lobos, who, with him, formed a musical triumvirate of their generation. Whereas the two other composers are generally more rhapsodic and improvisatory in their approach to composition, Guarnieri's music bears a strong affinity for the highly structured, well-worked traditional forms. Several of Guarnieri's piano pieces, however, were tape recorded as improvisations, then notated. Even there, his improvisations had a natural organizational flow. In his music one is very aware of the unity, sense of balance of parts, and an inner cohesion. He so infused the national elements into these forms, however, that in essence a new kind of synthesis between folk elements and existing forms was achieved. Because his nationalism passed so far beyond the gestation period, it was never a hindrance to his musical speech. His material evolved with an inner logic and natural flow of germinal motives that served to shape the structures themselves.

França has summarized Guarnieri's approach to the problem of folklore used with the traditional forms in an article from 1947: "The music of Camargo Guarnieri is characterized in the instrumental field by a happy compromise which he obtains between the great universal forms and native content."[4] Sá Pereira had already noted in 1929 that "Instinctively and not by calculation, Guarnieri became a national composer."[5] Mozart de Araujo believed that Guarnieri's earliest works should be considered "nationalistic" because they barely conceal their folkloric elements. He also noted that the composer passed smoothly and rapidly into a more refined transposition of these elements in his music. Araujo spoke at length of Guarnieri's nationalism in an address delivered in Santos in 1957:

> What must be considered in this transition of the nationalistic composer to the national composer is the absence of conflict or faltering or of any hesitation in his writing. The aesthetic evolution of this composer was processed and accomplished within a coherence and a unity of principles never evidenced by any other of our Brazilian composers.
>
> Guarnieri never put his proposition of being a Brazilian in opposition with the useless and fickle pretensions of being a universal composer. He understood from the very beginning that universal music is nothing less than the sum of diverse national expressions. He was also convinced that the more unlocalized the musical themes, the more can they be said to belong to all people and therefore also to Brazilians. Within his works of art, he incorporated these more general styles and characteristics. He understood very early that if we say a music is national, we must be basing our comments on the existence of determined elements that compose it and give it a different kind of character which distinguishes it from the music of other countries.
>
> The adoption of these principles does not indicate that the works of the Paulistan composer have been bound to the limits of what we term folklore. But if, as a composer, Guarnieri has passed beyond folklore, as an artist he does not withdraw himself from it. It is rather that, to him, folklore has become a storehouse or picturesque repository of themes that can be embodied in his works. For him, folklore is still a font for process, procedure, and stimulation. It is no longer an element of nature but simply an inference or suggestion of that element.
>
> Returning again and again with a rare sense to the use of folkloric motives in his works, Camargo Guarnieri never shows an a priori preoccupation with demonstrating a citation or of profiting from a motive. He has

such a good sense of equilibrium. Great artist that he is in search of aesthetic realization, I have never heard him speak of any irreconcilable conflict between what we call folkloric nationalism and essential nationalism.

Occasionally using in his works fragments of those sorrowful and pastoral *rodas* which were so well exemplified by his contemporary Marcelo Tupinamba, or using here and there themes from songs of the northeast of Brazil or the Baiano *condomblé* or the Recife *xangos*, the truth is that Guarnieri used this material with the same naturalness, and I almost say freedom, that he used the themes of his own making. If one analyzes works, it is evident that the folklore never interferes artificially. Rather, the elements are so transformed in the musical fabric that one could say that they become recreations of the composer. Without denaturing them, the elements are incorporated in such a way that it becomes impossible to identify them in the scheme of the piece. In this surely lies one of the most important characteristics of this composer within the entire historic scene of Brazilian music.[6]

Araujo seems to have caught most clearly the nature of Guarnieri's use and absorption of folkloric elements, a topic to which he continued to be very sensitive. The German-Brazilian Hans Joachim Koellreutter also expressed very clearly the complete assimilation of Brazilian elements in Guarnieri's music: "The music of Camargo Guarnieri is essentially Brazilian, not that pseudo-Brazilianism which shows in a great many authors called 'folklorists,' but in a radical Brazilianism in his intimate soul. It seems to me that Guarnieri will be to Brazilians what Bartók was to his people."[7]

As noted earlier, the various regions of Brazil each have their distinctive types of folkloric expressions; among the richest is the area of Tietê, where Guarnieri spent the first fifteen years of his life, virtually unaffected by other influences. Despite only two years of primary school and a few lessons with Virgino Dias, his early years were nurtured by the musical gifts of his own parents and the songs and dances and strolling groups of musicians of Tietê, where the contributions of many ethnic groups had merged. The famous "Paulistan thirds" in his works stem from the remembrance of the music he heard there as a boy.

What is unique about Guarnieri's contribution is that, in a sense, he specialized in the folklore of his own native São Paulo. The "Mode of the Northeast" (with its raised fourth and lowered seventh tones), the *baião* of Bahia, and the carioca *choro* hold a large place in his works, but no other composer has so often returned to the *rodas, modinhas,* the *toadas,* the Amerindian motifs, and the "Paulistan thirds" for inspiration as did Guarnieri. To trace the growing freedom with which he used the "Caipira" or "Paulistan thirds" is in itself an interesting subject. For example, their use in the *Toada à Moda Paulista* is completely diatonic. A number of the *Ponteios* have thirds with cross-relations and subtle chromatic alterations. The second theme in the opening movement of the Piano Sonatina no. 4 combines an evasive tonality with chromatically altered thirds. In the third movement of the Concertino for Piano, the thirds contract to seconds and expand to fourths in an even freer usage. In addition to the melodic types and his harmonies, the rhythmic life found in Brazilian music of all kinds permeates his work. Its use is facilitated and enhanced by the predominantly polyphonic fabric with its constant interplay of lines.

Mário de Andrade, who introduced Camargo Guarnieri to the larger musical world and continued to support him in numerous writings, gave an early warning about his too facile use of folkloric elements. Andrade was excited and thrilled with Guarnieri's total absorption of the Brazilian feeling and his ability to express it in erudite musical forms, but he continued to call him to greater refinement in his use of these elements. But for Guarnieri, the rhythms, forms, and qualities of the music with which he grew up were his own language. Not to use this language would have left him in a musical desert.

His Piano Sonatina no. 2 stirred up a controversy, not because of its folkloric feeling but because of the dissonance it utilized. It constituted the composer's first attempt at a less tonal style of writing, one that he claimed was atonal. This direction continued as a natural development of Guarnieri's musical language.

With the ongoing emigration of Europeans to Brazil, the German flutist-composer Hans Joachim Koellruetter arrived in 1937 and drew students to serial composition. Guarnieri had a great concern that what he viewed as "mechanical" composition would do violence to authentic Brazilian music and lead young composers into degenerate musical paths. He was not alone in his concern for the future of the art of music, nor was Brazil the only country struggling with such questions.

José Maria Neves dealt extensively with this period in his 1981 book *Música Contemporânea Brasileira* (Contemporary Brazilian Music), a period in which subjective expression, dodecaphonic procedures, and "music for the masses" in a socialistic sense were topics laden with political overtones. Ideas were shared in publications and gatherings of the Grupo Música Viva and other kinds of meetings, national and international. Koellruetter himself had published articles on the topic. Guarnieri's response to this question did not come out of a vacuum.

On November 7, 1950, this composer's famous *Carta Aberta aos Músicos e Críticos do Brasil* (Open Letter of Musicians and Critics of Brazil) created a major stir. It was a strong statement, illustrative of how harsh Guarnieri could be toward those who disagreed with him or did not meet his standards. It appeared in most of the country's journals and was sent to many composers, critics, and conservatories. It read as follows:

Open Letter to Musicians and Critics of Brazil

Considering my great responsibility as a Brazilian composer before my people and the younger generation of musical composers, and deeply worried about their present musical orientation under the influence of wrong ideas that lead them to dodecaphonism, a formal current which leads to a degeneration of the national character of our music, I resolved to write this open letter to the musicians and music critics of Brazil. Through this document I want to alert them to the great perils which seem to threaten our entire Brazilian musical culture to which I am strongly linked.

These dangers come from the fact that many of our young composers, through inadvertence or ignorance, are permitting themselves to be lead by false, progressive theories of music, orienting their original work in a feeling contrary to the true interests of Brazilian music.

Introduced into Brazil some years ago by elements which came from other countries where musical folklore is impoverished, dodecaphony found here a welcome from those with deprived spirits.

In the shadow of this evil method some young composers of great strength and talent established themselves, such as Claudio Santoro and Guerra-Peixe, and having unhappily followed this wrong orientation, they finally freed themselves from it and returned to a music based on the study and artistic-scientific use of our folklore. Other young composers, still dominated by the wave of dodecaphony (which unhappily received the support and sympathy of many disoriented persons), are suffocating their talents, losing contact with reality and Brazilian culture and are creating cerebral and fallacious music entirely divorced from our national characteristics.

In the face of this situation which seems to grow more aggravating day by day, compromising the destiny of our music, it is time to speak and cry out in order to alert and stop this formalistic and anti-Brazilian infiltration that, if received with tolerance and complacency today, will bring in the future a grave and insatiable damage to the development of the national music of Brazil.

It is necessary to tell these young composers that dodecaphony in music corresponds to abstractionism in painting, to hermitism in literature, to existentialism in philosophy, and to charlatanism in science.

This being the case, dodecaphony (as with other things that we are importing and so easily absorbing) is a characteristic expression of a politics of cultural degeneration, a branch of a wild fig tree of cosmopolitanism which threatens us with its deforming shadows and has for a hidden objective and pernicious work the destruction of our national character.

Dodecaphony is, from a more general point of view, a product of a culture that was surpassed and that degenerated in an inevitable manner: it is a cerebral artifice, anti-national, anti-popular, and taken to an extreme. It is chemistry, it is architecture, it is mathematics, it is all you may want, but it is not music! It is like a certain kind of saturated intelligence of dry souls who do not believe in life; it is a vice of the almost-dead, of mediocre composers, of beings without a country, incapable of understanding or feeling, of loving and revealing all that is new, dynamic, and good in the spirit of our people.

That this musical pretense would find friends in the midst of civilization and decadent cultures where they have exhausted the original fonts of folklore (as in the case of some European countries), that this deformed tendency lays its poisonous roots in the tired ground of a society in decomposition—that is acceptable! But it should not find a welcome here in America and especially in Brazil where a new and rich people with creative power has a magnificent national future to create with its own hands. To import and adapt in Brazil this caricature of music, this method of anti-artistic cerebral contortionism which has nothing in common with the specific national characteristics of our temperament and which is destined to nourish the perverted taste of a small and receptive elite of paranoiacs, I say is a crime against the country! It constitutes further an affront to our creative capacity and the intelligence of Brazilian musicians.

Our country has the richest musical folklore in the world, but it is almost totally ignored by many Brazilian composers who inexplicably prefer to burn the brain to produce music according to the apparently innovative principles of a false aesthetics. As monkeys, as vulgar imitators, as creatures without principle, they prefer to import and copy harmless novelties, pretending that they are original, modern, and advanced. They deliberately and guiltily forget that we have an endless font of folklore—a living expression of our national character—a music which awaits them to come and study it, to reveal it for the benefit of our Brazilian culture. They do not know or seem to know that we can only represent an authentic value, even an international value, in the measure that we know how to preserve and perfect the fundamental traces of our national physiognomy in all of our expressions.

The dodecaphonic composers adopt and defend this formalistic tendency because they did not take the trouble to study the treasures of our classical inheritance, the self-development of Brazilian music and its popular, folkloric roots. They certainly did not read the well-known words of Glinka, "Music is created by the people, and we artists merely arrange it." (These words have great value also for us.) Nor did they think of the opinion of the great teacher Honegger concerning dodecaphony: "Your rules are too naively scholastic. They permit a nonmusician to write the same kind of music that a highly talented one would write."

What will be the end of this anti-artistic trend which seems to strike predominantly our young musicians and their first works? It has the same intention here in Brazil as in other countries of the world: to attribute too much value to form, stripping the music of its essential element of communicability, to destroy its emotional content, to disfigure its national character, to isolate the musician, transforming him into a monster of individualism, and reaching the principal objective which is to justify a music without any country and which is entirely incomprehensible to the people.

As in all tendencies within degenerate and decadent art, dodecaphony with its methods, tricks, and recipes of making a-thematic music, its denial of the creative work of the artist, institutes an improvisation, a charlatanism, a half science as substitute for research, for talent and culture, and its denial of the rational benefit of past experience which is the basis for a realization of a work of true art.

Desiring absurdly to remain above and beyond the influence of social and historical facts of order such as manners, traditions, customs, and classic inheritance, attempting to ignore or disdain the indolence of the Brazilian people and the particular conditions of their development, the dodecaphonists try to smilingly accomplish the destruction of the specific national characteristics of our music, disseminating among our youth the theory of laboratory music created with a group of special rules, without any ties to our popular fonts.

Meanwhile, our people with keen intuition and understanding have known how to despise this falsification, this semblance of music which some have been able to produce. In trying to explain this nonacceptance on the part of the public, some of the most fervent experimenters allege that "our country is behind" and that they are writing music of the future, or that dodecaphony is still not understood by the people because the work has not been sufficiently promulgated.

It must be said once and for all that those do not escape blame who try to hide from our eyes their more profound motives of this divorce. I affirm without fear of error that dodecaphony will never be understood by many people because it is essentially cerebral, anti-popular, anti-national, and it has no affinity for the soul of the people.

Much still needs to be said regarding this dodecaphony and the pernicious work that its proponents are developing in Brazil, but I must finish this letter which is already long enough. And it must reach publication stage before I can feel that all has been said. I waited for better conditions for the pronouncements to those responsible for our music, considering this important problem which involves intentions more grave than we can imagine. These conditions did not occur, and what is noted is a strange and compromised silence. Personally, I think that our silence at this moment indicates agreement with dodecaphony. For this reason, this document has a personal character. I hope meanwhile that my fellow composers, interpreters, conductors, and critics will now sincerely show their urgent support of the ideas contained herein. This, then, is my patriotic call.

São Paulo, November 7, 1950
(Signed) Camargo Guarnieri

It is no wonder that this strong statement ignited an explosive controversy. Koellreutter felt that he, in particular, had been the target of many of Guarnieri's barbs, and he retaliated in the subsequent reviews he wrote of Guarnieri's music. Guarnieri's inclusion of terms like "patriotic duty" and his obvious espousal of "music for the people" added political overtones to the argument in a period where socialism and communism were fearful words and threats. Some wondered whether Guarnieri's brother Rossine, a writer with communist sympathies, might have written the letter, but the composer himself signed it and bore the repercussions. Lutero Rodrigues noted that, two years before Guarnieri's letter, the International Congress of Composers and Music Critics in Prague had also condemned dodecaphony.[8]

Long after the immediate controversy subsided, Guarnieri still bore the effects of his strong position. His overreaction spoke both of a certainty of his own paths and of an intolerance for the compositional preferences of others. This adamant position made it difficult for him, a composer of integrity, to explain the changes in his own style as he continued to develop. In subsequent years Guarnieri's work naturally evolved and created sonorities of the current vanguard. For example, some of his slow movements in orchestral works even have a sense of synthesized sounds, such as that of the Symphony no. 4, although such an observation would probably have surprised him.

Many have questioned whether or not he had changed his mind when, in his Piano Concerto no. 5 from 1970, he seemed to be espousing serial techniques. His response to his challengers was representative of the fine lines he had drawn on this subject. While working on this piece, he said on December 20, 1969, "I am not changing my ideas. I am in the present and my music is in the present. You will recognize it as my music; the personality of my music is always in the present."[9]

The seeming contradiction becomes clearer if one sees his 1950 indictment of serialism as a rejection of a technique used by unskilled, inexperienced composers, a mechanical means devoid of aesthetic intent. What he tried to prove to himself and others in his own use of serialism is that any technique in the hands of a mature composer can produce music that is more than a mere manipulation of tones.

As legitimate as his perspective may have seemed to him at the time, his *Open Letter* had placed him in a defensive position from which he could not seem to extricate himself. He felt the need to continue defending his philosophic positions, to criticize freely whatever seemed contrary to his way of thinking. In an interview when he was seventy, he confessed, "One person in the musical vanguard considers me a stumbling old man and says that I am against his music; I am against bad musicians! There are vanguard composers of worth, but most of them who compose are very ignorant."[10]

In March 1977 Claver Filho wrote a three-part series of articles in the *Correio Brasiliense:* "Guarnieri e o Dodecafonismo." In looking back on the *Open Letter,* he quoted Guarnieri as saying,

> The publication of the letter actually made me lose all hope in relation to most Brazilian composers. . . . If they all fight me on dodecaphony, in my defense of our artistic patrimony, it is because they cannot write national music, especially Brazilian music with the twelve-tone technique. Our music in essence is tonal and modal.[11]

In an interview in 1982 on his seventy-fifth birthday, Guarnieri admitted to being "a controversial or polemic person."[12] His intransigent defense of nationalism had the ultimate consequence of having his own works either defended or opposed, often vehemently, by others. This kind of defensive position came to mark Camargo Guarnieri's personality, and it is a pity that so much energy was expended in defense of what was so uniquely his gift. The sources of this inclination are all too human and undoubtedly stem from the intensity which also made him the strong, gifted, unique composer that he was. On February 22, 1987, the year which marked Villa-Lobos's hundredth and Guarnieri's eightieth birthdays, Luiz Paulo Horta noted in the *Jornal do Brasil:*

> The lack of understanding among the masters is a fact in the history of culture. Here in Brazilian terms, it is known that Camargo Guarnieri has misjudged the phenomenon of Villa-Lobos, resenting also the historical coincidence which has cast a shadow over their anniversaries. With all respect to Guarnieri, exception must be taken to his thesis [that Villa-Lobos only quotes folk music], which could have pernicious effects on the minds of the young.[13]

A person who had probably been closest to Guarnieri throughout his creative life and who had followed his development as friend, musician, and writer was João Caldeira Filho, music critic of the *Estado de São Paulo.* In the notes which he wrote for a recording which appeared in 1961, one finds what was then the best summary of Guarnieri's nationalistic works:

> In the panorama of various contemporary techniques such as atonalism and serialism, Camargo Guarnieri remains a Brazilian musician with a nationalistic thrust, which impels him toward the universal in music. He resides with the masters who used the well-tempered scale, that is in the company of Stravinsky, Hindemith, Messiaen, and many others. He can be atonal, but his atonalism is neither dodecaphonic nor serial, it is decisively thematic.
>
> In the whole field of national music established by Villa-Lobos, Camargo Guarnieri came to realize a nationalism fixed in certain elements (Caipira

thirds, the Amerindian character of popular melodies) and in the preference for the balanced, traditional forms in which his music is strictly cast. He has remained indifferent to the call of more or less extra-musical, descriptive ideas stemming from the immense flood of sensual tropicalism or the salient historical episodes. The work of Guarnieri is bare, dispossessed of all ornamental elements, but it is extremely alive.

The productions of Guarnieri represent an affirmation of constant growth in the national spirit. The aesthetic and technical elements are treated with an increasing liberty. Those elements which in the beginning served him as national themes are today the stimulus for creation; it is no longer the idea to be cited and used, but rather a moment of Brazilian sensibility to be treated sonorously. Camargo Guarnieri enlarges his harmonic concepts, the rhythmic dynamisms and orchestral timbres, but he does not do this at the expense of the formal intelligibility of his music.

Compositional balance is always evident in him with a subtly insinuated polyphonic style, which really marks the position of this composer: in the midst of all solutions, the music must preserve its melodic essence which is the soul of song.

The music of Camargo Guarnieri is of a national character, and contemporary culture has not extinguished its national distinctiveness. This music speaks of authentic things, the soul of which he has defended against mere compositional "processes," not being interested in the role of imitator or of being impersonal, amorphous, or of pursuing the latest novelty.[14]

What Guarnieri said when he was celebrating his seventieth birthday reflects both the rewards and difficulties of his choices: "You could say that, now at seventy, I can look back, and I am very happy to see that I have not betrayed my desire to be a national artist whose message is the soul of my people."[15] He was very sensitive, however, about being referred to as a "folkloric" composer, preferring the term "national" composer. In the same article referred to above, Luiz Paulo Horta draws an interesting comparison between the efforts of Villa-Lobos and those of Guarnieri as "national" composers:

> If Villa-Lobos invented Brazilian music—in the category we so pedantically call "erudite" (an unhappy name, especially inappropriate when dealing with the music of Villa-Lobos)—Camargo is one of those who knew how to extract the best consequences of this discovery. Twenty years younger than the founder, he matured his own style which has not been militantly national these past twenty years. He has a catalog which is so important and so varied.[16]

As one listens to his later compositions, there is no doubt that Guarnieri finally achieved a unique synthesis of his own Brazilianism, of classic forms, and of a universal musical language. Guarnieri was who he was and he could be no other. Likewise, his music reflects its author, unmistakably Brazilian. The true test of Guarnieri's value as a composer will lie in the ability of his works to be heard repeatedly over a long period of time by people of many cultures. If his music survives this test of time, all the arguments over unimportant details will fall into a welcome void. Camargo Guarnieri seems to have a better chance than most to achieve this kind of musical immortality.

Many may have disagreed with Guarnieri's holding to a national thrust, but no one could accuse him of being unfaithful to that in which he believed, or of not writing according to his own inner truth. As if to close his catalog of works with another bookend, he prepared a lengthy *Depoimento,* or "position statement," in 1985 when he was seventy-eight.[17] In it he explains once more what he considers to be the qualities of national music and the importance of respecting them. Shorter than his *Open Letter,* it covers similar ground, albeit more "tranquilly" as he indicated:

Depoimento [Statement]

Before being an individual, a composer is a social being, conditioned by factors of time, of race, and of environment. To deny this through snobbery or some intellectual attitude, to introduce into one's work strange stimuli in which the composer has not participated as a human being, is to produce a hybrid artificial work.

I am, and I want to be, a national composer of my country. If each human being has a responsibility on this earth, the composer surely must make a contribution within his means and abilities to enrich the music of the world, understanding this to include the sound of the diverse music of all countries.

In the case of young countries such as Brazil, this responsibility increases because it is not only to enrich the wealth of universal music, but to affirm a national Brazilian music. In order to have the right to universality, as did Italian, German, and French music of the past, Brazilian music must first of all exist as an autonomous entity. I believe that nationalism understood in this way is the only credo that can keep a composer in touch with the past, present, and future, avoiding the maladjustments that we observe to be so common in composers who embrace other schools of aesthetics. As the sociologists say, a person is at the same time the heir, carrier, and transmitter of culture.

Brazilian music, as a product of a young country, will have to look to its popular music for its specific characteristics. I agree that I speak here of music in a nationalistic school when already one could simply call it Brazilian national music as proposed by Mário de Andrade.

A nationalistic music presupposes a direct, systematic use of folkloric material. From this supposition comes a diversity of processes in the use of folklore in our erudite national music. This great diversity has not been able to form currents or tendencies. They are personal styles of working that a composer chooses because they seem to be well suited to one's own individual possibilities of creativity. I do not refuse to use a melodic line or folkloric rhythmic cell in my works; what I try to avoid is letting this element be extraneous to the work. The folkloric element must be integrated into the work as well as it is in the sensibilities of the composer.

From the viewpoint of the technique of composition, I must credit Lamberto Baldi's teachings, which were most helpful and which constitute the basic principles that I still hold to today. As to aesthetic orientation, it was in the company of Mário de Andrade that I learned to challenge, so to speak, the sacred rules of the three traditional schools of music. Mário de Andrade was a great theorist of Brazilian music, and his influence, I can assure you, was felt not only by me, a lifelong disciple of his, but on an entire generation of Brazilian composers who were his contemporaries. Even the younger composers of Brazil reflect directly or indirectly the influence of this admirable spirit whose teachings remain alive, even today.

Music is not an isolated phenomenon. A composer must meet and examine carefully the directions which the other arts are taking, look at that invisible thread which binds one art to another, a thread which many prefer to call "the spirit of the times."

As with all arts, music has its own materials: sound and rhythm. To pretend that this material can be treated as if in a mechanical laboratory or as a mathematical formula is above all to dehumanize the art. Theoretically speaking, if sound and rhythm do not have a homeland or inner basis, it is necessary to acknowledge that the mind and feelings of the artist are actually the laboratory where those elements are manipulated.

As the artist is à social being who realizes himself only by functioning in the group or organization to which he belongs, I conclude tranquilly that the technical processes might be infinite but not eternal. Art as an expression of human emotion, however, is eternal.

There are many schools of thought today on musical technique, such as twelve-tone, serialism, musique concrète, or electronic music. In Brazil as elsewhere, the acceptance of modern art raises always the same problems. In principle, some leaders direct a small chorus of fanatics for modern art which one day will become old. On the other hand, the reactionaries do not feel, do not comprehend anything new. The preference of the latter for Classic or Romantic music by composers who are universally recognized (Bach, Mozart, Beethoven, Wagner, or Chopin) does not imply a hostility to that which is deemed "modern." It is rather a question of almost total ignorance of the principles which guide the new schools.

If it is fine to acknowledge in Brazil a rejection of twelve-tone or serial music, can we not at the same time say that other "modern" trends can be admitted as a curiosity? In whatever form, the solution to the problem is in the diffusion of these trends. Only if these various kinds of music are given a hearing on stage will we have a chance to reject or accept them.

M. Camargo Guarnieri
1985

This *Statement* and the *Open Letter* give the clearest possible understanding of Guarnieri's own position on his nationalism. It is one of the principal elements that has given his music such a personal and profound power of expression and authenticity. Nationalism is his language, the strength and the beauty of his work, even as it was for Grieg, Rachmaninoff, Stravinsky, or Bartók, among many others. A composer cannot write with someone else's language, in a foreign tongue. One wonders why it is even a question to be raised. Aesthetic arguments are to music much as theology is to faith; the former might explain the latter, but they are mere explanations, not the heart of the matter. Words may divide, but it is the music itself which has the power to speak the guileless message across verbal boundaries.

What these two statements by Guarnieri attest to, finally, is his convictions, and the keen intellect and vast mastery of intellectual concepts that they represent. The man in whom these gifts resided was complex. Understanding who he was can cast light upon all that has already been said.

PERSONALITY

It is difficult to overestimate the influence of Guarnieri's early life on the development of his personality: born in a small village, surrounded by a rich culture of folk music and dance, and encouraged by musical parents to develop his musical talents. He was one of four boys in a closely knit Italian-Brazilian family and had the company of six sisters as well, and a loving mother and energetic father. He said,

When I had to leave school after second grade, I suffered because of the awareness of my ignorance, but [later] Mário and my brothers helped me very much. My brothers and sisters stayed in school. I was a barber and helped my father; therefore I could not study. I had a horror of being a barber.[18]

A few attempts at formal music instruction in his early years proved ineffective. With no formal classes to attend, and in spite of helping his father, he was left with extended blocks of time to pursue his own interests. Given his intellectual brilliance, curiosity, and musical giftedness, this could have been a boon or bane, and it proved to be a bit of both.

On the positive side, the lack of formal education, both academic and musical, left him free to explore his world, natural and musical. He spent hours each day improvising at the piano and learned both flute and violin from his father. He must have conceptualized musical content to a relatively high degree if he could produce a first well-written composition at the age of eleven. Not limited by outside influences, he could give free rein to his reflectiveness, improvisation, and sense of discovery. It was here that his own musical judgment and gifts became rooted as an integral part of who he was. Living in his own musical world, so to speak, Guarnieri developed a strong sense of purpose, dedication, and strength of ideas, which later in his life would often be perceived as stubbornness. If he had not been so focused on his particular perception of and approach to life, he would not have developed his personal and musical strengths to the degree that he did.

The lack of a formal structure to his academic education had its negative side as well, evident in his stubbornness. I believe that his building of a professional life with only two years of primary school education was a key element in the development of his personality. The move from Tietê to the strange environment of São Paulo at the age of fifteen alone could have been intimidating, but coming without a firm educational foundation must have increased his natural timidity. His desire to be among the students who attended the São Paulo Conservatory of Drama and Music suggests the need he felt to enter the musical mainstream, but family finances prevented his doing so. This lack of early interchange among his musical peers did not enhance his ability to share ideas with the normal give-and-take of a more social and intellectual setting. This finally changed, however, when he began classes at the age of twenty-one with Mário de Andrade, but he had formed himself well by that time. It becomes understandable that he was so devoted to Andrade, their meeting an experience which changed his life and gave him the emotional and professional support he seemed to need so desperately.

THE FEMININE PRINCIPLE

All of the above observations are the basis for a consideration of Guarnieri's strong emphasis on the "feminine principle" in his life. He often spoke of how women, or the feminine, were an inspiration for him. This relates directly to another statement he frequently made, that for him, "Music is emotion." Guarnieri was both deeply intuitive and highly intelligent. Because he married three times and with his great sensitivity, it is understandable that his many relationships with women would affect what he composed. It seems that he was always seeking the perfect feminine ideal but was not always able to sustain relationships once established.

This search for the beautiful and for emotional expression is evident in his music. No composer writes "just notes," but Guarnieri above all never wrote "just notes" apart from deeply expressive musical messages. His music could be playful, dynamic, genial, explosive, somber, or intimate. Nowhere is his intimacy felt more than in some of the slower *Ponteios* and *Improvisos,* or in the long, soaring solo violin lines. People are often deeply moved by the depth of feeling in these passages. Lifelong friend and writer Maria Abreu spoke of this expressive power of Guarnieri's music: "His music had a sweetness which recalled the magic of Stradivarius. One only had to hear him. The piano appeared to have no accents and to evoke mysterious vibrations, coming from the school of Cremona."[19] Guarnieri's daughter, Tânia, shared that when she practices his music for violin, people will frequently stop at the door, knock, and ask what the beautiful music is. It has an undeniable communicative power that touches people. Abreu also shared her insights into the importance of this feminine aspect of his life:

> The women in his life represent a fascination which he never resisted. Some may ask: which of them was most important? A response could be: all—or none. This is to say that the feminine presence had acted as a stimulus to the imagination of the artist, but not as an element integral to the realization of the musician. . . . One [reason] might be, probably, that he himself had a musical conception of love. As a musician, a master of thematic development, he was not able to transport his consummate art to the level of the existence of both.[20]

Another interesting aspect regarding his feminine consciousness is the fact that his principal interpreters have been women: Lidia Simões, Isabel Mourão, Laís de Souza Brasil, Cynthia Priolli, Zuleika Rosa Guedes, and Belkiss Carneiro de Mendonça. All of them worked with Guarnieri in preparing their recordings and performances. Most of his songs, likewise, are for the female voice. Abreu again shared her insights on the women pianists:

> But why women? Could it be that he preferred the feminine manner of playing? I don't believe so. The reason is more subtle. It is that, for Guarnieri, the familiar composer-interpreter relationship had to forge a spiritual unity. Under this aspect, it is the feminine aspect that gave him a harmonious understanding.[21]

In a brief article published upon Guarnieri's death in 1993, Abreu enlarged upon this aspect of Guarnieri:

In music, his emotions were transfigured. But in life, his passions escaped logic. He said that he was never able to resist the enchantment of the feminine figure—an ideal which was in the singular while his interpreters were many. "For me, to love is the state of grace. It is when I compose my best works." These works put order into emotional chaos provoked by impossible loves. Because of this and the technical resources which he possessed (like no other Brazilian composer), this musician imposed a discipline on his work worthy of a scientist or, even better, of a religious. A faulty man but an impeccable artist, Guarnieri never believed in doing things half way, even if it led him to embrace apparently opposite stances. On the one hand there was order and beauty, and on the other, extravagance, calm, and sensuality.

"When I die, who will revise my unedited works? I am afraid they will make mistakes." Guarnieri, who as an adult, never let the child within die. He was afraid of many things, especially regarding his music—written with scrupulous perfection—afraid that it would be changed. His greatest courage? This artist never made concessions.[22]

These reflections make clear that Guarnieri possessed an exceptionally strong and vigorous personality. He was a powerful combination of keen intellect and equally strong emotions. His great sensitivity was a cause of suffering to him in the course of his life, and his childhood insecurity, in a sense, never left him. Financial security was always a challenge, and being misunderstood was difficult. The integration of these two complementary parts of his own soul, intellect and passion, form the meeting ground where he faced the daily challenges and struggles of his creative life.

His strong positions on musical topics over the years, his complexity and the structural control of his art, his genial but robust personality, his playfulness—all these are to be found in his music, a faithful picture of the man. His gifts were developed at great personal cost to himself. The long journey that development of such a talent requires can create a kind of isolation for a composer, and this suffering, too, is evident in his music.

Lest one get the impression that Guarnieri faced only struggle, it must also be acknowledged that he could be very genial, as well as combative and harsh. The very strength of his early experiences and isolation in Tietê, and the intensive education by Mário de Andrade and Lamberto Baldi, helped him set a unique, firm direction from which he could not vacillate. The underside of this gift, however, also becomes for him his point of greatest suffering and conflict as a composer. His *Open Letter* is indicative of how his very gifts and convictions could bring out his stubborn defensiveness. He could be impatient and stinging in his responses to those who did not live up to his expectations, particularly in challenging his ideas or in the performance of his music. Yet he was also a faithful, warm, and generous friend who could not pass a Salvation Army bell ringer without giving a donation.

"Gone Fishing."
*Photo courtesy of the
University of São Paulo
IEB archives.*

All this is to say again that he was a very complex person, a wonderful man who was faithful to what he believed, and who had to work out his own life process and deal with his own limitations in the best and most creative way that he could. This he did.

ELEMENTS OF MUSICAL STYLE

Rhythm

The strong, incisive rhythms of the *cocos* and *emboladas,* the gentle undulating syncopations of the *toadas* and *modinhas* with their nostalgic qualities, the playful *rodas*—all these are found repeatedly in Guarnieri's music. The fifty *Ponteios* for piano are a particularly rich resource of these movement or mood types cast in miniature form. Francisco Curt Lange noted the "internal rubato" which these pieces contain, especially the gentler ones.[23] Guarnieri's kind of free melodic line over a light, flowing pulsation pre-dates the more popular *Bossa nova* by almost twenty years. Although there is no obvious direct connection between them, they both draw from a common deep, rich source. In turn, these are rooted in the complex, multi-layered drum beats of African music with their rhythmically free melodies riding above them. This rhythmic interaction of melodic line with accompaniment is always supple and sophisticated.

The twenty *Estudos* for piano would be a study in themselves of his rhythmic invention. Guarnieri achieves this not through any simple patterns, but rather through a web of contrapuntal accents. With lines going in all directions and outlining unhandy quartal harmonies, he frequently has two or three distinct rhythmic patterns holding the entire fabric together. The *Estudo* no. 7 presents cross-rhythms with persistent two-against-three in the right hand and three quarter notes in each $\frac{2}{4}$ measure in the left hand. These three gently undulating lines actually imply a constant poly-metric overlay of $\frac{2}{4}$, $\frac{6}{8}$, and $\frac{3}{4}$. The result is not a "heady" piece, but a wonderfully expressive interlude among his more aggressive works in this set. (See page 101.)

The larger symphonic compositions are also permeated with the dance forms, though on a grander, perhaps less intimate and personal, scale. The enlarged scope and use of more instruments allows for the polyphonic treatment that an entire orchestra can provide, resulting in a more complex rhythmic fabric. The varied timbres allow him to underscore and etch rhythmic cells with even greater intensity. At times, as in the Concertino for Piano and Orchestra, his orchestra seems to become one large guitar that rhythmically supports the soloist. His contrapuntal textures enable him to build rhythmic intensity to points of high climax. The dynamism of these works is grounded in their rhythmic fabric.

Another aspect of Guarnieri's control of rhythm is in its virtual absence, as in the seemingly motionless lines which hang in suspended, ethereal stillness. The slow movement of the Sixth Piano Sonatina, marked *Etereo,* and the *Lento e tragico* of his Fourth Symphony (*Brasilia*) are wonderful examples. The latter describes the absolute flat line of vision as one's gaze circles the horizon of the *planalto* where Brasilia was built. The expansiveness of the horizon, its seeming endlessness and uniformity, are portrayed by one long, somber line introduced by the violins. Such lines can feel almost mystical.

Form

Guarnieri adhered to the traditional forms more than either Villa-Lobos or Mignone. Beyond that, however, he conceived his music in a structurally coherent manner. His musical textures are highly organized, whether in fast or slow tempo, always giving a sense of clear direction and purpose. Because they evolve organically, his music is intellectually engaging.

He developed and regularly used a type of ABA form in which the B section was not new material, but rather a development of the A material. The middle B section frequently begins imperceptibly as a continuation of the opening material, grows to a climax, and then there is a welcome return, often harmonized in a new way, casting new color and light on the original theme, an example of apotheosis. Thus, many of Guarnieri's compositions, particularly for piano, are monothematic, a situation which lends itself to the use of contrapuntal techniques in which themes or subjects are developed through sequence, repetition, inversion, diminution and augmentation, fragmentation or extension, all of which are found in his music.

Ricardo Tacuchian has written:

> The technique of development is one of the most typical resources of the composer. In his hands, any motif possesses unimaginable possibilities. In all of his symphonic works, his themes, once exposed, are immediately developed. Little motives are used for an entire work, even when a second theme is presented. At times, a second theme with a character different from the first is formed from elements of the first. . . . This economy of material gives to the works of Guarnieri a wonderful unity which is one of the principal characteristics of his style.[24]

Guarnieri also gave new connotations to at least two existing forms. The word *ponteio* comes from the Portuguese *pontear,* meaning "to stroke," as with a guitar. He applied the term to his fifty piano preludes, which he called *Ponteios.* The *choro* has also accumulated several meanings. It originally referred both to the kind of serenade music a small group of strolling musicians would play in Rio's streets at night, and to the group itself. Guarnieri began using it to title his concertos for solo instrument and orchestra in which he drew more clearly upon folkloric material. He wrote *choros* for piano, flute, bassoon, clarinet, violin, viola, and cello.

Melody

Typical of Brazilian tunes is the descending melodic direction. This Guarnieri used to wonderful effect in one of his first pieces, the *Dança Brasileira,* which begins high and descends through a repeated-note figure.

Guarnieri's slower melodies are completely suffused with the emotional qualities of the *modinhas,* the melancholy *toadas,* or with Brazilian *saudades,* or longing. The rhythmic freedom and syncopated hesitancy of a tune often suggests a sensual dance with the accompaniment. His several hundred songs are replete with every possible emotion, and he mastered the setting of the Portuguese language into singable, understandable texts—a difficult art.

The use of modes is another means of conveying these feelings. The Mixolydian mode, with its flatted seventh degree, is common in Guarnieri's music. A modification of this is the "Mode of the Northeast" in which the raised fourth degree of the Lydian mode is also used. This peculiar, charming, and poignant mode is one of the most common and recognizable characteristics of Guarnieri's music. His *Ponteio e Dança* for Cello and Piano is a good example of use of the Mode of the Northeast.

Within his use of chromaticism, the frequency of cross-relations—that is, conflicting accidentals within a chord or contrapuntal lines—is striking. His *Ponteio* no. 45 seems to be a study in cross-relations in which he created a playful, teasing alternation between major and minor.

The interval of a fourth plays an important part in his writing, both harmonically and melodically, particularly in many of the *Estudos* for piano. Obviously such quartal melodies are not to be sung. The angularity which they create, especially in rapidly moving tempos, exudes a dynamic energy. In *Estudo* no. 9, he has the two hands running in parallel motion a ninth apart in an angular sixteenth-note figuration. Number 20 has each hand, in turn, dealing with rapid melodic ninths in a three-note pattern.

It is difficult to speak of Guarnieri's melodies without also noting that they are part of his contrapuntal textures and are subject to the kind of development common in polyphony. What American theorist Ludmila Ulehla wrote of twentieth-century melodies applies to many of Guarnieri's:

> Linear tonality replaces the all-encompassing harmonic tonality of the former musical periods.[25]

When this linear tonality occurs along with chromatic writing or atonalism and within a dynamic rhythmic framework, as is the case with Guarnieri, it can result in a very complex web of elements with melody leading the way. It is a fascinating aspect of his writing that cannot be fully understood without experiencing works in a variety of media from his catalog.

Harmony

Harmonically, Guarnieri began with tonal relationships that were quite familiar to his early audiences. He made easy use of the "Paulistan thirds," which were commonly used by guitarists to harmonize melodies. But this did not continue for long. Within a few years he had begun his search for his own language. For example, his 1934 Piano Sonatina no. 2 shocked many with its dissonance, achieved through his early attempts at nontonal writing. He intended it to be a venture into atonalism. From this example onward, his pursuit of atonalism was constant, though not consistent. His melodies continue to have a natural, continual flow, although his excursions into stronger atonal sonorities continued.

Gradually his language came to be marked heavily by quartal harmonies. The Piano Concerto no. 5 of 1970 consciously used serial techniques as an extension of the polyphonic techniques which were his language for the preceding forty-five years. This time, however, the thematic material was serial and not tonal. The use of cross-relations frequently makes tonality even more indecisive. The *Ponteios* have numerous examples of this. Belkiss Carneiro de Mendonça summarized: "Using the principal of dissonant harmony within a tonal sense, he used more and more chromaticism, until his music became atonal. Today he possesses his own language, resulting from a fusion of these three stages."[26]

Just as pertinent to his harmony, however, is Guarnieri's contrapuntal skill, which he developed to a high degree. He admired Bach, but his pieces resemble more closely the writing of Brahms, possibly because of their emotion-laden qualities. Paulo Rabelo, however, drew a direct connection between Guarnieri's contrapuntal writing and Brazilian folk music:

> Polyphony is much more representative of Brazilian music than harmony. The custom of accompanying music with the melody itself or with elements derived from it started in Brazil among popular rural singers centuries ago. In Brazilian urban popular music the countermelodies and thematic variations employed by serenading flutists and the melodic basses played by guitarists in the *modinhas* are characteristic of the polyphonic character of this music. Guarnieri was doubtless affected by this fact and became a remarkable contrapuntist. His textures are basically polyphonic.[27]

Developing the technique of counterpoint was important to Guarnieri, both for himself and in his teaching of students. The complex contrapuntal fabric was a natural expression for a man so intense. Thus, it came both from his Brazilian roots, as noted above, and through the development of his own personality and creative gifts. This aspect of his writing is a perfect illustration of the man.

Expression

Guarnieri consistently wrote performance indications, not in the customary Italian, but in Portuguese, which suggested their source in the people's music. For example, *Piu Calmo, Festivo, Molengamente, Dolente,* or *Com muito saudades* suggested a feeling rather than just a tempo. Because he drew upon the soul of Brazil, as expressed in its folkloric content, he plumbed a deeply emotional source to which he gave a transformed expression. Belkiss Carneiro noted:

> Whether he wanted to suggest melodies characteristic of the northeast or São Paulo, the pronounced rhythms of the rural *batuque,* the duet of serenaders, or the counter-lines of the guitars, Camargo Guarnieri showed in his work the presence of all of Brazil. He said in an interview that, at times, he did this even through his counterpoint, his emotionality, and his freedom of expression.[28]

Because music was emotion for him, this emerged as an important stylistic element. Whatever he wrote has about it an intensity than is unmistakable. More and more, his later works reflect the man in his later years. Life continued to be a struggle on many levels. He had said that people thought him to be very happy, but he was, in fact, sad. The struggle with his own life and personality, his firm resistance to fate, seemed to come through in the powerful, aggressive, percussive chords that punctuate climaxes and conclusions of some movements in his larger works. These points seem to scream, "No! No!" One can also hear in the slower movements a peace that he seems to have made with life. That this is all evident in his music testifies to the integrity and a certain wholeness of Guarnieri.

One of his finest interpreters, Lais de Souza Brasil, noted in a 1979 interview:

> Camargo Guarnieri possesses three well-defined characteristics that are reflected in his compositions: He is an intense and anguished person; he possesses a strong and sublime inner force in his symphonies, in the second movements of his sonatas, and in his slow and contemplative pieces; his third characteristic is his playfulness. This joyful side appears especially in the *Ponteios,* some of them only thirty seconds long.[29]

Many of his gentler pieces have a quality of improvisation about them. His early years in Tietê, where he improvised surreptitiously, bore him the fruit of a naturalness in the flow in his melodies. Of the larger works, however, he explained that he mulled them in his mind, sometimes for months as they took shape in a period of gestation. Then when he sat down to write, with pencil in hand, he sketched the entire work, "all parts at once."[30]

This was no ordinary, occasional composer who could thus conceive of major works with every detail. The creative tension, the isolation, the focus required to produce in this manner were considerable. He was in a world apart when he composed. Guarnieri, above all, knew this experience, and he knew where that gift came from. The responsibility of being true to it was an intensely conscious act for him. His *Depoimento* illustrated this conviction. He also said many times, "I compose for the same reason that I breathe."[31] And he composed almost until his breath ceased. After his death, an unfinished concertino for violin and orchestra was found in his studio.

All of these elements—melody, modes, rhythm, texture, harmony, orchestration, expression—in interaction are what create the style of Camargo Guarnieri. No one of them in isolation stands out, but rather the integration of his use of musical elements, infused with his own personality, marks his music as being completely distinct from that of any other composer. The skill with which he practiced his trade, the musical architectures that he created, the emotion with which he infused these—all speak of the special gift that he developed throughout his life.

FOUR

Music for Solo Piano

Camargo Guarnieri's music for piano shows the composer in his most natural medium. His early experiences of improvising at the keyboard served him well in the natural, easy flow of his keyboard works. Indeed, many of the *Ponteios* seem like improvisations, and some were actually created in that way. Both these short piano pieces and hundreds of songs nurtured his creativity throughout his long compositional life. They reveal his mastery of the small musical form.

Guarnieri liked to write these piano pieces in groups, as indicated earlier. For example, there are fifty *Ponteios,* twenty *Estudos,* ten *Improvisos,* ten *Momentos,* and ten *Valsas.* In addition there are twenty-eight individual pieces reflecting both the song and the dance types of Brazil. The composer also wrote eight sonatinas and one sonata. Almost all of these works are published, many of them are recorded, and most of them have had frequent performances as a result of the emphasis on the teaching of piano in Brazil.

INDIVIDUAL PIECES

Canção Sertaneja (Song of the Backlands). 1928.
[Chiarato, São Paulo–1955; RB–1955]

This is his first work for piano listed in his professional catalog. Guarnieri preferred not to include any works predating 1928. The source of inspiration for the piece, dedicated to his parents, was the singer of the *sertão* or backlands. There is the syncopated, chordic accompaniment with its melody etched on top, the chromatically colored shifting of this ostinato in and around a simple tonic-dominant harmonic alternation, and the flowing, subtle melody. This is one of his few pieces that uses a key signature, and the accidentals do nothing to dilute the strong tonal orientation of the piece. In a review shortly after this piece was published in 1928, Mário de

Andrade wrote, "The *Canção Sertaneja* confirms the talent of Camargo Guarnieri. It is a tender song, melancholy and very much our own, revealing the healthy influence of Villa-Lobos. It is a pleasure to play."[1]

Canção Sertaneja

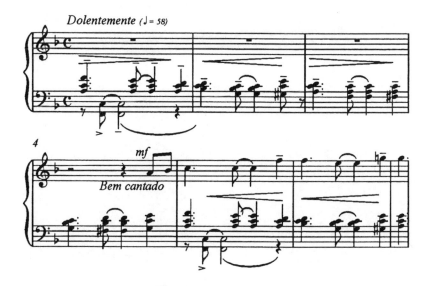

Dança Brasileira (Brazilian Dance). 1928.
[Chiarato, São Paulo–1930;
RB–1948; AMP–1949]

Written the same year as the *Canção Sertaneja,* the *Dança Brasileira* has remained a popular favorite. It is the one Guarnieri piece many North Americans are familiar with because its orchestral version, published in the United States, has been recorded several times in this country. With its typically descending melody of rapidly repeated notes, its rhythmic vitality is immediately appealing. His dance-inspired pieces come directly out of Brazilian folk culture, but he noted: "My dances are suggestions of atmospheres."[2] Guarnieri further explained the origin of this piece:

> I was born in a little town called Tietê. My house was on one of the slopes of the town which was circled by the Tietê River. Here in Brazil on May 13 we commemorate the abolition of slavery. From the time that I was a little boy, I remember hearing the rhythm of the dances of the Blacks in Tietê during the celebrations. The rhythm was incessant. My *Brazilian Dance* has resulted from this memory.[3]

Dança Brasileira

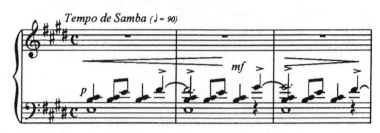

Mário de Andrade hailed this piece on May 6, 1928, in the *Diário Nacional* when he wrote his famous "By golly, this boy is predestined!" article. It read in part:

> It is a delightful work, very well constructed. It is inspired by ethnic elements (descending phrases, repeated notes, staccatos, our rhythms, lowered sevenths, etc.), but it does not quote directly from popular works. Well written, refined in its harmonization, ignoring a little some pianistic fingering, it is so very rhythmic with a clear, straightforward, and appealing spirit.[4]

Prelúdio e Fuga (Prelude and Fugue).
1929. Manuscript

This pair of brief, experimental pieces dated 1929 has not been published. The fugue shows a growing mastery of fugal technique, if not a clarity and directness.

Toada. 1929.
[Chiarato, São Paulo–1929; Kalmus]

The short, lyrical *Toada* from 1929 continues the style of the *Canção Sertaneja* of the previous year. The *toada* is a lazy, melancholy kind of song. Dedicated to Lavinia Viotti, his first wife, it has an intimate quality suggested in its chromatic movement. Guarnieri also transcribed this piece for orchestra in 1929.

Choro Torturado (Anguished Song). 1930.
[Chiarato, São Paulo–1947; RB; AMP–1947]

Composed in 1930 and premiered by Guarnieri's wife Lavinia, this piece contains some of the composer's earliest strongly chromatic writing and thickest textures. From the opening declamatory line to the final chord, the mood of the piece is one of relentless energy or *tortura,* thus its title. The rhythmic texture is extremely volatile with cross-rhythms and irregular groupings of notes and a generally strong accentuation. Harmonically the language is functional and tertian, but the great number of appoggiaturas, accented nonharmonic tones, and some bitonal passages give the effect of a prevailing chromaticism. The angularity of the accompaniment against chromatically moving melodies adds to the sense of restlessness which marks the piece. It falls into three main sections, the second being relatively more melodic and less agitated.

Guarnieri heard this piece performed by Brazilian pianist Guiomar Novaes in Rio in 1935. The story surrounding this event is related in the discussion of his *Tocata* for piano.

Dança Selvagem (Jungle Dance). 1931.
[Chiarato, São Paulo–1934; RB–1955]

This is a second of Guarnieri's three dances, written in 1931 and first performed by Lavinia Viotti. The title is reflected in the rhythm, which Guarnieri took from an ethnographic recording made by Roquete Pinto among the people of the backlands. The piece is frenzied from beginning to end, beginning *ff* and coming down dynamically only once to an *mf* before the rush to an *sfff* close. The melody is projected over quartal chords and appears irregularly over the unrelenting rhythmic pattern, which is shared by the two hands. The irregularity, the high dynamic level, and the constant occurrence of quartal sonorities, with those in the left hand of a different tonal orientation, give this piece a harsh, crude, and biting quality. As with most of these individual pieces, it is in ABA form.

Mário de Andrade, accustomed to reviewing new music in his regular column in the *Diário de São Paulo,* reviewed this piece on May 3, 1934:

> As for the *Dança Selvagem,* it represents Camargo Guarnieri in the most specific core of his personality: the use of chromaticism, the tonal liberty, the virulence of the accents, the beauty in its hidden themes, the richness and directness of the implacable rhythms. And also the bad habits—principally the abundance of appoggiaturas which the artist is constantly overusing. That which is most curious in this piece is the evolution of the rhythmic accompaniment. The composer achieves a gradual transformation of the beginning —rough, simple, hard, a subtle Brazilianism—and reaches the delightful syncopations at the end. Of all the works I have reviewed today, the *Dança Selvagem* appears incontestably the most significant and the strongest.[5]

O Cavalinho de Perna Quebrada
(Little Horse with a Broken Leg). 1932.
[AMP–1944; RB–1948]

This is one of the most charming piano pieces Guarnieri composed and is one of only a few with a descriptive title. He explained his reason for writing it:

> I wanted to write a child's piece for my son's birthday. Actually it is a difficult piece, and the left-hand part suggests the little horse with the broken leg. It is the only piece of mine in which the name of the piece was suggested by the rhythm. I gave it the name after I wrote it. On one occasion a young child asked me why the second half of the piece was slower. I was embarrassed and didn't know how to answer, but I said that perhaps the child who owned the horse felt sad about its broken leg.[6]

As suggested by Guarnieri's comments, the piece falls into two main sections. It was written in 1932 and published in 1938.

Lundu. 1935.
[Music Press–1942; RB–1947]

Cascudo wrote of the *lundu* in his *Dicionário do Folclore Brasileiro:* "The *lundu* is a song and dance of African origin brought to Brazil by the Bantu slaves, particularly those from Angola."[7] It was a lascivious dance in which the woman dancer approached the man, and efforts to seduce him were prolonged to a point of frenzy, delirium, and convulsiveness. Oneyda Alvarenga adds:

> The *lundu* was the first form of African music which Brazilian society accepted, and, thanks to it, the Blacks gave our music some important characteristics, such as a system of syncopation and the use of the lowered seventh

degree of the scale. In order to totally accept the *lundu,* colonial Brazilian society transformed it into a song, freeing it from the choreography which scandalized and irritated the pretenses of their whiteness.[8]

Guarnieri considered the *lundu* to be originally a song, frequently with humorous texts. In his *Lundu* for piano, one senses both the humor and the frenzy. The piece is hard-driving and very dissonant, attempting to capture the fanatic, ritualistic frenzy. It falls into an ABA form with the A section utilizing very independently moving lines. The rhythmic independence of the theme and angular, wandering accompanimental lines present a challenge to the performer.

Tocata. 1935.
[BR–1947; AMP–1947]

This piece has a rather dramatic origin. As a young man of twenty-eight, Guarnieri made his first 250 mile trip from São Paulo to Rio de Janeiro in 1935. He recalled:

> As soon as I got to the hotel, I decided to go to the Municipal Theater. I had to ask someone how to get there. When I arrived I looked at the playbill and saw that Guiomar Novaes would play a concert. I was surprised to see that she would play my *Choro Torturado.* I went to the box office, and, as I didn't have much money, I asked the ticket seller if he could give me a ticket. When I looked at him, I noticed that it was Otávio Pinto, husband of the soloist. He recognized me and said that there would be a seat for me in the orchestra section. Naturally he told Guiomar that I was there, and that night, after she played the *Choro Torturado,* she pointed to me. I stood up. It was the first time that a Rio audience had seen me, and I was deeply moved by their warm applause.
>
> I returned to the hotel that night and went to sleep, but during the night I dreamt that I was writing a toccata for Guiomar. I got up and, as I always carry some staff paper with me, I took some and wrote almost all of the *Tocata.* Then I went back to bed. When I awoke in the morning, I had really forgotten that I had written anything, and I was surprised to see what I had done because I had not anticipated writing anything. When I returned to São Paulo, I of course dedicated the piece to her.[9]

This *Tocata* is a difficult piece. The initial texture consists of double-note figuration for the right hand with a three-note ostinato in the left hand. The harmonic orientation at the opening is obscure, although it moves toward a C tonal center on the first page and then away again. A middle section centers initially around F with a new kind of right-hand figuration, which suggests a *samba* rhythm. This suggestion then becomes a reality and proceeds to constitute the major portion of the piece. The first part recurs in basically the same form. Although the indication for the piece is *Piacante ma com garbo,* there is nothing gentle about its technical requirements.

After its premiere by Arnaldo Estrela in Rio de Janeiro in April 1941, Andrade Muricy wrote:

> The *Tocata* of 1935 belongs to the genre of free toccatas of the moderns, of whom the pedagogue Czerny is an example, but especially Schumann with his incomparable *Toccata,* Op. 7. The *Tocata* of Camargo Guarnieri has a fierce passion about it, a change from his usual happy sportiveness. . . . This work is one of the most impressive in our repertoire.[10]

João Itiberê da Cunha attended the same program on which the *Tocata* was premiered. He had earlier decried some of Guarnieri's other pieces with his "Atonalism is witchcraft!" remark. Of this work, however, he had this to say: "The *Tocata* is a more significant piece, better in form and architecture, much more polished, in this program presented by Guarnieri. It is a work that should be in our repertoire."[11]

Eurico Nogueira França wrote in a March 17, 1945, article in the *Correio da Manha:*

> The *Tocata for Piano* is of transcendental difficulty, moved by a spontaneous and impetuous force as if a natural element had been unleashed. The novelty of the harmonic idiom in which it proceeds, which sounds splendid on the piano, the counter-melodies which rise, the capricious and systematic mutations of the compass in which is invested extreme dynamic variety, the effectiveness of the progressions and dynamic contrasts—all require a detailed musical analysis.[12]

Three years later, França repeated the above review, preceded this time by the following comments:

> The *Tocata for Piano* (which we heard tonight, after the Sonatina no. 3, the *Waltz in C♯ Minor,* the *Choro Torturado,* the *Dança Negra,* and the *Ponteio* no. 13) gave me the sense of a great work of universal musical worth, without doubt one of the most important pianistic pages yet written by this Brazilian composer. Within the free form of a toccata, and keeping in the legitimate tradition which flowed from Schumann (for whom Czerny's *Toccata* was the technical precursor), this work of Camargo Guarnieri is of transcendental difficulty.[13]

Toada Triste (Sad *Toada*). 1936.
[G. Schirmer–1942]

Dedicated to Guarnieri's second wife, Anita, this 1936 work is a delicate piece of writing with the quality of gentle, sustained breathing. It moves in subtle syncopation with thirds, sixths, and tenths over a dominant pedal point which finally grounds itself on the tonic in the seventh measure. The melody remains on the top of the texture throughout the piece, while the left hand provides a simple foundation and assists with a few passages of the melody in the middle staff. Harmonically the language is tertian, often extended. Mild dissonances are created through the movement of inner voices, and there are some cross-relations and unexpected chromatic alterations in the melody.

Francisco Curt Lange commented on this piece in his preface to the volume in which it was published:

> The indication *com muito saudade* permits the introduction of expressive elements, of a soft melancholy which is heightened by the appoggiatura. Despite its rhythmic quality, the *Toada Triste* is an exponent of the internal rubato which is so frequently discerned in Brazilian works.[14]

Ficarás Sozinha (Be Alone). 1939.
[Music Press–1942; RB–1948]

This is the first of a series of three shorter pieces which use a great simplicity of material within a gentle, yet sophisticated setting. The other two are *Maria Lucia* and *Acalanto*. All three are cast in the form of a repeated double period, and all use two treble clefs. This one was composed in 1939 and first published in 1942. In a review of the piece that appeared shortly after it was published in a North American edition by Music Press, Eurico Nogueria França wrote the following:

> A group of editions by Music Press prove again that Camargo Guarnieri, a musician before anything else, has the ability to soar into regions of music without an ethnic feeling, not being thereby less imbued with folklore as a composer, full of the songs of our country.
>
> If we begin, for example, with some of his pieces outside those limitations of geography, suddenly we are aware that the composer has led us back to Brazil! That happened, for example, with the little piece for piano *Ficarás Sozinha*, where a folkloric melody is treated moreover with an irresistible spirit, rising suddenly in the middle section. Does this folklore signify an intimate impulse or an intuition which strengthens our folklore? Does the composer want to lift folklore from its level, or is it that it is folklore which comes to nourish him in his creative work? Perhaps these factors all come together. Whichever it is, this time there is no other alternative in the music of Guarnieri. But more than the elegant and refined allusions, this wonderful native melody cannot but touch us and make us accepting and delighted.[15]

Maria Lucia. 1946.
[Music Press–1942; RB–1948]

As with the preceding piece, this is written entirely with two treble clefs and is also dedicated to the young daughter of a friend. It has no chromatics, which suggests a pandiatonic approach. Phrase lengths are somewhat uneven in its two-, sometimes three-line texture. Harmonically it begins vaguely as if on a supertonic chord in A minor, but then it touches other chordal points smoothly and gently, increasing its sense of harmonic indecisiveness. It uses grace notes on the top line in a way that suggests vocal inflections.

Dança Negra. 1946.
[RB and AMP–1948]

A world apart from the three preceding pieces, the *Dança Negra* resulted from a visit Guarnieri made to a candomblé ceremony during his 1937 visit to Bahia. He related that he had set out by taxi with a friend, Jorge Amado, for the site of the ceremony. The taxi climbed a long hill to a certain point, at which the driver indicated that they would have to walk the remaining distance. The two continued walking to the top in complete darkness and silence. They could hear the singing and dancing in the distance as they began to descend the hill on the other side. The sound grew louder as they approached: this explains the dynamic arch of the piece. Guarnieri explained: "It should start pianissimo and continue to grow until it reaches a maximum volume; then it should diminish."[16]

The left hand begins a subtle ostinato, which remains constant throughout the piece. Initially it fits the meter, but as the piece progresses, the pattern tends to be of more irregular length under the very regular modal melody. The static harmony provided by the ostinato, the simplicity of melodic material, and the five statements of the double period all contribute to the sense of morose energy and a swirling hypnotic effect.

There is a key signature in this piece: four sharps, but accidentals place the principal theme in C♯ major. The tonality remains very diatonically modal, though augmented octaves and other mild dissonances provided by the moving lines do occur in places. The climax is reached in the fourth statement of the period, where the melody is stated in chords over the most irregular of rhythmic patterns. The texture then thins out to a *pp* close.

The *Dança Negra* was premiered in São Paulo in 1946 by Lidia Simões. It was transcribed for orchestra by Guarnieri in 1947, published by Associated Music Publishers, and has been recorded numerous times. Guarnieri and this author have written manuscript copies of an arrangement of the piece for two pianos.

Acalanto. 1954.
[RB–1957]

The *acalanto* is a Brazilian lullaby that also exists in a more popular form as the *cantiga de ninar.* This particular piece was extracted in 1957 from the orchestral *Suite Centenário IV* for orchestra of 1954 that Guarnieri had written to observe the four hundredth anniversary of the founding of São Paulo. The orchestral suite had been commissioned by the Louisville Symphony Orchestra.

This piece has a two-line polyphonic texture with a simple, irregularly phrased melody over a two-measure left-hand ostinato based on A. It uses two treble clefs. Both melody and accompaniment begin pandiatonically, the left hand stressing quartal sounds in its ostinato, the right moving in A minor. The gradual introduction of chromatics in both parts and the widely spaced grace notes and cross-relations increase the tension between the two lines. Seconds, sevenths, and ninths occur frequently on the beats.

Em Memória de um Amigo
(In Memory of a Friend). 1972.
[Hans Gerig Köln–1978]

This 1972 piece, commissioned by pianist Caio Pagano in memory of his father, is an evocation of sadness. A single melodic line begins a gentle, circling movement, gradually moving into more angular skips of sevenths in keeping with the accompanimental sevenths, outlined by the quartal fragments in the left hand. The right-hand melody maintains a continuity above the left-hand fragments, which are occasionally punctuated with staccato single notes. The dissonant sevenths create a growing sound mass, leading to a climactic point where the melody is stated in octaves for a few bars, then increasing to ninths. After a *fff* climax, there is a return to the opening melody with a receding dynamic scheme which closes the piece with sevenths. Harmonically it is atonal; musically it is a poignant expression, both of emotion and of the distilled, intense style of the composer.

Fraternidade (Fraternity).
1973. Manuscript

This piece was composed in 1973 at the invitation of the Israeli government for the Arthur Rubenstein Competition. Because of the outbreak of war in the Mideast in 1973, however, the competition was postponed.

Guarnieri chose to use two themes: an original one of his own for the first section, and an Israeli melody for the middle section. The first section is relatively short, leading rather suddenly on the third page to the *Calmo* middle section in which is presented the Israeli thematic fragment. This builds to a grand climax. Beneath its final ringing chords, there enters a linear retransition to the *Tempo primo*. This final section gathers momentum through the use of octaves, and it finally culminates in an *ff* restatement of the Israeli theme in the final bars of the piece.

Saracoteio.
1978. Manuscript

The title means "Rambling," or "moving the buttocks as one dances," suggesting the delightful rhythmic quality of the work. This is a relatively long piece, seven full pages. It is unusual in that Guarnieri repeats a full thirty-five measures in the reexposition without alteration. The piece ends with a left-hand cluster of tones, indicated to be played with the fist. The piece, which remains unpublished, was premiered by Belkiss Carneiro de Mendonça of Goiânia in the Auditório de Escola de Música in Natal in 1978.

Ondeante (Undulating). 1981.
[RB–no. 19 of Volume 4 of the
Estudos–pending publication]

This is one of two pieces that Guarnieri decided in the late 1980s to insert into the final book of *Estudos*. His declining health suggested this as a way of completing the set of twenty studies. Thus *Ondeante,* composed in 1981, became *Estudo* no. 19, and another piece, *Saramba,* became no. 20.

The opening musical idea establishes a constant, gentle flow. Snatches of Brazilian syncopation continue to appear and disappear as Guarnieri explores the extreme ranges of the keyboard. Both the title ("Undulating, floating on water") and the *Tranquilo* indication suggest the gentleness of this piece, which involves both hands in its consistently undulating texture.

Toada Sentimental.
1982. Manuscript

This piece reflects again Guarnieri's early exposure to the folk forms of his native Tietê. Osvaldo Lacerda wrote the following in his notes for the 1985 recording of this piece:

> The two most important types of Brazilian song are the urban *modinha* and the rural *toada*. The latter exists throughout Brazil and reflects the musical characteristics of each region. The *toada* is from what is called the "Caipira Zone" in the states of both São Paulo and Minas Gerais and is one of the most captivating forms due to its quaint nostalgia, tenderness, and amorous sentiments. Camargo Guarnieri was born in Tietê where good music of rural

people was always cultivated, and he seems to have in his blood the spirit of the *toada,* so evident if one listens to many of his pieces which he wrote in this spirit, whether or not he actually called them *toadas.* This *Toada Sentimental,* written in 1982, is an excellent example of this genre, lifted here by Guarnieri to a high, artistic expression.[17]

This piece has the less commonly seen meter of $\frac{3}{2}$; most Brazilian music usually uses a duple meter, as does most of Guarnieri's music. It was completed on October 14, 1982, following the composition of two *Momentos.* This raises the question as to why Guarnieri would give it such an unusual title amid a group of pieces of very similar character. It might also have well been a *Ponteio,* but he called it *Toada Sentimental.* One suspects that his series of fifty *Ponteios* was complete, and as a group the *Momentos* are shorter musical statements. Perhaps it was the mood he was trying to clarify by the title. This piece was given its premiere by Cynthia Priolli in São Paulo in October 1983.

Saramba. 1982.
[RB–no. 20 of Volume 4 of the
Estudos–pending publication]

As with *Ondeante,* this 1982 piece was included as the last of the *Estudos.* Osvaldo Lacerda wrote:

> The *Delta-Larousse Grand Encyclopedia* defines *saramba* as "A species of percussive *fandango* generally danced by the Blacks, referring evidently to the *fandango* of the southern and southwestern Brazilians, not to the Spanish *fandango.*" The *Saramba* of Camargo Guarnieri was written in 1982, and, to my knowledge, is the only stylized example of this dance in our erudite music. Its choreographic character is emphasized by its obsessive and vigorous rhythms in both hands.[18]

With unabashedly Brazilian rhythms and typical Guarnieri energy, this piece is a triumph of joyful dynamism over any other mood in which Guarnieri may have indulged himself and his listeners. As suggested by Lacerda the piece fairly bristles with exuberance and excitement. Its ninety measures fly by.

SUITES FOR SOLO PIANO

Among Guarnieri's groups of pieces, there is one called a "suite," the *Suite Mirim* (Miniature Suite), and three other sets which could be considered suites: the *Cinco Peças Infantis* (Five Children's Pieces), *As Três Graças* (The Three Graces), and a *Série dos Curumins* (Series for Little Children), seven pieces for children. There is another very early work, the 1929 *Suite Infantil* (Children's Suite), which Guarnieri arranged in 1949 for piano solo from an orchestral piece, but it was never published or made available for performance. The *Cinco Peças Infantis* date from 1935, and the last of the *Série dos Curumins* were written in the 1970s. They are among his easier pieces, intended for children to play. Belkiss Carneiro noted of all these works:

> Even when composing easy pieces for children, Camargo Guarnieri uses a language which is not habitual for them. It gave him the opportunity to familiarize them with contemporary works, giving them a chance to know, very early, a new kind of composition as a foundation for future studies.[19]

In these works he challenged them to changing meters, polyphonic writing, and typical compositional techniques they would find in more difficult music as they progressed.

Suite Mirim
(Miniature Suite). 1953.
[BA–1955]

These charming pieces are all very Brazilian in their character and diminutive titles: *Ponteando* (Plucking), *Tanguinho* (Little Tango), *Modinha* (Little Song), *Cirandinha* (Little Round Dance). The word *mirim* in the Tupi dialect suggests "little," which explains the diminutive titles. All four movements are basically melodic, although their textures are very different from one another. The *Ponteando* is the most dissonant in its two-line texture, resembling in many ways several of the *Ponteios*. Harmonically and structurally, this piece is the simplest. The *Tanguinho* is probably the most accessible to non-Brazilian children, although its light "swing" feel is a challenge to maintain. It is essentially a two-line texture with a supple conjunct melody woven over a descending *samba* rhythmic pattern. The third is a dialogue of melodic fragments. The final movement is a cheerful children's song which makes use of the Mode of the Northeast with its raised fourth and lowered seventh degrees. Key signatures are not used, but each piece has a different tonal center. Although the four pieces constitute a well-integrated set, they can be performed individually.

Cinco Peças Infantis
(Five Children's Pieces). 1931–33.
[RB–1947 and RA]

This is an early set of five pieces for children, composed between 1931 and 1933. All use the G clef in both hands and afford the young pianist (in the second or third year according to the composer) some very sophisticated and expressive contemporary material. All the qualities which mark the larger, more complicated works of Guarnieri are present here in diminutive form. The fourth piece, *A Criança Adormece* (Sleeping Child), is an absolute gem, perhaps his most inspired piece for children. The expressive power achieved here with so few notes is exceptional. Andrade Muricy wrote of the set:

> Only the poets, musicians, and saints can revive the candor and imaginative freshness of the sons of men, as Kipling said. Music for children is really adult music, thought as children might, in a moment of pure contemplation. Camargo Guarnieri is a noble and virile artist, but in him there is the vigor of authentic youth. In these little pieces are hidden simple expressions, but dense in feeling, as is the *Criança Triste* [Sad Child]. . . and the most sensitive *A Criança Adormece* [Sleeping Child]. . . . These pieces truly reveal Guarnieri.[20]

João Itiberê da Cunha also wrote of these pieces shortly after they were published in São Paulo:

> With these pieces, Camargo Guarnieri has done a real service to teachers of piano who are looking for the best examples with which to start children in the study of a musical instrument. The *Cinco Peças Infantis* are truly delicate gifts. In the first, *Estudando Piano* [Studying Piano], the child learns all possible rhythms equally, without difficulty. The second contains a melancholic song—a sad *acalanto* [lullaby]. The third, *Valsinha Manhosa* [Clever Waltz], is delicious. The fourth is a tender *acalanto,* very well suited to habituate children with modern harmonization. The last *Polka* is joyful, and is of the dance genre which gives it its name.[21]

Guarnieri transcribed this set of pieces for string quartet in 1941, but it is not published in that form.

Série dos Curumins
(Series for Small Children). 1960–77.
[Irmãos Vitale–1977]

This series of seven pieces was written over a period of seventeen years from 1960 to 1977. All utilize only the treble clef in both hands, all are two-line textures, and each represents in miniature one of the folk forms common in Brazil, as suggested by their titles: *Brincando* (Playing), *Valsa, Flavinha, Valsinha Pretensiosa* (Pretentious Waltz), *Acalanto para Barbara, Valsinha* (Little Waltz), and *Dança da Pulga* (Dance for the Thumb). Their contrapuntal textures make them a challenge, even to a fairly good second- or third-year student. The series title *Curumins* suggests "servants" or perhaps useful pieces. Some of the pieces are dedicated to particular children.

As Três Graças
(The Three Graces). 1963, 1965, 1971.
[RB–1973]

Dedicated to Vera Silvia, mother of the "three graces," these pieces were composed on the birthdays of their three children—Tânia, Miriam, and Daniel Paulo—born of the marriage of Guarnieri and Vera Silvia. Like the other pieces that Guarnieri intended to be played by children, these three use only the treble clef in both hands. They are not among the most interesting pieces for children, and their contrapuntal two-line textures seem to provide more challenge than reward. However, what this particular set of pieces does reveal is the tenderness of the composer toward his three children.

The *Acalanto* for Tânia speaks of tenderness, simply, in a straightforward manner. The *Tanguinho* for Miriam is like a miniature Bach *Two Part Invention* in Brazilian style. Daniel Paulo's *Toada* offers a rocking rhythm to sustain a simple melody. These three pieces, slow-fast-slow, could be performed as a set or individually.

TEN *VALSAS* (WALTZES)

With the *Valsas* we enter the first category of pieces that Guarnieri conceived in groups. He intended to write ten waltzes, and that is what we have. The waltz is a very distinctive form of Brazilian music. Os Irmãos Tavares de Lima wrote in a newsletter put out by the publisher, Editor Vitale, that the European waltz had come to Brazil through the strong influence of Italian piano teachers between 1865 and 1870, although it had actually made an appearance as early as 1837.[22] It lent itself to an almost total transformation in Brazil into a nostalgic, expressive form, very much Brazilian and yet very distinct from other Brazilian forms. Mozart Araujo explains the development of the Brazilian waltz clearly:

> Guarnieri's ten waltzes do not reveal an intention to explore the popular character of the waltz. We see rather in them the desire to uncover the emotional character of a genre which has affected almost all of our national music.
>
> The Brazilianization of the waltz was a slow process, beginning about 1870. Its splendor and popularization happened between 1870 and 1940 approximately. During this period, whether looking at the quantity or quality, we find examples of all types of the Brazilian waltz: the slow salon waltz, the serenade type, in the waltzes of the serenaders, and those of the bands of musicians from the interior of the country.

The ethnic or national character, however, was not the most important element of these waltzes (of Guarnieri), as I noted above. Guarnieri was not content to leave an impression merely through the serenade or popular qualities of this typical Brazilian waltz, rather stressing first of all the emotional character of each which is evident in each of his expressive markings: *Lentamente, Preguicoso, Com moleza, Calmo e Saudoso, Choroso.* And in the midst of this interplay of sentiments and emotions arises the counterpoint through which the talent and sensitivity of Camargo Guarnieri were capable of revealing the entire history of our Brazilian waltz.

Many times I have said that I do not think Guarnieri is a nationalistic composer. I repeat once again that the Brazilian character of Guarnieri appears to come without his seeking it.[23]

Almost every Brazilian composer of the period between 1870 and 1940 has written in the waltz form, which developed such a distinctive character over the years. It has in common with the *modinha* a nostalgia which lifts it forever above any semblance of a dance movement. Guarnieri remembered hearing waltzes all his life, and that everybody played waltzes and *modinhas,* even in the remotest areas of the country. He said,

I think that the Brazilian waltz is characterized by a certain sadness. Generally all of these waltzes are in a minor tonality. I do not think there exists a waltz in major. Nowadays the waltzes seem out of date, but some years ago they were always played and were always in minor. They also had a two-part form. The first part was sad, and the second part moved a little more quickly. I do not remember seeing any Brazilian waltz in three parts: ABA.[24]

There are ten *Valsas* listed in Guarnieri's catalog of works. His very first composition, entitled *Sonho de Artista,* was a waltz, which perhaps gives weight to the power that this national form has had over his soul. The ten pieces, all published by Ricordi Brasileira, were written over a period of twenty-five years, which in itself is a curious fact for a composer who tends to cluster his works of one type. All are in ABA design and are in a minor tonality. The principal harmonic progressions associated with minor tonality form their harmonic structure. Many of the weaving lines are often excessively chromatic, making use of appoggiaturas and neighboring tone ornamentations.

Frequently an inner melody is shared by both hands. The lines often follow deviant paths. Combined with the general linear quality of the writing and the dissonances that occur, the total effect becomes one of longing, introspection, and less direct movement than is common in waltzes of other countries. Some feature a melody in the lower register to be played by the left-hand, recalling the *bordenejo* or lowest guitar string and the serenade types of music proper to the guitar. These pieces have definitely lost their dance character in favor of an idealized vehicle for a nostalgic, restless reflectiveness. They have been recorded by Belkiss Carneiro.

FIFTY *PONTEIOS* (PRELUDES)

If there is any one category of Guarnieri's piano music that might be considered representative of his "Brazilianism," the *Ponteios* would certainly qualify. Fifty pieces published in five books of ten each, composed over a period of almost thirty years (they were concluded in 1959), the *Ponteios* reflect not only the varied compositional techniques of the composer during those years but also, as Ayres de Andrade wrote, "the musical soul of the people."[25] Few of the *Ponteios* exceed two pages in length. Each is a well-integrated, perfectly structured musical expression that could only be Brazilian. Among them are found the intimate qualities of the *modinha* and *toada,* the simple children's *rodas,* the instrumental styles of the Caipira viola and violão, and the frenzied dances of African origin. These characteristic forms are never present literally, but, nonetheless, they breathe life into each of these brief pieces.

Of the title *Ponteio,* Guarnieri explained, "They are really preludes. They have a character that is clearly and definitely Brazilian. I thought it would be better to use a word other than 'prelude' to express this Brazilian character, so I wrote 'ponteio' and in parentheses 'preludio.'"[26] The word actually derives from the Portuguese *pontear,* which refers to the plucking technique used on the guitar. Guarnieri coined this use of the term. It has since been used by many other younger composers for pieces of a prelude or improvisatory character.

Gilbert Chase compared Guarnieri's *Ponteios* with the *Préludes* of Chopin. He wrote:

> There is the same concentrated variety of mood and expression, the same contrasts of lyrical tenderness and dramatic utterance, the same combination of harmonic subtlety and brilliant virtuosity. His music is intensely poetical, imaginative, emotional, full of that nostalgic quality which the Brazilians call "*saudades,*" and also possessing a large measure of the dramatic power and energy which one would expect from such a dynamic country as Brazil.[27]

With regard to the form of the *Ponteios,* Guarnieri explained that he considered nearly each of them to be monothematic with an exposition and then a reexposition.[28] Because of the irregular phrase structure, their varied lengths, the polyphonic textures, elisions, and chaining together of fragments, in many of them it is very difficult to distinguish if and where a middle section exists, or if, in fact, there is just a continuation of the principal material. Frequently a more active harmonic movement will herald the textural climax of the piece and then a reexposition of the theme. Moreover, the opening melody will often recur at the end of the *Ponteio* in the guise of a codetta. The brevity of most of the pieces also makes it impractical to speak in terms of a three-part form as such since each part may consist of only a few phrases. The point of form could perhaps be argued in some of the longer *Ponteios,* for example, nos. 32, 40, and 47. However, these three represent not the melodic *modinha* type, but a more aggressive type of figuration involving both hands, thus creating a more extended type of harmonic figuration that might be considered a middle section. Thus it would seem that the composer's explanation makes the most sense when considering the form of these pieces.

As to texture, it is impossible to find a "typical" *Ponteio* because of the great variety of textures that they represent: single-line melodies with ostinatos which may be linear or chordal, Schumannesque figuration with a melody within the texture, various kinds of accompaniments over or under rapid figurations, toccata-like interlocking chordal movement, chord streams running against flowing lines or other chord streams, rapid and fragmentary mirror writing of étude proportions, and mixed textures which occur in a call-response alternation. They also generally alternate in the collections between a slow and then a fast piece. Because they can be selected and grouped with great flexibility, this variety has contributed to

Ponteio #38

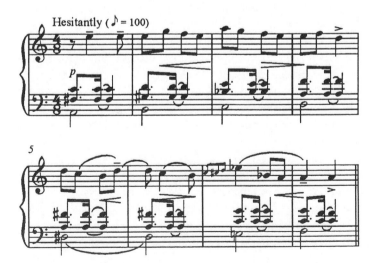

their great popularity in programming. *Ponteio* no. 38 is especially lovely. Its rhythmically supple melody seems to float freely over the gently pulsing accompaniment. Guarnieri follows Chopin's lead in beginning with harmonies that are already in motion, not on the tonic.

What all the *Ponteios* do have in common is what Francisco Curt Lange called "the internal rubato which is so frequently discerned in Brazilian works."[29] At times this is achieved through a subtle syncopation of a gentle melody over an accompaniment that maintains a rhythmic ostinato in its harmonically changing support. Frequently it is a direct result of cross-rhythms, polymeters, or hemiolas. The changing meters, seldom absent in Guarnieri's music, do not alter the basic rhythmic fabric appreciably, probably because of the linear texture and the phrase structure. Otto Deri gives two possible reasons for the use of changing meters: for purely rhythmic effects or for giving special inflection to a melody.[30] The second would more properly apply to Guarnieri. These changing meters do not interrupt the flow of the texture in any way. They are usually less discernible to the listener as a rhythmic characteristic than is the constant syncopation.

The relationship between the harmonic rhythm and the general tension embodied in these pieces is significant. The melodic *Ponteios* generally follow a pattern of little-to-more-to-less harmonic activity. The more stable harmonic sections utilize a pedal point which gradually begins to move, or they may begin with conjunct bass movement which slowly increases its intervallic progressions. An example of the latter type is again *Ponteio* no. 38. Bass movement by fourths illustrates the natural, expected flow of the harmony through large sections of Guarnieri's writing in these pieces. This occurs particularly at cadential points and in the middle section of the piece, where fragments of the theme are developed sequentially, thus achieving a greater sense of movement through the more active bass line.

Ponteio no. 31 illustrates several compositional techniques. The stability provided by a pedal point in the exposition offers a chance for an enriched harmonization on the return of the material. This is what Edward Cone refers to as "apotheosis: a special kind of recapitulation that reveals unexpected harmonic richness and textural excitement in a theme previously presented with a deliberately restricted harmonization and a relatively drab accompaniment."[31]

The *Ponteios* reflect a harmonic language that includes almost pure extended triadic harmony through chromaticism and bitonality to a form of atonalism, though Guarnieri's later works are more clearly atonal. Contrary to what one might expect, the thirty-year span does not show a preference for one or another language at any given time. Each volume will reveal examples of all of them. If there is any change at all in the course of the five volumes, it is toward a greater simplicity of texture, which in turn has its effects upon the harmonic density. For example, the first volume alternates with exact regularity the soft-slow with loud-fast pieces. The latter category in each represents harmonic language that uses strong dissonances, through either bitonality or strongly chromatic writing. In contrast, the slower pieces are more oriented toward extended tertian sonorities with chromatic inflections. Volumes 2, 3, and 5 seem to show a greater preference for the slower type of piece, which, in the last volume, leans toward greater chromaticism.

In virtually all of Guarnieri's *Ponteios* there is an ambivalence of tonal orientation, adding to the nostalgic mood that is characteristic of so many of them. This ambivalence is achieved in a number of ways. Seldom do even the most tonally oriented pieces begin on the tonic, with the result that there is an inherent suppleness from the very beginning. If the accompaniment is some type of linear or chordal ostinato, the chromatic inflections that alter it from measure to measure extend this sense of indecisiveness of tonality. In some cases the melody may be the sole vehicle of tonal orientation and may be somewhat vacillating because of chromatic nuances. What Ludmila Ulehla wrote concerning contemporary harmony and contrapuntal textures is well exemplified in many of the *Ponteios*: "Linear tonality replaces the all encompassing harmonic tonality of the former musical periods."[32] She writes further:

> Many of the indecisive intervallic structures are controlled by a melody line that has a degree of linear tonality. This overall tonal suggestion may be present within a motive or during a phrase. It is prompted by the stronger intervals that suggest linear roots. If the harmony below the melody tones is indeterminate, the melody itself may guide the whole movement of sound. In this respect, it suggests a shifting of the role of harmonic provider away from the bass and toward the melody.[33]

The choice of harmonic language itself may be purposely ambiguous. For example, the prevalence of quartal structures immediately dilutes harmonic exactness. Bitonality, whether linear or chordal, likewise poses an aural question. Cross-relations within vertical structures or moving lines may raise the question of mode. Finally, the independence of linear harmonic suggestion, which may or may not concur with that of its accompanying line, frequently makes vertical harmonic identification both difficult and impractical.

To consider harmony apart from the dynamics, tempo, and general tension of a piece would be to produce an incomplete picture. For example, one would only have to compare *Ponteios* nos. 12 and 14 to realize that textures that appear similar to the eye can be very different to the ear. Both of these pieces employ sixteenth-note figurations in the right hand harmonically foreign to the left-hand activity. In no. 12, however, the right hand constitutes the principal part and enters *decidido, f* in a rapid, bristling tempo. In no. 14 the figuration is accompanimental and is completely subdued over the *cantando* melody of the left hand, providing merely a suggestion of atmosphere, though it is strongly bitonal in relation to the melody. On the other hand, a toccata-like piece such as no. 47 sounds much more strident than the bitonality of no. 14, even though it uses only a root-fifth-octave melody sequence for the most part. The difference in this case is due to the rapidly changing harmonic rhythm, dynamics, and tempo.

In well over half of the *Ponteios,* the characteristics and elements already noted are subordinated to the melody. It is probable that Mário de Andrade would be willing to apply to the *Ponteios* what he wrote in reference to Guarnieri's songs in 1940: "Through their expressive force, their complete assimilation of popular elements, the originality of the polyphonic accompaniment and the beauty of the melodies, the songs of Camargo Guarnieri are his best contribution to Brazilian music."[34]

These melodic *Ponteios* embody the spirit of the *modinha.* Like the nostalgic Brazilian waltz with which it has so much in common, the *modinha* is almost always in minor. Guarnieri claimed that he had never seen a *modinha* in major. Unlike the waltz, however, it is in duple time. The changing meters do not appreciably alter the metrical preference for duple time.

The phrases normally begin in regular lengths of two or four measures, and then gradually develop into chains of shorter fragments, frequently sequential in treatment. Their suppliant quality dictates a preference for conjunct movement and a descending direction. Occasional use of grace notes is suggestive of the vocal inflections of much folk music.

Subtle chromatic nuances keep simple lines from sounding banal or expected (nos. 31 and 33 are good examples). As indicated earlier, the principal melodic idea returns for a reexposition, although the intervening material is most often an extension or fragmentary development of the main theme rather than new material.

Many of the melodies are modal in their orientation, although the chromatic nuances modify the modes as well as the major or minor tonalities in which they may be written. The modes most often used are the Dorian, Lydian, Mixolydian, and the Mode of the Northeast.

The more agitated *Ponteios* in which the melodies are not of the song accompaniment type are more angular and lie within right-hand chordal patterns, as would be expected. At times they begin in single lines, broadening into octaves or chords at more climactic sections. In all cases they are rhythmically free, proceeding with a suppleness like that of more simple *modinha* types.

All of the aspects discussed—form, harmony, melody, texture, harmonic rhythms—must be considered in each *Ponteio,* because no one aspect can give an adequate picture of the piece or the composer's style of writing. To the degree that each element is integrated into the fabric of a particular piece, the inner tension will be more or less fluid.

One cannot live with these pieces very long without responding to their balance, beauty, and power of evocation. Each is exquisitely crafted. Ayres de Andrade summarized all of these qualities:

> They would be simple piano preludes without major pretensions if they were not individualized and made valuable by a musical content which represents the varied aspects of Brazilian life. Other factors which make these pieces so valuable are their intensity of emotion and the versatility of their stylistic treatment. These *Ponteios* of Camargo Guarnieri form a vast and wonderful musical anthology of the regional expressions of Brazilians, raised to the level of artistic communication.[35]

The *Ponteios* have been the object of several doctoral research projects. One study was completed by Ney Fialkow, who summarized his insights in this way:

> [The *Ponteios*] stand as a fundamental contribution to the repertoire of today, and probably will continue to do so in the future, for several reasons: for the insights they provide into the Brazilian popular music practices of the early and mid–twentieth century; for the comprehensive character of their pianistic language; for the abstract and intellectual exercise they provide; and merely, perhaps mostly, for the sheer musical enjoyment that they offer.[36]

The *Ponteios* have been recorded in their entirety by both Isabel Mourão and Lais de Souza Brasil. Many individual *Ponteios* can also be found in other recorded collections. They are among Guarnieri's loveliest and most approachable works. One memorable hearing of these pieces occurred when Guarnieri and Vera Silvia visited Milwaukee in 1970. After dinner with friends one evening, we sat and listened to all fifty *Ponteios*. It was a wonderful experience, to listen and to see Guarnieri as he listened to each of them, something he said he had never done before. It was as if each recalled a precious memory of his long, productive life.

TWENTY *ESTUDOS* (STUDIES)

With the *Estudos* we enter a completely different realm of Guarnieri's music for solo piano. As a musical form, the étude has always provided the performer with the challenge of conquering a particular technical problem and ideally challenged the composer to infuse musical worth within the technical setting. Guarnieri has managed to do both in his set of twenty studies. The *Estudos* span forty years of Guarnieri's later life, a few of them among his final works. Again, they represent his penchant for writing groups of pieces. Three volumes of five *Estudos* each are available from Ricordi Brasileira; the fourth volume, nos. 16–20, is pending publication.

It is interesting to note that the first *Estudo* was composed in 1949, the year before Guarnieri wrote his famous *Open Letter* to Brazilian musicians. While his letter was written in defense of a truly Brazilian music, this first study is in no way related to any particular folkloric elements. It is, however, a distilled essence of everything Brazilian in its vitality and complexity, expressed through two very articulate lines which explore the entire range of the keyboard at very high speed. One wonders if he purposely attempted to move into a more "modern" mode of expression in this piece.

Estudo No. 1

The right hand maintains a constant flow of sixteenth notes. The angular design of its figuration involves the contraction and expansion of the hand as the pattern moves through the upper half of the keyboard. The left-hand accompaniment runs in regular eighth notes in a staccato line that falls into groups of three notes, causing the first of the group to touch at various rhythmic points in successive measures. Intervals of fourths and fifths predominate in both hands, and the independence of the two parts creates a fairly dissonant counterpoint. It strikes one as a perfect musical description of the seeming chaos, yet the ultimate organization of our cosmos, thus a musically prophetic statement of sorts.

Of the second *Estudo,* Frederick Moyer noted:

> It is a dramatic, extremely difficult piece in which the accompanying hand constantly spans the interval of a minor 9th. This piece is an incredible mental as well as physical challenge. The pianist not only has to play eight notes to the beat in one hand and three in the other, but the hand playing eight must syncopate in irregular groups of three's and two's. The left hand is sprinkled with extremely wide, rolled chords, sometimes reaching as far as three octaves.[37]

Estudo no. 4 is essentially a right-hand octave study, while no. 5 requires legato double notes in the right hand and a staccato left-hand accompaniment. If there is such a thing as a "Brazilian cakewalk," this is it. Number 6 presents a vigorous angular line duplicated by the hands two octaves apart. *Estudo* no. 7 is a gentler piece with cross-rhythms, suggestive of three contrasting meters.

Estudo no. 7

Number 13 is subtitled "Homenagem à Claude Debussy" and exploits *pianissimo* atonal and impressionistic sonorities. Frederick Moyer described no. 18, a study for the left hand alone, as "moving into the heart of sadness."[38] The last two are the pieces that Guarnieri incorporated as studies to complete the set of twenty: no. 19, *Ondeante,* and no. 20, *Saramba,* as indicated earlier.

Each of these pieces is of transcendental difficulty and a formidable challenge to any pianist. Most of them have polyphonic textures and a free, often atonal, language. They employ dissonant quartal configurations of chords or patterns that demand rapid hand contraction and expansion, frequently with the two hands pursuing independent directions of high rhythmic independence and vitality. Most of them are in rapid tempos and require forceful dynamics. Changing meters and irregular rhythmic groups are the norm. All maintain rigid continuity of technical device, challenging the pianist's endurance capabilities. They are definitely not material for the casual performer.

Their form is tripart, with the exception of nos. 6 and 8, which utilize an ABABA rondo form, and no. 7, which is in two parts. In nos. 3, 4, and 15, the middle section consists of an exchange of material between the two hands. Quartal sonorities predominate in many of these pieces. They reflect the kinds of harmonies and textures that appear in other piano pieces from this period of Guarnieri's life, the later sonatinas and the sonata.

The *Estudos* of Camargo Guarnieri deserve a wider audience than they generally receive, both within and outside Brazil. A 1997 recording of the complete set by Frederick Moyer (Jupiter Recordings, Lee, N.H.) is a major contribution to international piano literature. Within Brazil they frequently appear on required lists for competitions. For example, in the 1970 Piano Contest held in Santos, Brazil, a selection from the first two volumes was required a *habilite prova* for entrance. Music critic Maria Abreu has written of the pieces:

> The studies of Camargo Guarnieri, as those of Chopin, present problems of transcendental difficulty in artistic form; those of Guarnieri are the pianistic epitome of his works. There is nothing more complex or virtuosic in the range of Brazilian music than these studies. They should be recorded for their musical beauty as well as pedagogical value.[39]

Thanks to Frederick Moyer, these *Estudos* now have been recorded.

EIGHT SONATINAS
AND SONATA

Osvaldo Lacerda wrote, "There are actually nine sonatas for piano, although only one is called 'sonata;' the other eight are called 'sonatinas.' This diminutive term refers only to their length and their expressive power; their originality and compositional technique are the same as is evident in the Sonata."[40] Guarnieri himself liked to view these works as tracing his musical development, and well they do, since it was his First Sonatina that placed him decisively in the public eye. The Eighth is dated 1983 and reveals the dissonance and atonalism that came to mark his later works. All follow the three-movement design, beginning with the sonata-allegro form in which the composer was very much at home.

The first five sonatinas were performed at a concert at the São Paulo Discotec on March 5, 1964. The Second and Third are written entirely in the treble clef. The composer's slow movements are extremely intense, nearly bursting their bonds of pathos and feeling. The closing movements reveal textures similar to those found in the studies and some of the *Ponteios*. The Third and Sixth utilize fugues for final movements.

All of these pieces are published. They are frequently performed and several have been recorded. Sonatinas nos. 3, 4, and 6 are also published in the United States, making them accessible to North American performers. In this medium, so natural to the composer, he shows his ability to wed native content with classical form in an eminent degree.

Sonatina no. 1. 1928.
[Chiarato–1929; RB–1958]

Composed in 1928, this piece was dedicated by Guarnieri to his new mentor, Mário de Andrade. Andrade had publicly extolled the young composer at the publication of his *Dança Brasileira,* but other composers before him had used the dance forms. It was his successful utilization of the traditional sonata-allegro form for national content that sounded the signal for a new stage in the development of Brazilian music.

Much later Eurico Nogueira França noted that "The music of Camargo Guarnieri is characterized in the instrumental field by a species of happy compromise which he obtains between the great universal forms and native content."[41] This fact was not lost on the musicians of São Paulo in 1929 with the publication of the Sonatina no. 1. It prompted enthusiastic articles from both of his teachers, Andrade and Sá Pereira. Sá Pereira wrote:

> It was written a year ago (a year to be noted in the development of an artist who is evolving very rapidly), and it represents traces most characteristic of the author. That which commands and draws attention in the music of Camargo Guarnieri is the strong Brazilian atmosphere which he evokes. It is the power of localizing the listener geographically and placing him, whether he wants it or not, directly in the middle of Brazil. Instinctively and not by calculation, he has become a national composer, ignoring that which is justly a tendency in all other countries.[42]

Sá Pereira gave much credit for Guarnieri's development to Professor Lamberto Baldi, who, although being Italian, did not impose his own spirit on Guarnieri. Rather, he inspired him to search for his own style and language, thus supporting his national tendencies. Andrade also noted the great speed with which the young composer was developing, as evidenced in this work:

> One of the censures which has been made orally is that Camargo Guarnieri is moving too fast. I have the pleasure of converting this censure into a eulogy. In fact, Camargo Guarnieri is going very fast. When I celebrated the appearance of his *Dança Brasileira* last year, things were going so well, but I did not imagine that he would accomplish these things so soon. The Sonatina will take its place among the illustrious pieces of our national pianistic repertoire. It is structured beautifully with a lyricism that possesses a legitimate musical imagination, written by a patient artist who knows his business.[43]

Not only the use of folk forms, but Portuguese musical indications as well served as a type of musical manifesto for the young composer. Mozart Araujo referred to it as "forcing the note of his deliberate nationalism" and noted that it took even Andrade by surprise:

> This first Sonatina certainly received more publicity than any of the following. It foreshadowed his inclination toward traditional forms, the very distinctive chromatic nuances in gently moving lines, the beauty of feeling for the *modinha,* the ostinato-type accompaniments which so often form a peaceful basis for his melodies, the solid pianistic technique and passages that lie so well under the hands, and the rhythmic life which marks all of his music. It reveals both a mastery and a simplicity, and thus, a certain degree of maturity. This first work is not experimental by any means; it shows the basis from which the young composer will build his succeeding works in this form. It is one of his few works which does not use changing meters.[44]

The titles of the three movements suggest their Brazilian flavor: *Molengamente, Ponteando e bem dengoso,* and *Bem depressa, muito rhythmado e marcado.* The first is in sonata-allegro form, the second and third in ABA form. At the bottom of the page in the second movement, Guarnieri indicates the source of his thought: "The counter-melodic phrases should imitate the *bordenejo* of the violão." The third movement has a very vital, bristling texture in toccata style with hands interlocking in fifths, and later thirds, and with a rapid melody riding atop the figuration. The harmonic structures are primarily seventh chords, the entire effect one of brilliant, scintillating rhythm. Andrade wrote of this movement: "The Sonatina finishes with a dance, a piece of virtuosity which does not lose anything of its intrinsic dynamism and frank *batuque* theme."[45] This sonatina sent a strong message to Guarnieri's observers.

Sonatina no. 2. 1934.
[RB–1973]

Six years intervened before his next sonatina, an experimental work in which Guarnieri claimed that he was moving from a period of atonal experimentation into a nontonal style of writing. Dating from 1934, the piece was not published for almost thirty years. At its premiere in Rio de Janeiro in April 1941, Andrade Muricy wrote:

> This Second Sonatina is separated from the first by an abyss. The *toada* of the middle movement is sung as if by a serenader, as in the first work, but in a terrible and distant aesthetic climate. In this work the tonal color is white, neutral, frozen like a lunar landscape. All of its musicality is as if it is under a hard crystal and subdued. Secular habits of hearing congeal the movement between it and us. All of our auditory preconceptions are seized, stiff, hostile before the emotion which appears disguised, dissimulated and which we judge to be his perpetual worry with dissonance."[46]

Another writer was also obviously disturbed by the piece: "At first I resolved not to take notice of the Second Sonatina of Camargo Guarnieri because the only comprehensible thing about it is its division into movements: *Alegre con graça* (or without grace!), *Ingenuamente,* and *Depressa espiritoso.*"[47] Still another anonymous reviewer was less drastic in his comments: "The Second Sonatina seems like an experimental one to me, for in it we see a Guarnieri managing formulas and recipes in a laboratory which is of little help in the evolution of his artistic talent."[48] These comments seem almost amusing because the piece is a very charming work according to today's standards.

One must consider the contrast between these first two sonatinas in light of Guarnieri's life between 1928 and 1934. These were the years of the Constitutional Revolution under Getúlio Vargas. Guarnieri did not have regular employment and spent many hours of uninterrupted study, analyzing the scores of Stravinsky, Hindemith, Berg, and other composers, all of which are reflected in the more stringent language and intellectual quality of the latter piece. Nonetheless, despite the relative harmonic harshness, the first and third movements have a genial gaiety that one would not expect at a first approach to the piece.

All three movements are written completely in the treble clef, and all utilize ostinato patterns. Both hands have single lines except for the second movement, where a third line is added to the right-hand texture. Melodies are concentrated in their range and have in common their descending directions. They are in harmonic conflict with their ostinato accompaniments and provide fairly dissonant linear results. As in Bach's fugues, the re-peated-note type of theme is contrasted with the flowing line in the open-ing movement's first theme. The entire piece gives one the sense of com-pactness.

Sonatina no. 3. 1937.
[AMP–1945 and RB–1969]

This work was published both in Brazil and in the United States. Associated Music Publishers added the subtitle "In the G Clef" because the writing for both hands uses this clef, as does the preceding Sonatina no. 2. It is a com-pletely youthful, diatonic piece representing a deliberate return from the chromatic "nontonal" writing of its predecessor. This could have something to do with the fact that it was "practice writing" for a contest he planned to enter, one which held the prize of a scholarship to study in Europe. He would not have wanted to jeopardize his chances of winning it by an entry that may have offended the judges. It was not Guarnieri's favorite piece, but he could never say why, though he noted its classical spirit and clear form.

The piece seems to have pleased Itiberê da Cunha, who had reacted so violently to the Second Sonatina that appeared on this same 1941 program. He wrote, "This Third Sonatina happily is of another species, understand-able, full of good folklore and the pleasant aroma of the *modinhas,* spirited in its movement and curious in the fugue with its theme, so cheerful and well-written, without becoming unbalanced."[49]

Once again, the first movement uses sonata-allegro form, and its second theme is one of the rare uses Guarnieri makes of an actual folk melody, *O Cego* (The Blind Man), from northeastern Brazil and constructed in the Ly-dian mode with its raised fourth degree. The second movement breathes the spirit of the *modinha,* and the last is a fully developed two-part fugue, opening on the F major seventh chord that closed the first movement. The left hand leads, followed by the right, maintaining its two-voiced texture to the end. It is spirited, playful, full of surprises, and completely delightful to hear. The final nine-measure coda finds the original theme in the right hand and an augmented version of it in the left. It ends energetically with a joyful close to a very cheerful work.

Sonatina no. 4. 1958.
[AMP–1973 and RB–1977]

Twenty years intervened between the Third Sonatina and the Fourth, writ-ten in 1958 and published in 1973 by Associated Music Publishers, New York. Though it is also playful and spirited, this later work reveals a greater maturity of writing in its technical challenges, particularly in the outer movements, and a greater simplicity in the slow movement.

The Fourth Sonatina is a completely delightful piece, basically tonal with some rather pungent bitonality characterizing the final movement resulting from superimposed triadic structures. Modal melodies are prominent in the first and last movements. Each of the three movements is constructed economically and follows respectively the traditional sonata-allegro, ABA, and rondo forms. The themes themselves, restricted to very small hand spans of five fingers, require facility of the performer but seldom forceful dynamics. Patterns are developed sequentially.

The first movement requires a tight-handed approach and much rhythmic precision. It utilizes the outer fingers of the right hand in its short, falling, sequentially developed phrases. The strong Lydian quality of the first theme creates an ambivalence of tonal orientation, which pervades the entire movement. The chromatic changes, changing meters, and a certain harmonic vagueness all combine to give the second theme an extremely delicate gentleness and nostalgia. Caio Pagano noted that "The second theme is much in the *caipira* [hillbilly] style of improvisation."[50] Guarnieri's use of Paulistan thirds here seems to have reached a new level of subtlety, enhanced by the harmonic ambivalence and the freedom of the rhythmic and metric textures.

Sonatina no. 4
1st movement

This second movement, *Melancólico,* is a very delicate *modinha* and one of the tenderest slow movements among this group of pieces. Its single-line melody is set over a thin accompaniment line of short descending groups of notes. A middle section becomes slightly more expansive before the principal melody returns. The entire effect is one of supple fluidity and strong *saudades* (longing). It is a gem among the composer's short pieces for piano.

The final movement is playful from beginning to end. The hand patterns are again small in the principal theme, and the bitonality which they represent is quite concentrated. The movement develops into an ABA-C-ABA rondo form, with the B section having a gentle *samba* suggestion, and the C section almost archaic with open fifths creating a tambor effect under a rigid tune. Belkiss Carneiro noted that this theme has the rhythm of the *baião.*[51] As in the first movement, the flow of notes never ceases, and thus creates an excitement and exuberance within its delicate texture.

This Fourth Sonatina is a very joyful work, delicate in one way and pungently playful in another. Technically it is not an easy piece with its constant flow of notes within restricted patterns. It certainly reflects the personal joyfulness which one finds in Guarnieri's personality. The Brazilian elements are well represented in its content: Paulistan thirds, the even flow of sixteenth notes, *samba* rhythms, the *modinha,* and use of the modes. It is a work that should be heard more often.

Sonatina no. 5. 1962.
[RB–1962]

This work was composed as a required piece for the 1962 Radio Eldorado Piano Competition and was published the same year by Ricordi Brasileira for this purpose. Guarnieri was a member of the jury for this event, so he heard a number of performances of the piece that year.

It is very different from the preceding compositions in this genre. It is more linear, leaner, and more dissonant. Its texture is of almost classical transparency, and it marks a new level of tautness and stringency. The first movement, *Com Humor,* is in sonata-allegro form. Belkiss Carneiro observed both the strong feeling of the Northeast in the opening theme, which rises on its Mixolydian arpeggio, and its playful character:

> In the development, the composer plays with the elements of the first movement. He begins with the second theme, modifying it, making a little canon with parts of the first theme, creating a new design, constructing a descending line leading to the second theme which is impatient, agitated, and which finally arrives at the reexposition.[52]

Carneiro also quoted American pianist Eugene List after he heard Joseph Battista perform the lovely second movement: "Never has so much music been written with so few notes!"[53] This movement, *Muito calmo,* is a mere sixteen measures long and strongly recalls the *modinha* movement of Guarnieri's First Sonatina in its texture and feeling. The final *Com alegria—*

con spirito is in ABACAC form. Its excited, and exciting, material is well integrated into a continuous flow of sound. This is another charming work.

Sonatina no. 6. 1965.
[AMP–1973 and RB]

This sonatina marks a new phase in Guarnieri's emotional intensity. He seems to have crossed over some barrier, not only in this piece, but also in the *Estudos* nos. 8 and 9, which predate this work by three years, and in *Estudos* nos. 14 and 15, of 1969 and 1970, respectively. In a sense this piece grew up chronologically in the midst of the studies and shares their quartal language, as well as the way angular motives are structured and then blended into longer, restless lines.

In contrast to the classical texture of Sonatina no. 5, this piece combines thicker textures with stringency of language very similar to that of the *Sequência, Coral e Ricercare* for chamber orchestra that followed the sonatina by one year. One is tempted to recall some of Beethoven's later compositions in which there is a sense that perhaps the message is too powerful for the medium. This results in a certain understatement, control, and reserve, most evident in the second movement of this work. In the opening movement it can be sensed in the fragmentary character of the principal theme and the density that Guarnieri achieves by his concentration of these fragments. Perhaps most surprising, however, is to hear a pianist like Caio Pagano, to whom the work was dedicated, sensitively re-create the delicate opening page. Here the angular appearance of the lines belies the auditory experience of their suppleness. The last movement shows a forcefulness born of disciplined strength.

In 1938 Enio Squeff wrote in the jacket notes for a recording of the piece by Caio Pagano:

> This composer has persisted in leading us in ways characterized as nationalistic. But the "national" character of this Sixth Sonatina, written in 1965, causes one to think that in the polytonal counterpoint the ideological process of other times has given way to a complex texture where the fashionable *choro* is undeniable in the first movement (even to the accentuation in the second group of eighth notes), and nothing is more explicit than this! Abandoning the primary principal in the end for virtual nationalism, the national is here permeated with the universals of contemporary music.[54]

This is a major work in every respect, actually a sonata in length and seriousness of content. It represents some of the most advanced thinking of the composer to date. After the premiere of this sonatina in Rio de Janeiro in 1968, Ayres de Andrade wrote:

The Sixth Sonatina received its baptism in a *carioca* auditorium. It is a work which enjoys a prefect equilibrium of form and great unity in the sequence of its three movements. In the fugue which constitutes its last movement, there is a complexity of structure which the composer develops at times, but it does not constitute an obstacle to his spontaneous expression.[55]

What is of particular interest in this work is the way in which Guarnieri maintains his dissonance levels in the three movements. The first actually begins very graciously, gradually becoming more intense, and its fragmented lines and their contrapuntal treatment result in a high level of dissonance. The second movement, almost immobile, relies upon the crossrelations of its distantly placed thirds and tenths to create another kind of atonality. The driving dissonant counterpoint which marks the final fugue uses longer lines and maintains a uniform degree of atonality.

In each of these three movements, the textural and harmonic tensions are interdependent upon each other. In this work as in the studies, one no longer looks for or speaks of the *modinha* or the *samba;* yet their syncopations and rhythmic life are present. In this sonatina Guarnieri has come to a new level of musical speech, and repeated hearings constantly reveal new aspects.

Sonatina no. 7. 1971.
[RB–1978]

The seventh work in this genre was completed on December 5, 1971. It has been neither published nor recorded to date, but continues the compositional direction set by the previous sonatina. It has three movements, the first two of which are very intensely atonal. The third seems, to the eye, to return to the toccata style found in several of the *Ponteios,* a texture maintained without reprieve through the entire movement, which offers a severe challenge to even the most able pianist. As with the preceding work, it is really a sonata in content and import.

The first movement, *Ritmico e Energico, ff,* does not seem to follow the typical sonata-allegro form, but it is difficult to be certain because of the way Guarnieri develops his material. One might consider it an arch form with the themes exchanging places in the recapitulation: AB-Dev-BA. It is a driving, intense and brittle texture with no relief from its *ff* opening to its *fff* close. Quartal chords, both harmonic and melodic, almost force a fragmented texture since the pianist's hand cannot negotiate passages that are much more sustained or continuous. Belkiss Carneiro said of this movement, "It maintains a crescendo of emotional tensions, not with heavy depression, rather with a shout of passionate victory, which is present from the opening five notes, played two octaves apart, and which constitute the principal element of the first theme."[56]

The second movement, *Suavamente, pp,* is another of Guarnieri's almost suspended, immobile movements that fairly hangs in space. The principal theme is in the left hand and is a single intense line marked by both skips and half-step movement. The total effect is one of high dissonance, even within the very soft dynamic level and the slow movement of the lines.

The final *Requebrado* might suggest a gentle rhythm, but this closing movement of Sonatina no. 7 is anything but that. It is every bit as biting, technically demanding, and brittle as the first. Again the composer seems to be expressing something that virtually breaks the bonds of the form and medium. It is one of his most tour de force movements.

Sonata for Piano. 1972.
[Irmãos Vitale–2004]

In Guarnieri's mind, this work stood in a class apart. It was the first time in his then sixty-five years, with a large catalog of over six hundred pieces, that the composer created a piano piece which he entitled "sonata." As indicated earlier, his eight sonatinas could well be considered sonatas in their scope and difficulty level. However, Guarnieri himself thought differently. He was never satisfied that the character of the thematic material, particularly of the fifth, sixth, and seventh sonatinas, was substantial enough to warrant the name "sonata," though they are expansive enough and follow the sonata-allegro design. Belkiss Carneiro, who recorded the piece, wrote:

> The sonata is considered by many to be a monumental work in pianistic repertoire. Composed in record time, between the sixteenth and twenty-fifth of December, it constitutes the apex of the creative development of the composer, represented through the magnificence and balance of its form.[57]

In a June 1973 interview with Acyr Castro, Guarnieri revealed that he had dedicated this piece to Lamberto Baldi, the beloved teacher of his youth,[58] but the manuscript actually carries a dedication to pianist Lais de Souza Brasil. Baldi's memory seemed to call out of Guarnieri his best efforts, and the intention to dedicate this piece to him seemed to say that he had finally written a work worthy of this genre and of his teacher.

Guarnieri considered this sonata to be a synthesis of forty-four years of artistic life. In contrast to the eight sonatinas, this sonata perhaps gives even more evidence of breaking the bonds of a form through the intensity of its emotional expression. The first movement has many very lengthy measures of $\frac{5}{4}$ and $\frac{3}{2}$ which give the visual impression of complexity and rhythmic freedom. Likewise, themes recur in octaves, sometimes in double octaves, which suggest weight and intensity of content. In addition, all themes are drawn from one motivic source, making it monothematic.

Lais de Souza Brasil suggested to Guarnieri that the sonata is, in reality, a tonal painting of his own life; the composer agreed.[59] Though creative work will often reflect the personality of the creator, this work in particular seems to imbibe the great intensity of the man, the *amargurado* (bitterness) which continued to reveal the deepest regions of a very complex, intense, keen, and sensitive personality. There is no question that it is a major work, a landmark in Guarnieri's creative life.

There is a visible development of style from the Sonatina no. 5 to this work. One finds an increasing stringency, both in melodic phrases and in the structural forms themselves. The quartal chords of the Fourth Sonatina are still present, but when superimposed upon quintal harmonies a semitone apart, a greater density of texture results. More and more, harmony begins to serve a percussive function. In this work melodic fragments are angular and abrupt rather than soaring. This combination of fragmented, angular ideas and dense harmonic material gives the two outer movements a sense of energy, aggressiveness, and thrust which was becoming apparent in the Sonatina no. 6. The slow second movement loses none of the intensity; it moves with a latent explosiveness which erupts several times.

Guarnieri wrote the slow movement first, completing it on November 10, 1972. The first movement bears the date December 16, and the final movement is dated Christmas, 1972. The sonata received its premiere by Lais de Souza Brasil in Goiânia in May 1973, with subsequent performances within the month in both Santos and São Paulo. After the São Paulo performance on June 30, 1973, Caldeira Filho wrote:

Sonata
1st movement

The sonata of Guarnieri is monothematic; that is, the opening passage which traditionally has two themes (with exposition, development, and re-capitulation in classic form) uses only one theme. Actually, in the music of today, what is the technical or aesthetic need to present two themes and then re-present them again? Guarnieri fuses their expressive characteristics and develops his own one theme. The unity is compensated through the partial and successive development of parts, made possible through its aesthetic and structural richness. For this reason, someone commented after hearing the piece that Guarnieri's monothematic technique develops two themes. All is in this initial movement: a series of violent moments, created and characterized by the internal tension of the generating musical cell.[60]

If one could say only one thing about the first movement, *Tenso*, it would be that Guarnieri surely and powerfully expressed his intent. It has the sense of impulsiveness with a clear direction. To quote Caldeira Filho again:

The theme is concise, an energetic nucleus whose forces the composer can expand in a feeling structure that is very clear and involved with intense emotion. This game of movement—ascending, descending, successive, simultaneous—proceeds with a rich show of ideas, with eloquence, vivacity, and force. The reexposition is short, corresponding to the short theme. From another point of view, the linear directions reveal the aesthetic foundations of the sonata. The ascending impulse of the initial theme is met with the simultaneous opposition of the descending design in the left hand, an opposition which immediately effects a spirit which is indicated by the title of the movement. Even with one motive, such opposition appears essential to its aesthetics.[61]

One can safely say that the theme of the second movement is a transformation of the material of the first movement, if not of the theme itself. Caldeira Filho considers this *Amargurado* theme to be a second, contrasting idea. However, it is created out of the same intervals—fifths which turn back in seconds—thus making it difficult to distinguish its distinctiveness. What matters is the level of expressive intensity that Guarnieri has achieved in this movement. To cite Filho again:

Monothematicism is normal in slow passages of a sonata. Guarnieri uses a second, contrasting theme in his *Amargurado* which assumes richness and varied figurations. Not withstanding the double melodic message it gives, it is at once both violent and melancholic, arousing the listener, for bitterness in only one part.

How could one speak of the pianism of Guarnieri and his most intelligent interpreter, Lais de Sousa Brasil, to whom the work is dedicated? Her interpretation lifted the mind to the realization of the inseparability of two things: the idea and its realization. All was possible because of her understanding and high level of sensibility. She reached the limits of the work in the second movement which soared as a moment of sweetest mystery: a succession of a few notes, the stammering of a child, a world of tenderness, an example of maximum efficiency in the relation of sound and idea. What could the composer have possibly imagined, what was so sweet and so bitter that could have inspired him?[62]

The third movement in particular exemplifies the most powerful writing of a gifted composer. *Triunfante, Energico* is a fugue in three parts. In light of the autobiographical nature of this piece, Guarnieri here stated very clearly his personal triumph over the vicissitudes of life. This final movement opens with a series of dramatic, attention-getting percussive chords which alternate with very *subito,* soft, ethereal polytonal chords. This brief dialogue appears several times in this opening introduction to the main portion of the movement. As if without warning, the mood changes rapidly as the *Rude, energico* fugal theme is stated by the right hand. It is again marked by intervals of a fourth or fifth with repeated notes that add emphasis at the ends of phrases.

A fitting coda to this intense, monumental work begins with an exact recall of the chords that opened this movement. In addition to the ethereal chords interspersed in its early measures, short fragments of the fugal theme also are included. This sequence of material recurs several times before the final percussive and defiant octaves end the work. In leaving this sonata of Camargo Guarnieri, the insights of Caldeira Filho, renowned critic and longtime friend of the composer, are again recalled:

> In this line of liberation [from tonal and harmonic concepts], he separated himself from the expressive use he had made of intervals. They are not only a difference of the distance between the two sounds; they are principally the movement, the transit of perception from one frequency to another. This movement is a mental phenomenon derived from sensorial stimulation. It has a dynamic value for this reason and it has an aesthetic unity. The coming together of formal unity with nature is a work of art.
>
> Guarnieri feels profoundly the stability of the movement through indications of tempo or speed of execution. For this reason, his titles are not *Allegro, Lento* or *Presto* but *Tenso, Angustioso,* and *Triunfante Energico.*
>
> In music of this genre, words fail to help; whatever the connotation or approximation, it is deservingly associative, never structural. And when, in the game of images the listener feels "It is as if" or "It appears that," the associations and similarities are in him or her, not in the composer.[63]

Sonatina no. 8. 1982.
[RB–1988]

Slightly more light-hearted than its predecessor, the sonata, this last of Guarnieri's pieces in sonatina form is nevertheless a major contribution to the category. One gets the sense of constantly moving, playful lines, always with their own sense of direction which move toward a desired point.

The texture is linear, the harmonic language quartal/atonal. The melodic units build or recede from climactic points through sequential treatment, and the changing meters neither restrain nor prepare the ear for the feeling of a very free but controlled rhythmic fabric. Unexpected accented passages are followed by more serene predictable ones (if Guarnieri's music can ever be described as predictable). Integral to the entire structure of the music are the hand patterns which require an agile technique. Proper fingering is treacherously urgent!

To play this piece well, a pianist needs not only an intellectual understanding of the rhythms, harmonic language, and form, but also a high degree of ability to internalize the rhythms and project the complex fabric of rhythmic figures and contrapuntal movement which is so different in each hand. Each new phrase will frequently mark a shift in accentuation.

Guarnieri's scores, particularly his solo piano music, cannot be approached casually. They require a serious performer, and perhaps having a few Brazilian genes helps. After the premiere by Cynthia Priolli in November 1983 in the University of São Paulo's Amphitheater, Lea Vinocur Freitag wrote, "In the first hearing of the Sonatina No. 8, the dissonances were balanced by the flow, underlining the independence of the left hand."[64] Oswaldo Lacerda wrote extensively for the record jacket notes of the 1982 recording:

> The sonata is a most interesting and perfect form of music, and to succeed, it needs much creativity and technical control on the part of the composer. The fact that Guarnieri has these qualities in a high degree ensures the success of his sonatas.
>
> There are actually nine "sonatas" for piano, though only one is called "sonata." The other eight are called "sonatinas." This diminutive term refers only to their length for their expressive power, originality, and compositional technique are equal to that which is evident in his sonata. His Sonatina no. 8 was written in 1982 and was dedicated to Cynthia Priolli. It has the traditional three movements:
>
> *Repenicado* presents some rhythmic and melodic processes of the *choro*.
>
> *Profundamente Intimo* has a meditative, wandering character.
>
> *Dengoso* recalls again some processes of the *choro*.[65]

The indication *Repenicado* means "like the stroking of all the strings of a guitar in one motion." This first theme suggests a playful stroking back and forth in the upper register, effected by a single line that flows between the hands. The second movement is an extremely introverted tonal picture in which a single line moves flexibly, with an almost dazed, wandering quality, over a descending left-hand figure. The movement is so very short that what is referred to as a B section is merely a few measures. The *Dengoso* is also comparatively short with its fifty-eight measures in which Guarnieri again uses his own brand of ABA form, as he did in the first two movements. The texture is restless with a contrapuntal writing that insinuates no definite tonality, as it rises and falls, contracts and expands in angular movement.

With these nine works in sonata-allegro form, we here leave a monumental contribution to the piano literature, not just of Brazil, but of the musical world. There is no doubt that the piano received some of Guarnieri's most precious musical utterances which reveal the scope of his development as a composer.

TEN *IMPROVISOS* (IMPROVISATIONS). 1948–81. [RB–1988]

This group of ten pieces reveals Camargo Guarnieri in those moments when his musical feeling was given full play. They are not the large, commissioned compositions over which he needed to spend a great deal of time planning and designing in his mind. Nor did they demand his utmost concentration, intuition, perseverance, and technique to serve his own personal craft of writing. Rather, these pieces reflect the times when he just sat at the piano and let his fingers give voice to what was in his heart. Often they were created and recorded as improvisations at the houses of friends, to be transcribed later. Cynthia Priolli wrote in her introduction to the printed edition of these *Improvisos* that "Guarnieri lives in an attitude of constant openness to his emotions, and his greatest desire is to be known as one who felt and not just heard. All of these pieces are, in truth, states of the soul, amorous confessions or technical solutions in pianistic form."[66] Osvaldo Lacerda wrote in his notes for a recording of these pieces:

> I've had the privilege many times of seeing Guarnieri sit at the piano and create without any previous preparation unforgettable moments of reflection, magic, and musicality. These are, to use a well-known expression, true confessions of a soul which electrify anyone who is present.[67]

The fact that these *Improvisos* were written over the period of thirty-three years confirms the unpressured source from which they arose. That there are ten again reveals Guarnieri's penchant for presenting his works in groups. A few of these were published individually as they were created, but the complete set of ten was published by Ricordi Brasileira in 1988.

Of these ten *Improvisos,* all but nos. 5 and 10 are slow and expressive. Number 3 bears a unique similarity to Chopin's *Prélude* no. 4 with its pleading two-note descending motive: C–B. The emotion comes from the same source, but the subtle syncopation of Guarnieri's piece sets it apart.

In these works it is interesting to note that Guarnieri's typical ABA form of his small pieces seems to become even more of a monothematic structure. It is a fine line between the two possibilities, one which is much less important than the pieces themselves. They have been recorded by Cynthia Priolli, who publicly premiered the set in 1983. Of that performance, Lea Vinocur Freitag wrote, "The *Improvisos* are studies in contrasts of tempos and conceptions, translated with care by the pianist."[68]

Ten *Momentos*
(Moments). 1982–88.
[RB–1989]

With the *Momentos,* we come to the last group of Guarnieri's music for piano. Six of them were recorded by Cynthia Priolli in 1985. They suggest that the composer again intended to respect the collections already in existence, the *Ponteios* and the *Improvisos,* all of which have similarities of form and temperament. However, the *Momentos* are much shorter pieces, truly "moments" in his own reflective life, but springing from the same spirit as the ten *Improvisos.* Osvaldo Lacerda wrote of this set, "The title of these pieces explains them very well: they reflect 'delicate moments' of musicality and beauty which reflect, as in all the writing of Camargo Guarnieri, various facets of the Brazilian soul."[69]

These pieces were all composed between 1982 and 1988, and all but nos. 3, 6, and 8 are slow and expressive. Because all of them contain only between eighteen and forty-one measures, most of them fewer than thirty, even his typical ABA form is distilled. One can hardly speak of an exposition and development of an idea in the short space allotted to them. All expose a principal theme, extend it in a quasi development, and then restate it, but in very brief form. It is not only the form that is concentrated, but also the musical expression. They are among his last musical utterances and continue to reflect the very intimate, strongly sensitive personality of Camargo Guarnieri. In this set of ten *Momentos,* Guarnieri distilled to the purest form the kind of expressive communication that marks his *Ponteios* and *Improvisos.* These are brief musical feelings from the heart.

As with Beethoven's and Brahms's last works that reveal a distillation and pure objectivity of emotion, the last *Momento* speaks a transcendent language not accessible immediately to a casual listener. In this piece one senses emotion too profound to utter, yet it lies hidden within the texture, dissonances, rhythms, and inner life of its lines. The entire piece is written in the treble clef, which affects its intensity by the tessitura of its parts. The reexposition appears in measure 16, but only the final three measures break free of the restatement to gently close this chapter of the composer's life.

Momento no. 10 was the penultimate piece that Guarnieri wrote for solo piano. (*Estudio* no. 18 was completed the following year.) That it is dedicated to this author seems significant in that one of his last "musical words" was to me, and I am making a definitive written word in tribute to him. The day he completed this piece in 1987, we were both sitting at the dining room table in the Guarnieri apartment. Around the corner in another room, his daughter Tânia was practicing one of his violin sonatas. Guarnieri was recopying this manuscript, and I was sorting through my writings, occasionally checking a detail with him. With a smile, he handed me this final *Momento* with its dedication. The three aspects of music—composition, performance, commentary—came together at that significant moment.

FIVE

Music for Piano and Orchestra

Guarnieri's ten compositions for piano and orchestra span fifty-six years, 1931–87. The works are interesting, not only in tracing the development of the composer, but also in the succession of changing styles which they represent.

The Concerto no. 1 stems from his exploratory period and reflects the stringent language of the early 1930s, as well as some Amerindian influences. The Concerto no. 2 also uses a theme of Amerindian inspiration, but it is much more expansive in its treatment than is the preceding work. This second concerto, written in 1946, was followed by a set of variations, a *choro,* and a concertino, all of which use very different compositional materials. The Third Concerto of 1964 is a harsh, powerful work, and the *Seresta* of the following year is a further development of these qualities. The Fourth and Fifth Concertos represent increasing degrees of serial organization, Guarnieri's first formal explorations outside the traditionally evolved textures. The last work in this group, *Saratí,* was completed in the early part of 1987.

The Concerto no. 2 was published by Associated Music Publishers in 1954; the other concertos are being published by Ponteio Publishing Company, New York City. All of the works have been performed. The Concertino has enjoyed special popularity and is in the repertoire of Brazilian pianists Lais de Souza Brasil, João Carlos Martins, Roberto Szidon, Cristina Capparelli Gerling, Caio Pagano, and Ney Fialkow. In one sense, these compositions represent some of the few works for piano and orchestra written in Brazil. Many of the younger composers have turned to the more abstract titles and forms of avant-garde expressionism, as well as electronic music.

Concerto no. 1. 1931.
[Ponteio–New York, 2004]

Dedicated to Guiomar Novaes, this work has all the earmarks of a first attempt, although it likewise reveals some of the qualities which mark Guarnieri's later works. Composed in 1931 when Guarnieri was just twenty-four, it was given its first performance in São Paulo by João de Souza Lima in 1936 at the first of three free concerts sponsored by the Department of Culture, newly organized through Mário de Andrade's efforts. Guarnieri conducted the orchestra of the Department of Culture. The *Correio de São Paulo* carried the following review:

> What really left the audience moved and full of magic was the Concerto for Piano and Orchestra in its first hearing by the prolific young and genial Mozart Camargo Guarnieri, author of over 150 works. This piece, to which the extraordinary Souza Lima brought all of his love and his technical power, honors the Brazilian musical art and reaffirms a master who, to this day in his power and creative sensibilities, distinguishes himself in both the national scene and even in the world, by his profundity and cultural integrity.[1]

It was performed the following year on July 7, 1937, during a congress called in São Paulo by Andrade devoted to the topic "Portuguese as the National Sung Language." João Souza Lima again was the performer. Andrade Muricy had both praise and constructive criticism for the piece:

> It was defective in its modern preconception, apparently anti-virtuosic (and in reality anti-concerto for piano and orchestra), an attitude which has prevailed among many contemporary composers. The first movement has an indefinite form and is more in a genre of its own. It appears to be a fragment of a symphonic poem. It is less organic and loses a little in its fantasy quality. The soloist's part is very restricted, more like that of a symphony with piano.
>
> Actually though, this concerto for piano is an admirable piece. The orchestra is full of dense sonorities and is as tasty as sweet nectar and has the scent of tropical fruit. Its warmth is very personal and new. Both the second movement and the Finale are beautiful. The *Andante* is a proud Brazilian nocturne, fresh with an exalted tropical humidity, especially in the long trembling sections which reflect our racial feelings.
>
> Camargo Guarnieri is creating works at this time which are really comprehensible to both critics and to the public. He can be natural and spontaneous; he does not have to want to be Brazilian. He is Brazilian![2]

It was performed again in 1944 by Lídia Simões Prado, after which Caldeira Filho wrote:

> Really, the surprising thing here is the richness and abundance of ideas expressed in a parallel richness of writing. It could be said that there is a waste, because our ears could not comprehend in one hearing everything that he offered, nor at the same time can our musicality respond to such a multi-

plicity of stimuli. On the other hand, it is felt, as in some of his other works, that there is a more self-critical tendency to eliminate the relatively useless things, resulting in a better stylization of essentials. In 1931, Camargo Guarnieri managed to conquer the initial difficulties of composing, revealing in this concerto a complete dominion over technique and musical language. Later we will sense the powerful presence of a free and independent musical personality.[3]

This work also had a performance in the United States with Leon Barzin conducting the National Symphony Orchestra.

The Concerto no. 1 is one continuous piece of three connected movements. There is a tenseness in the harmonic and thematic material that does not lend itself to expansiveness, and therefore the work has the appearance of lacking thematic development. This lack of expansiveness, even of the harmonic scheme, is partly responsible for Muricy's "anti-concerto" comment. A few measures into the work, a fragment of the principal theme becomes a motif and dominates a substantial part of the first movement. Only one other musical idea of equal aridity appears in this first movement. There is really no extended development or interplay of contrasting themes. Thus, the composition lacks the kind of soaring sonorities commonly identified with a concerto. Likewise its harmonic language is generally open and dry with dissonances serving percussive purposes.

The "long trembling line" of the second movement, referred to above by Muricy, is actually a very simple melody that appears over an orchestral accompaniment based on a rhythmic ostinato. The piano part becomes somewhat more expansive in a middle section and is followed by a return to its original mood and spirit.

The third movement, *Depressa*, begins with the piano's sixteenth-note figuration, which constitutes the principal theme of this movement. It is stated over the same rhythmic pattern that appeared in the first movement. Allusions to previously heard themes and fragments gradually begin, constituting a coda of brilliant *ff* passage work.

Concerto no. 2. 1946.
[AMP–1942]

The Concerto no. 2 also draws upon Indian sources. It has the advantage of fifteen more years of experience on the part of the composer. The germinal development of the Indian motif occurs in what might be considered a series of loosely woven variations, although that is not indicated by the composer. The spirit of the movement is harsh, but simple and straightforward. It possesses all the soaring lines, solo bravura passages, and orchestral interplay of the great concertos of the late nineteenth and early twentieth centuries. It is also very Brazilian, not only in its thematic material and rhythmic structure, but also in its representing a more mature assimilation of these elements than did its predecessor. It is scored for full orchestra and piano, and it falls into three movements. Harmonically it is very tonal, with the first movement theme being developed within a modal framework.

The second movement, *Afetuoso, molto espressivo,* is strongly diatonic and has a scherzo for a middle section, which provides more rapid, fragmentary harmonic color. A D♭ harmonic pedal point and a supple, easygoing syncopation provide the basic material, over which is stated an utterly simple theme by a solo clarinet. A flatted third and seventh in the melody give it a strong blues quality, intensifying its nostalgic character. The first four notes of the theme are transformed in the middle section of the movement into a rollicking scherzo. Piano and orchestra "ping-pong" the theme back and forth, giving the impression of much more harmonic activity than is actually present. The $\frac{6}{8}$ meter frequently has groupings of $\frac{3}{4}$, which intensifies the rhythmic interest. On its return, the principal theme is carried by the strings, while the soloist provides a lacey filigree above it. The movement comes to a complete, peaceful end. Caldeira Filho wrote of it:

> It is one of those rare moments of expressive grandeur, of authentic Brazilian lyricism, saturated with its own spirit and atmosphere. It is in these slow passages that Camargo Guarnieri seems most profoundly integrated with the land and its people, or better still, it is he who reveals the land and the people at the same time. We consider these moments of the composer among the most profound and the most authentic of Brazilian expressions.[4]

The last movement, *Vivo secco,* contains the slightly more pungent language of quartal chords, bitonality, and some cluster chords. The solo writing is more aggressive: angular seconds, ninths, and fourths appreciably increase the dissonance of this section. The piano soloist opens this movement with hammered chords of irregular accentuation, preparing for the entrance of the first of three themes of strong ethnic flavor. The concentration of these sounds and dynamic reiteration in their percussiveness create a fairly strong sense of dissonance. Lais de Souza Brasil wrote of this movement:

> Impetus is the idiom of the third movement: a *Vivo* with three themes in the form of a rondo. Evoking the *frevo,* the first two themes lay a perfect foundation, the melodic quality of the second supported by the rhythmic character of the first. The third theme, *Scherzoso,* equally vibrant, is the necessary calm respite and intensification of the return to the primitive dance, always more excited until the climactic final coda, crowning this major work.[5]

This concerto won the Alexander Levy prize offered by the São Paulo Department of Culture in 1946. Shortly afterwards, Eurico Nogueira França, lifelong friend and supporter of Guarnieri's creative efforts, reflected on the importance of Guarnieri's contributions. In particular he noted the composer's affinity for the classical forms as a vehicle for his own native expression. When one realizes that he had few models, his work gains even greater importance. His two older colleagues, Villa-Lobos and Francisco Mignone, pursued more spontaneous, free-form procedures. França wrote in part:

> In the historic panorama of Brazilian music, Camargo Guarnieri, one of the youngest of our great musicians, is an excellent representative of what I would call "classicism." He achieves a magnificent balance between idea and form. All the classical virtues of musical construction are found in his work: complexity of sound structure that does not mask the transparent simplicity of lines, the power of thematic elaboration which gives the music an inner unity, and an admirable sense of proportion.[6]

This Second Piano Concerto was premiered in the United States on April 16, 1947, over CBS Radio with Lídia Simões, dedicatee, as soloist under Guarnieri's direction. This performance established him as a major composer in North American musical circles. It was played again in São Paulo the following October and was well received by the public. After this performance Caldeira Filho wrote:

> One of the most beautiful moments was the return of the *Afetuoso* after the *Brincando* of the second movement; it must not be forgotten that in this resides one of the aspects of Camargo Guarnieri's mastery, that the desired effect results from the contrast established with the preceding section in such a way as to produce this contrast. The second concerto is a very vigorous work, revealing new aspects in the writing of Camargo Guarnieri. It is developed in the spirit of Romantic writing, or better, it is more expansively lyrical, showing every possible relationship that an orchestra and piano could have within a concerto.[7]

Variações Sôbre um Tema Nordestino
(Variations on a Theme of the Northeast).
September 27, 1953. Manuscript

This is Guarnieri's only titled set of variations and one of the few examples of direct use of a folkloric theme. He composed the work in collaboration with the choreographer Milo as a ballet score. The Brazilian artist Flavio de Carvalho did the visual designs and still includes them in exhibits of his works. The ballet, *O Cangaceiro* (The Bandit), deals with the life of a bandit in Brazil's colorful but poverty-stricken Northeast.

The theme upon which the eight variations are based is utterly simple, in two parts in the Lydian mode. Each variation ends with several measures of transitional material drawn from the second half of the theme, stated by the orchestra, each time on a different tonal center. The harmonic language of this work is consistently dissonant. It follows nonfunctional resolutions of chords and makes extensive use of nontertian structures, quartal harmonies, and bitonal relationships. Thus it goes beyond the Second Concerto in its tightness, both of harmonic language and of structure. The theme, *Lento, poco piu mosso, triste,* is in two parts and is first stated by the orchestra.

Variation I—Violento, ff. The theme is not particularly obvious in this variation. The soloist enters with a figuration based on fourths, as the orchestra injects fragments of the theme and supports with its own quartal harmony, which is different from that of the soloist. The piano establishes a driving *samba* rhythm, but then the last eight measures are a soft orchestra *Andante* based on the second part of the theme and tonally centered on A.

Variation 2—Dolce, calma, p. This variation is completely subdued with soloist and orchestra alternating phrases of the melody. The accompaniment is mildly dissonant with independently moving patterns, cross-relations, and bitonal suggestions. Again, there is the *Andante,* this time thirteen measures long, ending in F.

Variation 3—Sómbrio, íntimo, pp. The established rhythm remains constant through this variation. The piano's harmonization of its line is unconventional and is in bitonal opposition to the orchestral part. A climactic section ensues in which the piano has full chords doubled in both hands, followed by arpeggiated flourishes over the orchestral material. The climax subsides into a twelve-measure *Andante,* this time in C.

Variation 4—Misterióso, p. The mood of the preceding *Andante* is carried forward into this variation where a fragment of the theme serves as a dirgelike motif that simmers in both solo and orchestral parts. The texture expands to a climax and then recedes again. A ten-measure *Andante* is in E♭.

Variation 5—Con alegria, mf. The piano bursts in on the preceding interlude with an angular line in double sixteenth notes while the orchestra carries the theme. The writing is generally boisterous for both soloist and orchestra. A seventeen-measure *Andante* is in D minor.

Variation 6—Appassionata, p. The section begins softly over an E-major harmony with the melody in E minor. There is a *pp, luminosa* restatement of the theme. The *Andante* has gently moving, obscure harmonies, but it ends finally in F minor.

Variation 7—Contemplativo, p. A somber, Chantilly version of the melody is made more abstruse by its harmonization, which utilizes many chromatic alterations, strong bitonal relationships, and a nontonal fabric. The slow connecting section this time is marked *Lento* and is a nine-measure diminuendo into the last variation.

Variation 8—Furioso, ff. The piano opens with a chordal figuration similar to that which it had in the first variation. The theme is not immediately discernible. The piano writing is generally virtuosic with bravura double octaves, leading to a strongly rhythmic section, and then a sudden *Lento* in which the piano softly restates the theme two octaves apart. The orchestra has a very soft series of low pizzicato G's in the final measures, maintaining a subtle indefiniteness of tonality to the very end.

These *Variations* were premiered in Rio de Janeiro in 1954 by Lídia Simões, for whom they were written. The Municipal Theater Orchestra was under the direction of Nino Stinco. Guarnieri conducted the work on December 1, 1954, in São Paulo with its Municipal Symphony Orchestra for the celebration of the four hundredth anniversary of the founding of the city. The work was performed in Washington, D.C., by Yara Bernette and Howard Hanson with the Washington Symphony Orchestra in 1962 at the Inter-American Festival. It is also in the repertoire of other Brazilian pianists including Lais de Souza Brasil, who performed it in 1998 in São Paulo.

Choro.
1956. Manuscript

The *Choro* follows the *Variations* after an interval of three years. It represents a return to a more chromatic tertian language, as is also evidenced in some other works of this period—the *Choro* for Clarinet and Orchestra and some of the later *Ponteios.* The piece won first prize in the 1956 Latin American Music Festival in Caracas, Venezuela. It has had numerous performances: Albert Farber under Carlos Chavez and the Orquestra Sinfônica de Caracas; Arnaldo Estrela in April 1957 under Souza Lima and the São Paulo Orquestra Sinfônica Municipal; in Milan, Italy, on February 23, 1958; in São Paulo in July 1963 by Caio Pagano; and in Carnegie Hall by Cristina Ortiz.

In calling the piece *Choro,* Guarnieri was using a name with a developmental history. In the folk music of Brazil, *choro* refers both to a group of instrumental serenaders and to the music they performed. Such groups were common in the urban and suburban areas of Brazil's cities in the early and mid–twentieth century. Villa-Lobos used the term for the first time in concert music and applied it to his pieces of a rhapsodic character. Guarnieri uses the term as a substitute for "concerto" to indicate the more national character of the work. His first *Choro* was for violin and orchestra and was written in 1951. This one for piano was his second.

The harmonic language of this piece is basically chromatic-tertian, with some use of the modes. The second movement contains some mild bitonal writing, which heightens its nostalgic mood. Structurally the first two movements contain germinal developments of fragments derived from the principal themes. The first and third movements are in sonata-allegro form, and the third has a very syncopated rhythmic structure. The first breathes a gentleness and freedom of spirit which distinguishes it from the normal, hard-driving concerto tempo, but the third movement has the typical bravura concerto writing.

Concertino.
1961. Manuscript

The Concertino is one of Guarnieri's most popular and charming works for piano and orchestra. It received its world premiere in the United States on August 2, 1961, with Jõao Carlos Martins and the Little Symphony Orchestra of St. Louis. It has since been performed numerous times in Brazil by Lais de Souza Brasil, Sônia Munoz, Roberto Szidon, Ney Fialkow, Caio Pagano, and João Carlos Martins.

Composed in 1961, shortly before his marriage to Vera Silvia, to whom it is dedicated, the Concertino received the 1963 Silver Medal awarded by the Associação Paulista de Críticos Teatrais as the "Best Symphonic Work" of the year. It is completely ingratiating, straightforward, buoyant, and very joyous. In general, the solo writing is delicate and in keeping with its diminutive title, though the last movement has bravura texture in places. Harmonically the piece represents a return to the simple fonts of modality with judicious use of bitonality, and to extended tertian sonorities, particularly in the rhythmically tense portions of the piece. The three movements utilize respectively a sonata-allegro, ABA, and a rollicking ABACA rondo form.

In the *Festivo* first movement, the orchestra begins a subdued but rhythmically precise reiterated chordal accompaniment over a low D pedal harmony. It is as though Guarnieri were treating the orchestra as one huge, strumming guitar. Over this simple, somewhat static foundation enters the piano solo with a genial kind of melody that uses the Mode of the Northeast with its raised fourth and lowered seventh. The simple melody is doubled at the octave. The second theme is more brusque, angular, and fragmentary but is again doubled at the octave. A coda actually serves as a transition to the next movement. It gradually decreases momentum, slipping into D minor, the key of the second movement to which it is connected.

Concertino
1st movement

The *Tristonho, dolce, p,* has the soloist immediately beginning to intone the gentle *modinha*-like melody over an orchestral imitation of a guitar. The chromatic language of this movement is very similar to many of the *Ponteios* in which phrases are repeated sequentially. The orchestra moves the theme up a half step and is joined by the piano for an impassioned version of the final phrase. A sudden *Vivo* marks a scherzo-like section. A fragmentary dialogue between the piano and orchestra ends in a retransition. On the return of the *Tristonho* theme, the cello leads the orchestra as the soloist weaves new material above it. The phrases continue to breathe more and more gently until the final *ppp* repose.

The third movement is an exceptionally joyous one. It brings into play three themes from three varied folkloric sources. The first theme is in the style of a *frevo,* a joyful carnival street dance from Pernambuco. The second is a *moda Paulista* melody in thirds. The third theme, with its repeated notes and fragmentary dialogue treatment, suggests the *embolada,* which is a "patter" or dialogue song form in rapid tempo. The cross-relations give the second theme an in-key–out-of-key feeling, resulting in a more abstruse harmonic language than is utilized by the straightforward first theme. The piano wrests the first theme away momentarily from the orchestra, which quickly recovers it, and again leads directly into the third theme stated by the piano. In the *Grandeoso* coda the piano presents the third theme in toccata style. The orchestra then begins a final statement of the first theme in augmentation under the piano's continued toccata-style third theme. This develops into a final rush of brilliant double octaves, leading to the *fff* close in D major. The exuberant, spirited pace which this composition maintains, the lovely contrasting middle movement, and the well-balanced structure and interesting textures make it a delight to hear and rewarding to perform. It conveys a sense of effortlessness, joy of life, humor, and sincerity, all of which make it a very appealing work.

Concerto no. 3. 1964.
[Ponteio–New York, 2004]

This Third Concerto received its premiere performance in Rio's Cecilia Meireles Auditorium on May 25, 1967. The composer conducted the Orquestra Sinfônica Nacional with Laís de Souza Brasil as pianist. There were six music critics present on this occasion, from whom came a variety of reactions. Two critics commented on the excessively difficult writing for the pianist. One of them, Sula Jaffe, noted that "It is a work of transcendental difficulty. . . . This concerto is not among the most original of Camargo Guarnieri's works."[8] Andrade Muricy agreed somewhat in his own review:

> The Concerto no. 3 is decidedly virtuosic and neo-Romantic. It was presented with an impulsive virility, served by a real torrent of pianistic percussiveness. At a few rare moments, we were confronted with the Camargo Guarnieri of my own preference: lyric contemplation. This virile score does

not reach, to my mind, the definitive aesthetic synthesis that his Fourth Symphony or the opening of the *O Homen Só* reached with such exceptional ease. This is extraordinary pianism in Guarnieri's habitual manner in which we recognize a composer using his own very personal language. In this concerto, everything affirms the qualities of vigor and impetuosity with which he imbues it in his unique way—the most refined of all our greatest composers. It enables him to easily control and maintain the energy to the end. The soloist, Lais de Souza Brasil, ardently defended the pages with notable brilliance and security, transmitting its integrity and its pugnacious character with a percussiveness which the work requires.[9]

The newspaper *O Globo* in Rio carried the following comments: "It is a completely brilliant work, a summary of nationalism excellently orchestrated. It is truly an inestimable contribution to the enrichment of the repertoire of this genre less favored by contemporary composers."[10] Another composer-critic, Edino Krieger, supported these positive reactions in his review:

> The first world hearing of the Third Concerto of Camargo Guarnieri was a culminating point of the concert. It is perhaps the most important work in its genre in all of our national repertoire. Its extraordinary vigor carries a violent impact from the first *fortissimo* attack of the orchestra, establishing with the listener an élan of auditory interest which runs through all three movements. This same imperative character is reinforced by the presence of the instrumental soloist from her first intervention in ascending chords and incisive rhythms in toccata style.
>
> Camargo Guarnieri reached in this example one of the highest moments of his many works, producing in each bar a sensation of great vitality and tranquil control of technique that characterize his personality and define his condition as a consummate master.[11]

From these somewhat varied reactions, one distills the impression that the Concerto no. 3 is an extremely vigorous work conceived on a grand scale. Commissioned by the Rio de Janeiro Radio Ministério de Educação e Cultura, it was dedicated to the pianist Yara Bernette, later rededicated to Jaime Ingram. Guarnieri intentionally set out to structure the first movement of this work in a new way. He uses the sonata-allegro form, but it turns into an arch form with a retrograde presentation of the themes in the recapitulation. The two remaining movements are in ABA and rondo forms, respectively.

In contrast to the Concerto no. 2, written eighteen years earlier, the themes of this work are much more extended, varied, and sophisticated. The harmonic language likewise is more dissonant from the very beginning. Whereas the Second Concerto depended upon the imposing quality of the Amerindian motive, the Third presumes nothing and purposely maintains a more complex, stringent texture throughout, not reneging on its primitive intent.

Whereas the closing rondo of the Concerto no. 2 possessed a direct rhythmic drive, this movement possesses both a more dense rhythmic fabric and a higher level of dissonance. Combined with the fuller piano texture, it can easily give the impression of harshness and rough vigor, and it apparently did to some who heard its first performance. It has definitely moved beyond all Guarnieri's previous works for piano and orchestra, both in its musical language and in the forcefulness of its dynamic structure.

Seresta.
1965. Manuscript

In retrospect, the Third Concerto appears to have been a turning point in Guarnieri's writing, something akin to an overloaded circuit whose energy needed to be directed through subsequent channels. Within one year the tensions that came through almost violently in the concerto, stretching the limits of its dynamic structure, were to work an almost complete transformation in the composer's approach to this medium. This fact seemed to be lost on all, except for a few critical ears who heard the first performance of the *Seresta* in São Paulo on November 5, 1965, under Robert Schnorrenberg and the Pro Música Orchestra of São Paulo with Ana Stella Schic as soloist. This is due to the isolationism that existed among the cities of Brazil, a narrow contentment with local happenings. The absence of music journals in the country at that time also fostered the situation, as did the dearth of university music departments that could serve as centers of musical interchange, a situation which has happily changed. Thus, three years after the 1965 performance of this piece, musicians in Rio were still unaware of Guarnieri's evolving musical language. It seems pertinent to quote at length the excellent and perceptive 1973 review by the critic Caldeira Filho:

> The *Seresta* is recognized as marking a new phase in the composer, characterized by a liberation from nationalism and harmonic tonality. In an artist of this stature, it is not possible to have a liberation from this or that element—the liberation is total or it does not exist at all. I have just one reservation: Camargo Guarnieri did not turn suddenly to this new path in this particular work. He came to this process gradually as can be proven, among other things, in some of his *Ponteios* and the recently heard *Canto II for Violin.*
>
> Any liberation from nationalism is relative. To the degree that the author is separated from nationalism which is thematic, folkloric, or regional, so

much more does he touch a nationalism which is cultural, indestructible, and personal to the true artist, the means by which he opens the doors of universalism. We cannot forget what Mário de Andrade affirmed: "There is no universal music; there is only national music which is universal."

In the *Seresta* the evasion of harmonic tonality or tonal preconceptions appears to us to be relative. Its advanced harmonic conception revealed is not a creation of a soul which didn't exist before; it is really a lucid and highly artistic elaboration of conquests made earlier through the language of sound. Guarnieri's own thematic liberation appears to be less an abandonment than a greater concentration of the compositional processes, not only in the phrase or period but also in the motive, the cell of musical thought. Even the orchestration has new aspects, and all this is intimately related to the liberation of those elements.

All this new life that constitutes the *Seresta* and confirms its historical significance is based on the permanence of that from which Guarnieri knows he cannot be freed—the form. To a spirit so clear and reflective, form is a necessity of expression, it is the integrating element and coordinator, proponent of intelligibility and of all the material of construction used in the work of musical art. His concept of form is seen not only as a plan; it extends to sound, rhythm, and durations, because all of these are submitted to the plastic tendency. The *Seresta* can be seen as a synthesis of universalized modifications which are given, in the personality of the composer, a point a reference for their expansion.[12]

The liberation noted here is evident in almost every aspect of the score. The orchestra itself is different: strings, harp, xylophone, and timpani. Among Guarnieri's pieces in this form, the texture of this one is the most fragmentary. Thematically the distillation of fragments is extremely frugal, particularly in the first movement. Even the name of the piece seems a contradiction, since it is the Portuguese colloquial expression for serenade, a type of improvisation very common in Brazil. Guarnieri claimed that the title actually referred to the second movement; the first and last movements frustrate any thought of a sustained, entreating, or nostalgic serenade melody. Harmonically there is the constant ambivalence of quartal structures, very dissonant contrapuntal writing, and a bitonality which emphasizes chords only a half step apart. Consequently the overall impression of atonality is very strong.

The harsh quality of the piece is evident in the very first bars of the opening movement in which the piano begins with an angular figuration stressing ascending fourth chords. It is almost serial in organization, but not quite. The thematic material in general is very fragmented, but highly unified. Both soloist and orchestra maintain a continual interplay of these fragments.

The second movement in three parts is another example of Guarnieri's ability to create pensive, suspended sonorities. The orchestral "oom-pa"–style introduction sounds deceptively naive after the highly sophisticated first movement, but it leaves the soloist completely free to unfold a long *molto espressivo* line. In contrast to the first movement, the themes of this second section are much longer and very supple, almost seeming not to know where to end. The slow, reflective tempo helps to create a motionless quality.

The fragmentary texture of the first movement is balanced in this last movement, where two brief melodic fragments, both of only five notes, are exposed in turn and developed. They reappear simultaneously in the coda, creating a structural web of great intensity and unity. The movement opens with a driving timpani line with shifted accents and clusters of orchestral tones which appear irregularly but with great rhythmic precision.

A toccata-style texture is maintained throughout the greater part of the third movement. The orchestra's reiterated triads also serve a percussive function. A final coda begins a *tutti forza* drive to the final measures. Even as Guarnieri moves further away from folkloric themes, there is still an indefinable quality which marks the music as his own. The melodies, the contrapuntal skill, and the fragmentary dialogue could belong to no other.

The *Seresta* received the 1965 Silver Medal from the São Paulo Association of Theater Critics as the best chamber music work of the year. When it was performed in Rio in 1968, it received the Golfinho de Ouro from the Museum of Image and Sound. The piece had been commissioned by the Sociedade de Cultura e Artística of São Paulo.

Concerto no. 4. 1968.
[Ponteio–New York, 2005]

Following his 1950 *Open Letter* in which Guarnieri denounced what he saw as destructive tendencies of the dodecaphonic system of composition, it may seem strange that in this Concerto no. 4 he would turn to a mild form of serialism. In terms of the works leading up to this one, however, it was almost an inevitable development, another stage in the gradual dissolution of tonality that he had begun in the early 1930s. In fact, some people have questioned why it took him so long to arrive at this stage. Guarnieri himself claimed that he did not changed his ideas. In acknowledging the serialization to be found in this work, he stated, "I am in the present and my music is in the present. You will always recognize it as my music because the personality and expression of my music always reflect the present."[13]

This Concerto no. 4, like the Third and the *Seresta,* is basically a harsh, vigorous work. Whereas the third attained its dissonance through a homophonic concurrence of bitonal, percussive sonorities, the Fourth, more like the *Seresta,* has a much more linear quality. Bitonality and dissonant intervals are still responsible for the harshness, but not because of closely spaced chords and clusters of sound as in the Third Concerto. Many of the melodic lines avoid repeating previously used notes within short phrases, giving a semblance of serialization, or atonality at least. The themes of the first movement actually are serialized in their design. There is also less obvious use of ostinatos in this work. Both the first and last movements are monothematic, and the second is in an ABA design.

In the opening *Resoluto,* an orchestral introduction consists of low-placed chords with a pandiatonic melody. Open fifths add starkness to the quality. The piano soloist enters with a serialized theme in octaves. It is a continuous melody which presents a row, followed by a retrograde version, then an inverted statement. The orchestra continues its percussive texture but adds a fragmented version of the original row and a transposed statement, accompanied by the piano's jolting *samba* rhythm. Manipulation of the tone row continues throughout the movement. A harsh, dense climax begins to recede in the piano's ascending figuration and the subsiding chordal activity of the orchestra. The movement comes to a complete *ppp* close.

The second movement, *Profundamente triste, pp,* is not serialized, but is strongly atonal with bitonal relationships prevailing at any given point. Quartal sonorities and ninth chords are common. A climax diminishes quickly into the middle section of the movement, a $\frac{6}{8}$ *Vivo,* where the piano explodes into a tarantella-like passage distributed between the hands. The piano remains rhythmic and decorative throughout this section. Suddenly the orchestra begins a series of several snappy tunes that provide polymetric situations. The first is in $\frac{2}{4}$ over the prevailing $\frac{6}{8}$ meter; the second in $\frac{6}{8}$ utilizes hemiola; and the third is a gaúcho theme from Rio Grande do Sul, again in $\frac{2}{4}$ over the established $\frac{6}{8}$ meter. The orchestra has a comical "wahwah" response to this second theme, featuring pungent ninth chords that create a high degree of dissonance within the *scherzando* texture. At a *Tempo primo,* an abbreviated version of the first theme is stated, this time in the orchestral part. The movement ends *ppp* with bitonal sonorities above a low E.

Like the second movement, the third, *Rápido,* is atonal but not serial. The texture continues to accumulate force until the final *fff* close on E with tones added to the chord.

This Fourth Concerto was premiered by Roberto Szidon with the Porto Alegre Symphony Orchestra under Guarnieri on September 6, 1972. It had its first São Paulo performance on July 22, 1975, with Lais de Souza Brasil as pianist. After the São Paulo performance, Caldeira Filho offered the following review:

> The three movements—*Resoluto, Profundamente Triste* (with a rapid section inserted, corresponding to a scherzo), and *Rápido*—are played without

interruption. Guarnieri reaffirms here the originality which marks him. To begin with, in the strings he uses only the violas, cellos, and basses, dispensing with violins. The first impression one has is that he is a master of instrumentation for individual instruments and of orchestration that deals with the orchestra as a whole. He provides interesting effects with instruments or families of instruments, which provoke an evolving musical atmosphere. But then, all of Guarnieri's music soars toward a sound aura completely integrating the expressive context. Does he not exemplify, as we have had many opportunities to observe, the difference between sound and music?

The piano part of this concerto is very rich in color and in instrumental discoveries. The piano soars at times with extreme delicacy in contrast to other sections where it is transformed into turbulent sonorities, breaking through the orchestral sound. The effective use of higher registers should be noted, especially at the beginning of the second movement. A lovely dialogue between the piano and the harp is so enchanting. Broadening the dialogue, he gradually brings in the rest of the orchestra and achieves a splendid example of his aesthetic power over the timbres, a compositional technique that is his and which characterizes him as a creative personality.[14]

Concerto no. 5. 1970.
[Ponteio–New York, 2005]

Like the Fourth Concerto, the Fifth is serialized. Unlike previous works, however, it is also cyclic in the treatment of its thematic material. The five-note motif which opens the work forms the germinal material for all three movements. As in the previous concerto, the serial procedures result in a sectional development, though the first movement manages to adhere to the sonata-allegro design. The second movement is monothematic in Guarnieri's typical ABA design, and the last movement is an arch form ABCBA, with the first theme being derived from the composer's opening motive.

The Fifth Concerto was commissioned by the *Jornal do Brasil* for the II Festival de Música da Guanabara. Guarnieri began writing the work in São Paulo in January and completed it during his few teaching days at the Federal University of Goiâs in Goiânia in early February. It was performed during the festival in Rio de Janeiro on May 16, 1970; Lais de Souza Brasil was the pianist with the Orchestra of Rio's Municipal Theater, conducted by Mário Tavares. This concerto was one of a series of pieces commissioned from established South American composers and performed with the winning entries of younger composers. The idea of inviting established composers to submit works resulted from the misunderstanding at the previous competition in which Guarnieri was one of the more seasoned composers to have his music booed by the young audience. He rose to the occasion in providing this marvelous work. The review in *O Globo* gives an indication of both the experimental nature of many entries at this festival and of the reception of Guarnieri's piece:

> The same public who enthusiastically applauded the experiences of the young heard also—perhaps with less expectation, but with devotion and merited respect—some newer fruits from those great names which have made musical history, the voices of these masters, such vigorous, inexhaustible, unshakable branches, two very great composers of the Americas: Camargo Guarnieri and Domingo Santa Cruz.[15]

Guarnieri said that, in writing this work, he proceeded in a way unusual for him. He wrote the second movement first, and then the first and third movements. This second movement gives evidence again of the authentic, almost organic quality of Guarnieri's writing. He who never touched an electronic synthesizer could create acoustic music that simulated this kind of electronic sound. The *O Globo* review quoted above commented particularly on this second movement:

> Among the most beautiful pages in the catalog of Guarnieri is the second movement, *Sideral,* which presents a special interest in its timbres, almost electronic in effect, but with the elements always subordinated to the musical tradition: queen melody and her harmonic court.[16]

Eurico Nogueira França wrote that "the names of the three movements give some idea of the expressive meaning of the music, although the language shows an evolution of the composer toward a growing feeling of modernism."[17] As Guarnieri had said, it is music that is clearly his own, and listeners will always recognize it as such. One hearing of the piece will bear out his point. The national rhythms, the peculiar ethereal qualities he achieved in his pensive slow movements, the instrumental usages—all are obviously here, but combined within the serial technique.

Guarnieri's choice of a cyclic motif for this concerto produced certain situations not present in his previous works. In earlier pieces where he used more conventionally structured themes came both the opportunity and the necessity for development of their longer lines which were natural to his contrapuntal abilities. Even in the Fourth Concerto in which he used serialized themes, there was still ample room for contrast of lines and manipulation of material in traditional ways. In this Fifth Concerto, however, he purposely limited the melodic language and forced upon himself a greater distillation of the resources contained within just five notes. Thus, from the explosive, fanfare quality of its original statement came the more agile Theme I and the slightly more extended, questioning line of Theme II.

The opening *Improvisando* movement wastes no time in keeping the material moving. It begins with an orchestral announcement of the five-note cyclic motif, after which the piano speaks its *improvisando* line, utilizing the quartal structures enunciated by the orchestra. Fourth chords, sevenths, and ninths constitute the principal harmonic material of the entire piece. The nature of this brief fragment indicates the source of the dissonant material which follows: the opening upward skip of a seventh and the following descending half steps and a third. The half steps become prominent in vertical structures of an octave or ninth span with small clusters at both ends. There is a gradual decrease in activity with a final high C♯ sustained in the strings, connecting the first movement to the second.

In the second movement, *Sideral,* through an extension of the melody and a compacting of its tones into harmonic structures, Guarnieri was able to create an entirely different kind of musical atmosphere. This movement is perhaps the greatest success of the entire piece in that he transformed such an unpretentious theme so completely. Perhaps the secret lies in the fact that, as he confessed, he wrote this movement first, and only later pared down the basic elements of the theme to construct the two outer movements. Guarnieri wrote of this movement:

> The second movement, which is monothematic, is constructed with a formal plan of exposition development re-exposition. What becomes important is the search for a quality compatible with the designation of *Sideral.* The theme, which in the first movement had an energetic character, at times violent, now becomes calm, contemplative, more introverted. It is noted that in the middle of this movement the calm and contemplative character is transformed, becoming aggressive. All happens as if a dark cloud came over quickly, and then disappeared.[18]

Under the high C♯, which is sustained from the first movement, the soloist enters with the principal theme of the second movement, again spun from the five-note motif. The accompaniment is structured from the quartal chords, also essential to the fabric of the work. A *Mais calmo* gradually leads to a complete, peaceful repose. The use of the vibraphone at the ends of phrases in this section adds a particularly effective, ethereal quality to the suspended feeling of these closing measures.

The intention of creating a dance atmosphere in the final movement, *Jocoso,* is undeniable. It is scintillating from the first arresting clangs of the *agôgo* (a percussion instrument). What is particularly interesting here is the quality of the second and third themes. There is no doubt that the first theme arises directly out of the cyclic motif. The second, however, is not so much a theme as it is a percussive commentary, designed to accentuate the importance of the first theme, a supposition which is borne out by the close relationship of its second half to the cyclic motive. Likewise, the third theme seems in context more like a toccata figuration based on the principal motif. As noted in the discussion of the beginning of the piece, the cyclic motif with its ascending major seventh and descending half steps and third provides all of the basic material, including the quartal structures which result from superimposing the first, second, and fifth notes of the motif. Thus, particularly in the final movement, there is a continuing feeling of climax and generalized *stretto* created by the constant interplay of these related elements. The fabric attains an inner organization toward which so many of the composer's earlier works have pointed in their monothematic organization.

What intensifies in this piece is the concentration of material seen in the very short theme, pregnant with possibilities. The use of a serial technique surfaces here as an inevitability in Guarnieri's music. He described the motif of the piece: "In the course of the piece, it appears with different aspects and characteristics. The cyclic character becomes apparent in the piece where it has an interior necessity greater than is permitted merely by one elaboration."[19] Sensing that people might question his use of serial procedures, he tried to clarify the matter:

> The processes, or better, the actual solutions, that are combined with the sensitivity of the composer are used always in the function of a real interior necessity, never with the intention to shock, to be exotic or to write "music of the vanguard." All is presented as a function of feeling, a sincere message, emotional, from one who believes in the importance of the expressive power of music.[20]

Because this work was premiered in Rio along with almost thirty other new compositions, no extensive commentaries appeared in journals following the occasion. However, an interviewer questioned him regarding his aesthetic position. In response to what his opinion was of Webern, Stravinsky, Schoenberg, and Villa-Lobos, Guarnieri replied, "They are geniuses, and geniuses can do whatever they want!" His response to his use of serialism again stressed expression: "I use all resources of expressiveness. But I always situate them in a musical context."[21]

Its first performance in São Paulo two years later in 1972, Caldeira Filho gave the work its due in an extensive article:

> Guarnieri avoids sectionalizing the form in this piece, binding the first two movements together. One thematic idea is enough for him; its potential manifests itself throughout the long work, giving it a cyclic character. The suddenness and sculptural energy with which it appears, like a sudden bursting forth of music in the terrain of the imagination, gives an immediate sense of improvisation. The first movement is actually entitled "improvisa-

tion" or *Improvisando*. All aspects of the idea will be later revealed. Its gentleness is not diminished as its power expands and it seeks to conquer all possible sound space.

This is not the case with the second movement, *Sideral*. The last bars here use a serial technique. A popular joyful spirit is imbibed and synthesized in the *Jocoso* last movement. The entire work is developed with an indefinite tonality, one reason for the flexible syntax in the composer's language, clothed with a varied orchestration with moments of unexpected sounds and sonorities.

Some of these indications, among others, show that the challenge to Camargo Guarnieri was to give shape to his emotion, his great creative impulse toward which he has remained sincerely faithful. Almost too intense, it is this emotion which breaks the structural molds of more traditional themes. The metamorphosis of the generative cellular idea and the varied aspects it offers create new auditory stimulations of new aesthetic dimensions, greatly expanding the process of perception and enriching it with numerous associations and connotations.

This concerto is affirmative, not conditional. Its very nature demands the complete participation of its components and makes of the piano not a means of virtuosity for the soloist but an equal partner integral to the structure and the general expressiveness.[22]

This Concerto no. 5 marks a new level in the work of the composer. Lais de Souza Brasil has been its principal exponent in its premieres, both in São Paulo and Rio de Janeiro and in the United States, where she performed it on December 8, 1973, with Guarnieri conducting the Chicago Symphony Orchestra.

Saratí For Piano, Strings, and Percussion.
1987. Manuscript

Guarnieri subtitled this work "Three Movements for Piano and Chamber Orchestra." He was putting the final touches on the work on the morning of his eightieth birthday, February 1, 1987, and he completed it shortly afterwards. It was commissioned by the Ministry of Exterior Relations in honor of Guarnieri's birthday and premiered by Cynthia Priolli during the Tenth Winter Festival of Campos do Jordão with the University of São Paulo Orchestra under Guarnieri's direction on July 12, 1989.

Saratí is the name of the building in which Guarnieri had his penthouse studio on Rua Pamplona for most of his creative life. Here he spent the greater portion of his creative hours. He had no exact, clear reason for naming this piece after the building, yet it suggests a stability, a steadfast rootedness in his Brazilian culture, as well as in this homey, quiet place high above the heart of São Paulo.

With Lais de Souza Brasil, Chicago, December 1973. *Photo by M. Verhaalen.*

The work represents a distillation of Guarnieri's use of formal structures, revealing once again how germinal ideas continue to open and link together as primary units in his larger pieces. In scope, it is probably shorter, less seriously aggressive, more reflective than his previous works in this genre, revealing a creative mind able to express in one more, varied way the essence of his artistic gifts.

The first movement, titled *Caprichoso e bem ritmado,* is only ninety measures long and is monothematic. As with other works from this same period, Guarnieri uses his principal material as an opening fanfare. Here it takes the form of a ten-measure introduction. The piano then spins a longer line drawn from this introductory material. The strings support and occasionally interrupt this theme. Following varied versions of the theme, a restatement leads into a cadenza for the soloist. A descending line gently leads into the second movement.

A brief *Calmo, Muito Sentido* of fifty-two measures constitutes the second movement. A cello assists the piano in projecting the very expressive, pensive texture. After a short contrasting section, the piano has a final *Cantando amplamente,* full-sounding passage before receding to a gentle *Suave lentamente,* which brings the movement to a close.

In the final *Alegro bem ritmado,* another arch form, there is an orchestral introduction, after which the piano soars intensely with an emotional melody in right-hand octaves over a very active left-hand accompaniment.

Mais depressa signals a race for the ending. The ascending fourth chords are fragmented, alternating between soloist and orchestra as the texture builds into the final climax. It then ends the work on definitive, punctuated octaves. Whether defiant or merely firm, these final hammered tones became a signature for Guarnieri, particularly in his later years.

There is no question that Guarnieri left behind him a rich loam of music for piano and orchestra. Thankfully, most of these works are becoming available through Ponteio Publishing Company in New York City. Each of these pieces is substantive, strong, and powerfully expressive. They are intended for neither the casual performer nor amateur conductor. Having Brazilian genes is not a prerequisite for their performance, but one must be prepared for the challenge—and the reward.

SIX

Songs and Smaller Choral Works

Mário de Andrade wrote in 1940, "I do not know who in Brazil can compose songs better than Camargo Guarnieri. Through their expressive force, their complete assimilation of popular elements, the originality of the polyphonic accompaniment, and the beauty of the melodies, the songs of Guarnieri are his best contribution to Brazilian music."[1] Were he alive sixty years later, Andrade would probably still held to at least the first half of this statement. True to Dinhora de Carvalho's quip about his being a "congenital melodist," in his songs Guarnieri could let flow the endless stream of melody which rose through him from his Brazilian roots.

It would be hard to find another country with a greater wealth of, or feeling for, popular song. Compared with the United States, Brazil reverberates with popular music that has developed from the rich mixture of folk music from all parts of the country. In addition to the numerous popular songs of everyday, there is the store of carnival music which increases each year, the rural and urban *toadas,* and in particular the *modinhas,* an older song form contributed by the Portuguese but blended into a unique new expression in Brazil.

Guarnieri composed almost three hundred songs, most of them for solo female voice and piano, some with orchestral accompaniment, and others for choruses of equal, mixed, or children's voices. Occasionally he used the Indian or Afro-Brazilian dialects. Many songs utilize the poetry of folklore itself, but the vast majority draw upon texts of Brazilian writers, such as Mário de Andrade, Manuel Bandeira, Sylvia and Susanna de Campos, and his own brother and sister, Rossine and Alice. His styles of writing vary not only with the kind of text but also with his own development as a composer. Many of the songs are published, but many also remain in manuscript form. Some have been recorded.

With such a variety in one medium, it is impossible to treat all adequately here. There is sufficient material and reason for a future, more detailed study of his song literature. What this chapter will attempt to do is give a general idea of the songs with some discussion of examples from representative stages of his development, and comments from some of his contemporaries who have heard performances of these works.

The qualities of song are intimately related to the language they use. Brazil's folk and popular music are in Portuguese, but that was not always the case with the Brazilian art song. Throughout most of the nineteenth century, Italian was the sung language because of the heavy infiltration of Italian singers and Italian opera. In addition, Brazilian Portuguese pronunciation offered peculiar difficulties to challenge Brazilian composers of art songs

Alberto Nepomuceno (1864–1920) was the first to seriously attempt to set Portuguese in his songs. As with other aspects of the national movement in music, it was Andrade who gave the strongest impetus to the use of Portuguese by his organization, in 1937 in São Paulo, of the Congress for the National Sung Language. This Congress was devoted completely to the problems of using Brazilian Portuguese in erudite music and of coming to some agreement on an official dialect among the various ones prevalent in the country. In preparation for this Congress, several specialists prepared papers on the various aspects of the subject. Andrade himself did a lengthy analysis of selected songs of the principal composers who had already attempted to write songs in Portuguese; this study, *Os Compositores e a Lingua Nacional* (Composers and a National Language), is published in volume IX of his complete works, *Aspectos da Música Brasileira* (Aspects of Brazilian Music).

Andrade noted in this study that the principal problems facing composers were the following:

1. The irreconcilable conflict of the spoken and sung styles of diction
2. The phonetic accommodation peculiar to Portuguese
3. The nasal quality of some sounds which are difficult to project, particularly on high pitches
4. The hiatus and diphthongs which cause special problems where there are repeated notes on the same pitch
5. The ligation of words and syllables.

In his frank, inimitable style, Andrade wrote of Guarnieri, "In the beginning of his career, Camargo Guarnieri was a disaster, but he had enough interest to study in 1928, the year in which he composed his first works of erudite music. The first song, *Lembranças do Losango Cáqui* [Remembrances of a Khaki-Colored Military Beret], is a phonetic disaster because there is not one ligation of words in the whole song."[2] Andrade's logic, his honesty and understanding of the problems were of great service to Guar-

nieri and other musicians in their efforts to develop a national song repertoire. His main plea was that they study their own language and its unique
characteristics.

Having two writers in his own family, Guarnieri acknowledged a lifelong interest in poetry, and his own catalog of works reflects this. Seven
songs were written in 1928, his first year of serious composing. Throughout his life the songs usually outnumbered works in other genres. The texts
he preferred were those with a love theme. França has described the peculiar
qualities of much Brazilian poetry: "It appears certain that Brazilian poetic
language is more apt to use strong color and amorous eloquence than the
in-between sentimental tones or fixations or nuances which, to the sensibilities of our people, seem to be a characteristic form."[3] This is evident in
Guarnieri's choices of texts for his songs.

His first song referred to above, *Lembranças do Losango Cáqui*, has a
rather melancholy text taken from the writings of Mário de Andrade: "My
God, how white she was! She almost looked like snow. Perhaps I do not
know how snow is; I have never seen it! I do not like snow! I did not like
her." The song shows many of the characteristics that continued to mark
Guarnieri's work for solo voice: the ostinato accompaniments, the strongly
defined mood, and the use of the modes, Phrygian on F# in this case. The
right-hand figuration becomes increasingly more melodic in the interludes
of the piece. Andrade, who lamented the completely syllabic setting of the
text, wrote after its publication:

> Frankly, this new work of Guarnieri is very interesting and worthy of praise,
> but it does not seem to me to have the value of his *Dança Brasileira*. The
> problems are also more complex, and people cannot expect a youth to con-
> quer them when he is still in his formal training period. . . . In *Lembranças*,
> Guarnieri met the problem of treating the voice freely in recitation style and
> in nationalizing the mood of the piano accompaniment. Actually he created
> a piece which is pleasant to hear and to sing. He knew how to express the
> text as he understood it. It seems that the national solution which he pre-
> sented, however, is not sufficient. The characteristic accompaniment is not
> enough.[4]

This particular piece, given a through-composed setting, is dedicated to
Lidy Chiaffarelli Cantú, daughter of the head of the piano department of
the São Paulo Conservatory and for some time wife of Guarnieri's former
teacher, Cantú.

Another song of 1928, *Toada do Pai do Mato* (Father of the Forest
Toada), was given a strophic setting in which the rhythms were adapted for
each verse. Andrade noted that Guarnieri met the text-setting problem
more successfully in *As Flores Amarelas dos Ipês* (Yellow Flowers of Ipês,
1928), where he found three vowels together.[5] The setting of the *Toada*'s

short text is through composed with a patterned accompaniment. The voice part is independent, but it moves smoothly and expressively and is strongly diatonic. Vasco Mariz noted that *As Flores Amarelas dos Ipês* is "an ingenuous and coy miniature without great breadth."[6]

The *Prelúdio no. 2* (1928) is based on the poetry of Guilherme de Almeida, a text which exalts the beauty of one's own country: "How beautiful is my land! Stranger, look at that palm tree—what a beauty it is!" Guarnieri here used his typical accompaniment, a shifting ostinato pattern. Over the strong *samba* rhythm, the right hand dialogues with the melody of the vocalist. There are chromatic nuances, but within a diatonic framework. Harmonically the piece has a certain suppleness and ends with the fifth in the bass. Andrade pointed out a few places in this song which he considered difficult to sing because of the syllables of similar sound on repeated notes. He wrote in a review of the piece:

> The delicious *Préludio no. 2* reveals one of those moments in which the composer shows that he can be delicate and pleasant. It has an excellent balance between the piano and the voice; the lines of the instrument are laced with elasticity and rhythmic flexibility. It is without doubt one of the most beautiful pieces to come from the author.[7]

A final piece of 1928 is the *Trovas de Amor* (Songs of Love), which uses folkloric poetry. Andrade gave it a review when it was published:

> The verses are *coboclo* [country-style] in sentiment and diction. Camargo Guarnieri uses these *coboclo* elements of popular Brazilian music well, elements which in general are more characteristic than the urban elements. From a national point of view, these songs go far beyond the *Lembranças,* which begins a series. They are more characteristic, very national in sentiment. They are strong and easier to set because of the use of the strophic formula and the *coboclo* sentiment. . . .
>
> Another point is the vocalization at the ends of phrases. It is curious to notice this in the songs of Brazilian composers who want to make national music; recently Lorenzo Fernandez used the process, and now Guarnieri uses it in his *Trovas* in which all phrases end with a sustained vocalization on the last syllable as is found in the *aboios* [songs without words] of the Northeast. The piece is a good one, the artist is young, and he is the best hope of Brazilian music in São Paulo, but more than once I get impatient with waiting. May the time pass lightly for those who will remember the work of this youth when he reaches his maturity![8]

All of these songs of his first year of serious writing are marked by a fluency, a sensitivity and feeling for the horizontal line, and a high level of pianistic accompanimental design. Melodies are predominantly conjunct, and frequently the piano has a melody which dialogues with that of the singer. Harmonic language is diatonic with chromatic nuances. Ostinato accompaniments are present as are key signatures in a few of the pieces. In *Prelúdio no. 2,* Guarnieri avoids the use of a strong bass line, a technique which will appear in many of his later works when he wants a supple, groundless texture.

One can see why Mário de Andrade was such a gift in Guarnieri's life. Andrade, Eurico Nogueira França, and Vasco Mariz were there to support his efforts with their regular critiques and encouragement. It was an important time for a young composer and for a country that was waking up to its own rich cultural and creative resources. Had it not been for these three music critics and a few others, the musical history of this vital period in Brazil's cultural life may have been lost forever.

In 1930 Guarnieri began to include some other instruments in his accompaniments. His first piece for mixed chorus, *Canção* (Song), was written in 1930. The most popular and still well-known piece of this year was the *O Impossível Carinho* (Impossible Love) based on the verses of the great Brazilian poet Manuel Bandeira: "Listen, I do not want to tell you my desire, only of my tenderness." Guarnieri shared the excitement of his experience when Andrade invited him to play this piece for Bandeira one evening. Then only twenty-three, he recalled his nervousness as he sat down at the piano:

> Manuel Bandeira was a very frank person, and he told me that he did not like music. Mário said I should play the piece for Manuel, so I sat at the piano, Manuel on one side and Mário on the other. I played it. When I finished, there was dead silence. Finally Manuel said, "Play it again." When I finished it the second time, he said, "Play it again." So I played it a third time, not knowing what he was thinking. Finally, he said, "This is not your piece, it is mine!"[9]

For the first time, in this sensitive love poem, Guarnieri utilized a much longer introduction, balanced by a coda. Vasco Mariz noted: "It called the attention of the Brazilian musical world to the young composer who is a true singer about love. It is a true love song with an ethereal atmosphere and pure melody, a great lyric realization and one of the finest Brazilian *Lieds* we possess."[10] After its first performance in Rio de Janeiro in 1941, Andrade Muricy noted the broad conception of the piece which made it difficult to interpret.[11] Koellreutter (with whom Guarnieri would tangle in 1950 over their conflicting music aesthetics) wrote after the same program:

> Among the songs of this young Brazilian composer there are true gems, pieces of great expressive power and profound sentiment. Guarnieri, sensi-

tive to the most delicate subtleties of poetry, seeks always to create an adequate ambiance for their expression. What I admire especially in the songs of Guarnieri is the absolute sincerity with which he writes. This is felt in the personality of the composer. Camargo Guarnieri lives for music, thinking only of art, not tolerating any concessions.[12]

Guarnieri produced two major choral works in 1932: *A Morte do Aviador* (Death of a Pilot) and an opera, *Pedro Malazarte.* In addition, there were several songs in Portuguese and a few which used the Afro-Brazilian dialect, of which *Den-Baú* is a wonderful example. Other works from this year include fifteen songs for children's voices (which have been lost) in one to four parts, another lost manuscript for SATB, *Prenda Minha* (My Gift), and a men's choral piece, *A Glória de São Paulo,* a martial hymn stemming from the turmoil São Paulo experienced that year over the constitutional question.

Den-Baú uses an onomatopoetic text and creates a stunning effect with its joyful energy. Amid a discussion of using Portuguese in songs, Guarnieri wrote it to prove that one could sing in any language. The syllabic text comes in a rapid patter. The toccata-like accompaniment fairly bristles with rhythmic life, and the square phrases of the AABB form utilize the Mixolydian mode but are basically simple in keeping with the playful nonsense of the text. The accompaniment stresses the middle range of the keyboard, alternating a simple I–V progression, moving finally to a low F in the last measures of the piece. Mariz noted that this piece was a curious experiment for Guarnieri because he wrote the melody and then superimposed the words with an excellent phonetic effect.[13] Guarnieri denied that this was his procedure.

Guarnieri's experiments in atonalism, described earlier, also influenced his songs. *Solidão* (Solitude), written in 1933, is rather typical of the songs of this period. Still in manuscript, the piece evidences its more strident harmonic texture in the ostinato accompaniment with its stress on the major seventh, the chromatically moving lines, and the harmonic independence of the voice part, all of which mark a new stage in the development of his musical language. All four songs of 1933 represent efforts at atonal organization. The texts are short, accompaniments independent of voice lines, and the piano textures vary from ostinatos and dissonant contrapuntal lines to complete independence of all parts.

In addition to his SATB *Coisas deste Brasil* (Things of Brazil), in 1936 Guarnieri began his first group of songs, the *Treze Canções de Amor* (Thirteen Love Songs). These thirteen songs use verses of various poets including four by his brother Rossine. All pertain in some way to love. Musically they do not represent any cyclic attempt, neither in style nor in key scheme, but they were intended to be sung as a set. The fact that they were written over a period of a year and a half suggests that Guarnieri wrote each with a fresh-ness and spontaneity that might not have been present had they been con-ceived as a cycle. The majority of pieces in this set are of a reflective nature. All imbibe the syncopation of Guarnieri's style, although nos. 7, 8, and 12 are more like tangos. In all of them the accompaniments are very continu-ous, usually with their own melodic lines, which dialogue with those of the soloist. Strangely, the modes are barely evident in this set. A few have the simple serenade alternation of a V–I harmonic scheme. Ayres de Andrade wrote of them:

> Guarnieri has a way all his own of treating the voice with accompani-ment. When the vocal melody displays a spontaneous simplicity, the accom-paniment offers a contrast in an extremely reflective treatment, which the composer gives to both the harmonic and pianistic aspects. It can be said that among the two contradictory forces which operate in art—reason and sentiment—Camargo Guarnieri confers on both equal rights of expansion, offering them distinct fields of display as if fearing some conflict of more se-rious proportions in virtue of the rights of each.
>
> A more detailed observation indicates that in the style of Camargo Guar-nieri, the spirit of unity is stronger than is seen at first. If the melody seems to fluctuate at certain moments as if unprotected and free, at the same time the importance attributed to the accompaniment becomes responsible in a momentary transfer of the interest in musical episodes from the voice to the piano. In many of the little poems, the melodic lines approximate our old *modinhas*. The composer seems to fashion such melodic forms.
>
> In each of the *Thirteen Love Songs* we meet the signs of a frank and full lyricism. These moments, which are true effects of living emotion captured by creative gestures of the music, constitute the best periods in the pages of the composer's songs. This seems to me to be the great expressive force in the language of Camargo Guarnieri.[14]

With the assistance of Mário de Andrade in 1935, Guarnieri organized the Coral Paulistano, a mixed-voice chorus dedicated to singing the music of Brazilian composers. With the impetus of the Congress of Portuguese as the National Sung Language held in July 1937 in São Paulo, Guarnieri pro-duced a series of his own choral works. He submitted one of them, *Coisas deste Brasil,* in a contest sponsored by the São Paulo Department of Culture under his pseudonym "Paulistan de Curuça." The jury, composed of Agostino Cantú, Arthur Primeira, and João de Souza Lima, met on Decem-ber 13, 1937, and awarded Guarnieri first prize. His work for a cappella mixed chorus consists of three songs that utilize the poetry of Gregory de Mais: *Reprovações* (Reproofs), *A Gente da Bahia* (People of Bahia), and *Mais Mestres Caramurus* (More Caramurus Masters). After a March 1938 concert of the Coral Paulistano which included these pieces, Caldeira Filho wrote:

Guarnieri reveals a real virtuosity in treating the voices of the choral group. Atmosphere is easily attained in the opening *Reprovações;* the character is incisive in certain effects in the second number as in the strengthening of the word *A-ri-co-be.* In *Mais Mestres Caramurus* we note a lowering of the emotional level in favor of tonal precision; the introduction uses a litany-like theme which increases the anticipation and justification of this final number.[15]

Egbê-gi is another SATB chorus, written in 1936. Based on a motive collected by Manuel Querino, it praises the *macumba* ceremony of Brazil's Blacks. In sharp contrast to this is the *Ave Maria* of 1937, which is completely homophonic, nonsyncopated, a cappella, and in a traditional harmonic setting.

In mid-1938 Guarnieri left Brazil for study in Europe, at which time his principal compositions were songs. On his arrival he had two opportunities to present some of them in concert. On February 28, 1939, the Revue Musicale in Paris saw a program completely devoted to Brazilian song literature, and Guarnieri's works constituted the last portion of this program. Present were such important personalities as composers Florent Schmidt, Marcelle de Manziarly, and Claude Delvincourt, his teacher Charles Koechlin, and other musicians. A second concert was given with the Paris Symphonic Orchestra.

When Guarnieri returned from Europe in November 1939 due to the threat of German invasion, some were eager to determine whether or not he had acquired any European influences in his music. The concert of January 12, 1940, which included *Três Poemas* (Three Poems) on a text of his brother Rossine and set with orchestral accompaniment, was carefully scrutinized, particularly by Andrade:

> The dynamic element unites the pieces in an increasing gradation of intensity. *Tristeza,* inspired by the urban *modinha* with its low guitar melody and the counterpoint of the urban *choro,* permits a more expansive polyphonic conception. The vocal part is distinct from that of the orchestra, which sounded dispersed to me at first hearing; but Guarnieri has achieved an erudite transposition here of our popular *modinha,* more refined, more subtle, and well constructed.
>
> In *Porto Seguro* (Secure Harbor) the vocal line has an extraordinary forceful expression of the text, without losing any of its Brazilian character. Inspired by the Caipira *moda,* the composer interlaced the splendid and incomparable phrases of the guitarist's thirds. The orchestration is very simple. I do not hesitate to say that this piece is one of the most perfect solutions of erudite national song.
>
> The *Coração Cosmopolita* (Cosmopolitan Heart) is formed according to our principal melodic rhythmic *emboladas* of the Northeast.[16]

Andrade ended his review with the conclusion that Guarnieri had returned from Europe in his full maturity and had become one of the strongest and most profound forces in contemporary national music. He was content to see that the European experience had not robbed him of his Brazilianism. Two other songs dating from 1939 received comment from Andrade Muricy:

> Camargo Guarnieri sings as he breathes—full of amplitude, liberty, flexibility, force. Some of these songs are the best in all of chamber literature. Among them is *Cantiga Triste* [Sad Song] written on the verses of Juvenal Galeno. It is a first-class work. A touching gravity, sentiment of authentic melancholy are here expressed with gripping reality. The *Modinha* on verses of Manuel Bandeira is another wonderful piece.[17]

Among the art songs that use contemporary poetic texts, Guarnieri frequently returned to the folk texts. His *Três Canções Brasileiras* (Three Brazilian Songs) of 1948 are one example. The first in this set, *Quando Embolada* (Lulled), has a simulated guitar accompaniment with a leading bass line and uses his favorite Mode of the Northeast. The song also illustrates Guarnieri's strong chromatic writing. *Embolada,* in the title, clearly roots these pieces in the Brazilian culture.

Songs continued to flow through Guarnieri's pen, from his heart. And the reviews kept him encouraged and writing. A piece premiered in a 1950 concert in the Municipal Theater in São Paulo, the *Serra do Rola-Moça* (Rola-Moça Mountain Range) was dedicated to Jennie Tourel. Based on a poem of Mário de Andrade taken from his *Nocturne in Belo Horizonte,* it is probably one of Guarnieri's more powerful works. Lutero Rodrigues wrote in the program notes for a 1988 performance with the Symphonic Orchestra of the University of São Paulo:

> The work [*Serra do Rola-Moça*] was composed in 1941, about two years after Guarnieri returned to Brazil, interrupting his studies in France because the Second World War was imminent. It was the beginning of the creative maturity of the composer, a phase in which his expression was very expansive, producing a great number of works, many of them winners in national and international competitions.
>
> This piece begins, as if it were a premonition, with the same music that will be heard at the most dramatic moment of the work. After establishing a great calm, the singer begins the narrative, sometimes interrupted by the orchestra, gradually growing through a rapid ascent to the most dramatic moment in all Guarnieri's compositions. The orchestra assumes various functions: accompaniment, uniting different narrative passages, atmosphere, and reinforcement of the text with its musical allusions.

Quando Embolada

The effective interaction between the singer and the orchestra present throughout the work, in my opinion, is the principal reason that caused the composer to call it a "Poem for voice and orchestra" and not a "cantata."[18]

Serra do Rola-Moça begins with an upward rushing arpeggiation that arrives at a *ff* dramatic introduction of a principal musical idea. This retains its intensity until it melts through descending sequences to a *pp Piu Calmo*. The music supports a tale of two lovers who meet tragedy on a mountain trail. Guarnieri does a little tone painting to express the text, "They laughed, oh, how they laughed," to express the joy of the lovers as they ride their horses on the way to their marriage ceremony. Near the end of the piece, the opening motif becomes a whispered cry of disbelief, echoed by the French horn and supported by the other instruments. A D-major cadence suggests the end of the tale, only to have the orchestra suddenly interrupt with a *ff Tragico* outburst that leads to the final act of the despondent man who, whipping his horse, follows his lover over into the abyss. A final return of the refrain closes the work softly, casting a poignant new light on why the mountains are now called "Rola Moça." Caldeira Filho wrote of this dramatic work:

> Interesting is the melodic line through which the composer carries the vivacity of the poetic rhythm. The expressive inflections of the soloist strengthen the strong suggestive power of this poem, magnificently set with its play of timbres so well adapted to secure the impression which he wanted to convey.[19]

Guarnieri began to show a tendency to group the songs he wrote, rather than have them appear as individual pieces. Although some were written over a period of years, they would find their way into print in one collection. For example, the *Três Canções Brasileiras* unites three songs, one from 1939 and two from 1948, all published by Ricordi in 1955. The national flavor is very strong in all three, in both text and setting. The *Quatro Cantigas* (Four Songs) is another set, based on the poetry of folklore and composed between 1949 and 1956. They are published by Ricordi with piano accompaniment, and Guarnieri also made an orchestral transcription. These four songs, like the previous set, respect the simplicity of their origin and reflect it both in melody and accompaniment.

Dating from 1954 are the *Cinco Poemas de Alice* (Five Songs of Alice), published by Ricordi. These were also transcribed by Guarnieri for string quartet accompaniment in 1963. All five poems, verses by his sister Alice, are rather short. Guarnieri seems to have bestowed on them a special care and tenderness, alternating their moods but increasing the dynamic tension through the course of the five. Vasco Mariz considers these *Cinco Poemas* one of Guarnieri's finest vocal works:

The *Cinco Poemas de Alice* are all excellent music. My preference is given for their notable power of expression in the rich accompaniments. In full possession of his artistic powers that seem to be at a height here, Camargo Guarnieri is reaching a grand phase in his production, perhaps the climax of his career.[20]

From 1951 come the *Oito Canções* (Eight Songs) based on the poetry of Suzanna de Campos, entitled *Para Acordar Teu Coração* (To Awaken Your Heart). This set was published by Ricordi in 1955. In all these pieces, the piano accompaniments are continuous, providing a secure basis for their melodies. The Lydian and Mixolydian modes and Mode of the Northeast are used, and the harmonic language is basically tonal with some chromaticism. A few pieces have syncopated rhythmic fabrics, but most are fairly regular in both melody and accompaniment. An opening phrase will frequently return at the end of the piece, suggesting ABA form. More often, however, the melodies are through composed. Although there is a variety of mood among the eight pieces, most are reflective and gentle. Mariz wrote of this set of eight songs:

> They are miniatures which confirm the reputation of their composer as the true singer of love songs within our national *Lied.* The representative touch of the great Paulistan composer here identifies a master. This cycle has had a great acceptance in Brazil as well as in the exterior. It has been heard various times in Argentina.[21]

Duas Canções de Celso Brant (Two Songs of Celso Brant) of 1955, published in 1958 by Ricordi, indicate the beginning of a new phase, which is seen in the more sophisticated piano accompaniments. The first song, *Meus Pecados* (My Sins), has a very flexible melodic line with syncopations. The accompaniment is full and independent of the voice part. The *Como O Coração da Noite* (As the Heart of the Night) has many of the same traits. Both are love poems and are dedicated to soprano Lia Salgado, wife of Guarnieri's close friend Clovis Salgado, former Minister of Education.

Adoração (Adoration) of 1956 illustrates the interaction of solo voice and accompaniment, this time in an imitative manner. Gone is the intense chromaticism. The pure Lydian mode enhances the plaintive quality of Suzanna de Campos's text: "Who can help me feel again your look, with my hand pressed in yours?"

Duas Canções (Two Songs) of 1956 are based on the poetry of Silvio C. de Oliveira and likewise reveal a growing development in their accompaniments. The melodic treatment of the texts is quite different from many of Guarnieri's earlier songs. In these two he repeats melodic phrases more often, almost as if they were little antiphons. This gives the songs a reflective intensity rather than the expansiveness which marked previous songs.

Adoração

Guarnieri wrote music for the film *Rebelião em Vila Rica* (Rebellion in Vila Rica) in 1957. The following year he extracted an orchestral suite from the score and two folk songs: *Amo-Te Muito* (I Love You) and *Elvira, Escuta* (Listen, Elvira). They are completely square and folklike in structure, and simple in their harmonic settings. In both Guarnieri simulated the guitar in the piano part by giving the left hand a countermelody and the right hand the off-beat chords.

In the late 1950s Guarnieri produced many more songs. They show an increased fullness of accompaniment, as well as a more integral relationship between the voice and piano. What Marlos Nobre, *carioca* composer and former student of Guarnieri, wrote on the record jacket of a recording of some of Guarnieri's songs applies more and more to the songs of this period and the succeeding years: "In the search for good texts, a phonetic adequacy will be evident in the marriage between voice and piano, with the latter never simply being an accompanying instrument."[22]

The early 1960s saw a shift in emphasis to orchestral works, with the songs reappearing again in the latter part of the decade. This interim saw rather dramatic changes in the harmonic language of the composer as evidenced in the *Seresta* for Piano and Orchestra and the *Sequência, Coral e Ricercare* for small chamber orchestra, to mention only two examples. These changes or developments are also apparent in the songs that follow. For example, the songs of 1967 reveal the stronger atonality that Guarnieri had begun to use. The piano parts that had been melodically independent in many songs now also take on an harmonic independence. Melodies retain a certain linear tonality but at times are in harmonic conflict with the accompaniment. Larger intervals, common to much serial and atonal writing, become more frequent in vocal lines. As always, however, the moods of the pieces are an accurate reflection of the texts.

The songs of 1968 are quite different from those of 1967 in that there is a general thinning out of the textures and densities. The *Música e Letre de Modinha* (Music and Words of the Modinha) on the poetry of Afonso Arinos is dedicated to Yeda de Araujo and was completed June 6, 1968. Its mere thirty-one *Sem pressa* measures cover a repeated period which gives expression to the two verses of the poem. There is considerable agreement between the voice and piano part, both harmonically and melodically. The tune flows in fairly continuous lines and simple direction. The piano part is chromatic, linear, and marked by subtle harmonic nuances. It ends with a tertian chord which is extended upward to a point of dissolution.

Also from 1968 are three very short pieces, *Três Epigramas* (Three Epigrams), all dedicated to Edmar Ferretti, who has performed many programs of Guarnieri's songs. They are given very simple treatment with rather thin piano accompaniments and conjunct melodic lines.

Guarnieri arranged and wrote numerous songs for children's choirs. Two songs date from 1968: *Escravos de Job* (Slaves of Job), which uses a folk tune, and *Biborá da Cruz,* based on Paulistan folk music. Both are for two voices and use imitation. The melodies are very square in C major with no chromatic alterations, and the piano provides a contrapuntal setting.

In 1969 Guarnieri wrote three very contrasting songs: *Ave Maria, Cuziribâmbo,* and *Súplica* (Supplication). The *Ave Maria* was composed for the wedding of Wanda Cunha Goldfeld. It has a traditional setting. *Cuziribâmbo* uses an Afro-Brazilian folkloric text and is dedicated to Florence and Alan Fisher. Fisher, the American consul in São Paulo for a number of years, was the photographer of a wonderful series of still photos taken while Guarnieri was conducting. The *Súplica,* also dedicated to Florence Fisher, uses the poetry of Niles Bond in both English and Portuguese. Its *Calmo* and *Sentido* markings suggest its plaintive quality.

The *Cantiga de Ausência* (Song of Absence), dated July 17, 1973, is once again based on the poetry of Guarnieri's brother Rossine. The verse extols the bittersweet pain of love and desire. The density of the chromatic writing in this song is virtually without relief, following the sentiments of the text. Full-spread left-hand chords with several interweaving lines above them create a tense fabric for the nontonally oriented melody.

Five weeks after the *Cantiga* was completed in 1973, Guarnieri suffered the unexpected loss of his father. A very strong reciprocal relationship spanning some eighty years had existed between these two men. Guarnieri's sense of loss was expressed in a choral work for four mixed voices, *Em Memória do Meu Pai* (In Memory of My Father), in which he used a text from Hebrews, chapter 13, verse 6: "The Lord is my helper and I shall not fear. The Lord is my helper." Written on the day of his father's death, August 24, 1973, the piece breathes the simple hope and peace that follow a long and fruitful life. It uses the Phrygian mode. A few homophonic phrases are interspersed among the linear, contrapuntal textures that Guarnieri had begun to develop in his religious compositions.

On August 28 of that year, he completed a simple *Ave Maria* for solo voice and organ. Unlike his other religious works, this one has the organ doubling the melody. The tonality is again modal (Aeolian), but the texture is less tense and dissonant in its counterpoint. The phrases flow simply and freely.

Along with several other songs, Guarnieri used the Latin *Ave Maria* text again, this time in a two-voiced setting with organ, written for the marriage of a friend on May 19, 1974. As with his other recent religious settings, this one is almost entirely devoid of Brazilian syncopation and is completely modal in its counterpoint with no accidentals. Beginning in the Dorian mode on D, the middle section moves to C (Ionian mode). The piece ends simply in the Aeolian mode on A. The text is treated in a direct manner without repetitions. Maximum richness of texture is achieved through the independence of the two imitative voices from their accompaniment.

In 1975 Guarnieri combined twelve songs under the title *Poemas de Negra* (Poems of the Negress), all with verses by Mário de Andrade. These included seven preexisting songs and five new ones. Also dating from 1975, on a text of Manuel Bandeira, is *Es na Minha Vida* (You Are in My Life). The next year brought two works, *Amor Mesquinho* (Pitiful Love) and *Migalhas* (Crumbs), and 1977 three: *Oferta* (Offering), *Vocalise,* and *Poema Interior* (Interior Poem), the last two using texts by Renata Pallotini. The composer likewise produced three songs in 1978: *Despedida Sentimental* (Sentimental Departure), *E Fico a Pensar* (I Think), and *O Que Podia Ter Sido* (What Could It Have Been?). The first was also on a text of Andrade and was recorded by Lenita Bruno and Guarnieri for Funarte (MEC/ FUNARTE, 1983). *Que Pena* dates from 1980, *Desejo* (Desire) and *Eu Te Encontrei* (I Met You) from 1982, and *Miniatura* (Miniature) from 1983. His last song is *Acalanto para Luísa* (Lullaby for Luísa), from 1989, which uses a text of his own. This song and the 1983 *Miniatura* were premiered posthumously in São Paulo on May 5, 1994.

In reviewing these selected songs within Guarnieri's total vocal output, it is evident that the song was a very personal medium through which he expressed his most profound sentiments. Songs also reveal the composer's development, perhaps more obvious in his other works, but nonetheless very present in these intimate pieces.

His harmonic language came through periods of experimentation, particularly in the late 1930s, and again after 1950, reaching a more intense fabric of harmonic dissonance in his later songs. Noticeable, too, is the growing cooperation between vocal and piano parts, with the latter gradually assuming a more integral function, even though at times it is more independent of the melody than in earlier works. Contrasting harmonic orientations of the two parts also become an expressive means. Guarnieri sometimes used the violão (guitar) style with a bourdon lower line counterpointing the vocal line. Just as often, however, the entire piano texture was a subservient but equal partner to the melody.

Guarnieri showed a preference for short poems, which seemed to give him ultimate flexibility. As indicated above, the verses were usually love poems of strong sentiment. He used folkloric poetry, as well as that of the principal Brazilian poets. Melodies often used the modes, particularly the Mixolydian mode; the Mode of the Northeast and Lydian mode are less visible among his songs. Folkloric texts have suitably simple tunes, whereas the more carefully worked poetry provides him an opportunity to spin the longer lines for which he is so well known.

From the time of Mário de Andrade's early praise for Guarnieri's affinity for song, critics have noted the ease with which he produced vocal works, usually pointing out that in song he was free to express his strongly Brazilian melodic gift. Luiz Heitor wrote that Guarnieri had a command of the "subtle sublimation of popular melodic, harmonic, rhythmic, and polyphonic processes. He is the transfiguration of Brazilian music, diaphanous, catching the inspiration eternally drawn from the substance of the land, but free of national servility."[23] Eurico Nogueira França likewise mentioned that "The songs of Guarnieri are characterized by an intimate appealing lyricism."[24] Caldeira Filho was more explicit in trying to define exactly those Brazilian qualities which so many writers have attributed to Guarnieri:

> One characteristic of his music is the unconscious disappearance of the pre-occupation with rhythm, and especially of syncopation. For some, syncopation is the sum and substance of Brazilian music. For Guarnieri, it appears that syncopation was merely a suggestion of an atmosphere which was invoked within him and was no more than one simple detail. Now the melodic line is less angular, more elastic and robust, and especially more Brazilian. This Brazilianism is more than mere syncopation or very national melodic inflections. There is found in the quality of certain themes the ingenious use of the Caipira [Paulistan] thirds, and the profound significance of the *modinha* with its languor of the serenade which we attribute to it. In the songs, the composer brilliantly conquers the difficulties entailed in creating an emotional atmosphere within the restricted limits of the vocal tessitura.[25]

There are a number of singers who have made efforts to program Guarnieri's songs, including Cristina Maristany, Alice Ribeiro, Lia Salgado, and Edmar Ferretti, who, in 1968, recorded an entire disk of the songs with Guarnieri at the piano. Marlos Nobre wrote the notes for the record jacket. He perhaps has summarized as well as anyone Guarnieri's position in the field of Brazilian song:

> It is in the chamber songs, particularly for voice and piano, that the art of Camargo Guarnieri acquires his most individualized and personal projection. This is without detriment to his symphonic, piano, and chamber works, all of which are of excellent form and proven worth.
>
> It appears to be in the genre of the chamber song that the personality of the Paulistan musician is found completely at ease, expanding naturally, creating with a fluidity and security which characterize the art of the great masters. It is felt that today Guarnieri has reached a total control of technical problems as seen in this phase of his maturity, a phase in which the music flows freely from him without flaws or impurities.
>
> The category of his songs increases from year to year, attesting clearly his preference for this genre in which he has created what must justly be termed the national *Lied*. It is clear that the solutions which he found, the language he used, will not be the only way to be tread by other Brazilian composers. However, the idea of the model he has given will be used in the general orientation of a composer in the creation of his own songs.

The phonetic aspect of his songs is the decisive factor in their success, and it is noted that they are easy both to sing and to understand. The secret of this is the search for a certain rhythm for the inflection of each syllable, for the adequate phrase within the general dramatic line of the text.[26]

The last point, phonetic appropriateness, has been mentioned by sopranos Lia Salgado and Edmar Ferretti; both claim that Guarnieri's songs are very easy to sing, that they flow smoothly. From his first "disastrous" attempts, as Andrade put it, Guarnieri quickly learned. As his historic importance is recalled, one realizes that he broke much new ground, capturing the song form from the Italian language which had dominated Brazilian composers throughout the nineteenth and early twentieth centuries, bringing it home to a new flowering in Portuguese. França noted that, whether or not his songs will be considered his best compositions (or whether this is even a fair comparison to be made), there is no doubt that that songs of Camargo Guarnieri are a tremendous contribution to Brazilian vocal literature.

From a "disastrous" start through over sixty years of using the song form as his most personal expression, Guarnieri's songs will remain an important, precious legacy. Another close observer, Vasco Mariz, has the last word: "Guarnieri is the most prolific of our national composers for voice, and he has accomplished this with the greatest ability and good taste. His contributions to the national *Lied* repertoire are enough to immortalize him!"[27]

SEVEN

Dramatic Choral Works

I n this category of Camargo Guarnieri's compositions there are two one-
act operas, seven cantatas, a psalm, and a mass. One might think his Italian ancestry would have inclined him more frequently toward the operatic
form, but actually the opposite was true. He seemed to function best within
the abstract musical design in which structural principles could be the de-
terminants of form and content, except for the songs as noted in the preceding chapter. His choral and dramatic works are among the least performed.

These pieces span most of his compositional life. *Pedro Malazarte,* a
one-act opera written in 1931, reveals Guarnieri's preoccupation with the
incorporation of national elements in his work at that time. *Morte do Aviador* (Death of a Pilot), a tragic cantata dating from 1932, is set historically
within his experience of the Constitutional Revolution. *Sêca* of 1958, a
cantata based on the poetry of Sylvia Celeste de Campos, expresses the anguish and despair of Brazil's Northeasterners who repeatedly endure the
drought cycles of that region. Two more cantatas, *Colóquio* (Conversation)
of 1959 and *O Guaná-bará* of 1965, also speak of the land, the first giving
emphasis to the Genesis theme from Scripture, and the second to the
founding of Rio de Janeiro.

A lyric tragedy in one act, *Um Homen Só* (Only a Man), written in 1960,
is a tense psychological study of one lonely man and his struggle with his
world. *A Caso do Vestido* (A Case of a Gown), a 1970 cantata, was a favorite
of Guarnieri's. In 1972 he turned to a purely modal setting in polyphonic
style in his *Missa Diligite* (Love One Another).

The 1980s saw the creation of four choral works: three more cantatas
and *Psalm 23*. The cantatas are *Auto de Todo Mundo e Ninguem* (Story of All
in the World and None), *Canto de Amor aos Meus Irmãos do Mundo* (Song
of Love for My Brotherhood of the World), and *Cinquentenário da Universidade de São Paulo* (Sesquicentennial of the University of São Paulo).

Pedro Malazarte.
Comic Opera in One Act.
1931. Manuscript

This work is based on a libretto by Mário de Andrade. The idea of creating a national opera had been discussed in 1928 by Andrade, Lamberto Baldi (Guarnieri's composition teacher), and Guarnieri. Andrade agreed to write a libretto, and three days later he handed it to Guarnieri. The young composer studied the text and made several unsuccessful attempts at sketching a musical setting before he laid it aside. He picked it up again in late 1930, and this time something clicked for him. He had had two years to develop his own skills and gain confidence in his ability. He began writing on January 1, 1931, and by February 6 he had completed the work.

Guarnieri had planned to write a full orchestral accompaniment, but Andrade convinced him that a smaller chamber orchestra would be a better balance for the small scale of the work and its three characters. The final scoring was for pairs of flutes, oboes, clarinets, bassoons, trumpets, and a string quartet. The result was a group which was flexible enough to keep the texture clear-cut and rhythmically precise.

The opera has national ties, not only in its theme of racial miscegenation, but also in Guarnieri's use of folk forms and songs. The story itself employs only three characters: Malazarte (baritone), a Baiana woman (mezzo-soprano), and her husband, a German-Brazilian called Alemão (tenor). Malazarte chances upon the Baiana woman in her home and is delighted to learn that her husband has gone to the city. The woman prepares a fine meal for Malazarte, only to be surprised at the unexpected arrival of Alemão. Malazarte explains his presence, and Alemão treats him most graciously as a friend and welcome guest. While Alemão has an after-dinner snooze, Baiana begs Malazarte to take her away with him. By this time Malazarte has grown to respect Alemão and advises her to remain with her husband. Alemão awakens, and there follows a symbolic little situation in which he barters with Malazarte for a black cat before leaving. Renzo Massarani explained this folkloric reference:

> The figure of Pedro Malazarte is not really an authentic folkloric person, although he has lived in the devilish histories all over Brazil. Andrade has taken from him the fiery, sagacious temperament, keeping only the spirit of the legend of the corvo [black vulture, which is a symbol of evil, bad luck, and death], substituting it in the opera with a black cat. It is not an opera which exhibits the virtuosic abilities of the singers, but rather, the principal feeling is one of a sociological and cultural nature.[1]

Structurally, the work opens with a typical orchestral overture which is particularly light-hearted. The first scene opens upon the Baiana woman fretting about the things she is not permitted to do. A mixed chorus enters, humming a brief interlude following the Baiana's irritated reflections. The chorus then comments upon the situation, a role which it maintains throughout the opera with reference to all three characters. Orchestral interludes are interspersed periodically through the forty-five-minute piece. One interlude strongly resembles the *Dança Brasileira* of 1928, both in melodic structure and in delicate spirit.

Duets and trios in the operatic tradition are completely absent. Each of the characters has at least one representative aria although the vocal range is rather limited, making the projection above the orchestra difficult in places. Most of the solo singing consists of fragmentary dialogue among the three characters, while the ensemble aspects are relegated to the chorus. The lines of Alemão are distinctly sedate, respectful, and calm, for he represents, as Eurico Nogueira França noted, "the heroic figure common throughout the country."[2] The chorus, true to its function, has the final commentary and closes the work.

Guarnieri uses the full spectrum of colorful orchestration. Woodwinds and brasses are used to full advantage in the contrapuntally conceived texture, alternating fragments of the rollicking thematic material. At times the strings and winds are used antiphonally. The modes are prominent, especially the Mixolydian mode. Melodies frequently hover between the fifth and flatted seventh tones, giving them a peculiar ethos, a suspended, pensive quality. At such moments, Guarnieri likes to thin out the lower tones, adding to the sense of suspension without a firm foundation.

França noted, "There is a substantial feeling of Brazilianism in the music of *Pedro Malazarte* as there is in all of Guarnieri's music."[3] First there is a very strong rhythmic quality which undergirds the entire work and sets it properly right in Bahia, the source of so much of rhythm in Brazilian music. Secondly, Guarnieri utilizes two Brazilian folk forms, the *modinha* for the song of the Bahian woman, *Morena! Sultano!* (Black Woman! Sultan!), and the comic dialogue or patter of the *embolada* of Malazarte, *Sou Malazarte!* (I Am Malazarte!). There are two actual folk songs that also appear: *Mulher Não Vá* (Woman, Don't Go), sung by the Baiana, and the chorus's closing *Ciranda Cirandinha*. Although the opera was composed in 1931, it did not receive a complete performance until 1952 in Rio de Janeiro. However, the orchestral overture to the work was performed in São Paulo in 1935. Andrade wrote after this event:

> It is a very short piece that does not last even three minutes but touches
> on three themes, which is positively too much for such a short piece. The

first is a comfortable and gracious theme of repeated notes which, in the opera, accompanies the dinner scene. It is presented initially by the oboe and trumpets, and repeated by the strings after a contrasting motive which expresses the hero's theme. The second theme is exposed and comes from the scene in which Malazarte tells of the death of his father. The third theme, a charming one, is entirely ruined in the overture by its orchestration (and its performance which was cold and without feeling for its Brazilian rhythm). It arises in the trombone and English horn under the pizzicato of the lower strings. This appears an unhappy solution to me, but I reserve the right to change my opinion.

Incontestably, Camargo Guarnieri has not yet achieved the skill in handling the orchestra that Francisco Mignone has. The piece presents highs and lows in symphonic effects—excellent moments, as at the beginning, but others less happy, as near the end. But it would really be an evasion to decide details of criticism which are exclusively orchestral in a little piece so short and which is only the beginning of an opera buffa. It must be heard. It has a happy linear quality in its three themes which are exposed, and it makes one want to hear the whole work.[4]

One must read these comments of Andrade realizing his own great involvement not only with this particular work, but also with the evolution of the young composer.

When the complete opera was performed in 1952, twenty-one years after it had been written, it is not surprising that many noted the immaturity of the work. Such a time lapse leaves a composer open to criticism of a kind different from that given a fresh, new work. Such was the case with comments of Antônio Rangel Bandeira, who labeled it a work of youth with a libretto that was too limited, which in turn limited the composer. Further, he wrote, "In truth, the work of Camargo Guarnieri is substantially dramatic. It has nothing comic in it, playful or ingenuous. It is a very serious work."[5]

Eurico Nogueira França praised it as a great success, the first truly Brazilian opera. He noted that Andrade had written in his *História de Música Brasileira* that he "considered the comic opera the happiest aesthetic solution to the lyric genre, even to the convention of song, to express the daily sentiments and actions which are justified by the humorous effect he wants to obtain."[6]

França didn't seem to miss the grand arias, ensembles, and choruses of the late Romantic operas. Nor did he mind that it was not distinctly humorous. He was willing to accept it, not for what it was not, but for what it was, "an autonomous creation of the composer who has studied and assimilated our Brazilian popular music. Camargo Guarnieri never treats the work as a folkloric opera as some other composers have done.[7] Renzo Massarani likewise felt that it was truly Brazilian and would have been a success, even if it had not had its roots in philosophical and sociological concepts.[8]

Pedro Malazarte received a second performance in São Paulo in 1954, and a third in Buenos Aires in 1969. The December 12, 1969, issue of Rio's *Jornal do Brasil* quoted the *Buenos Aires Musical:*

> *Pedro Malazarte*, recently presented by the Little Opera Company in President Alvear Auditorium, was music which followed the intrigue of the text in a manner not grand but pleasant in its folkloric quality. The composer managed the text naturally and gave the appearance of spontaneous lyricism which is one of the strongest characteristics of the score.[9]

In 1994 the opera was presented four times in São Paulo and subsequently had three more performances in Belo Horizonte, and three in São Paulo.

A Morte do Aviador—Cantata Trágica
(Death of a Pilot—Tragic Cantata).
Cantata for Soprano, Mixed Chorus, and Orchestra.
1932. Manuscript

Dedicated to the memory of Gomes Ribeiro, who died for the cause of freedom for the Paulistans, it again uses a libretto by Mário de Andrade. More than any other city, São Paulo resisted the revolution that Getúlio Vargas launched in 1930. Guarnieri himself had served as a civil guard at night, watching for the expected arrival of Vargas's forces. Gomes Ribeiro was a pilot who gave his life in defense of the city and subsequently became the hero of the text, which Guarnieri began to set to music although this work was never finished. The incomplete pencil manuscript has an overture, followed by three sections. There is a chorus representing the Paulistans, and a part marked "Descraça" (Misfortune), which carries the narration of the tragic events. The original version of the cantata for voices and piano was almost complete, but only the first part of a second orchestral version was finished. Other things intervened, and Guarnieri never finished the orchestration, nor was the piece ever performed. The intended forces were soprano solo, chorus, and orchestra.

Sêca (Dryness). Cantata for Solo Voice,
Women's Chorus, and Orchestra.
1958. Manuscript

Northeastern Brazil is unique in the world for its intensely arid climate, which has given rise to a peculiar psychological type of Brazilian, typified in the *cangaçeiro*—a type of robber. The drought cycles there have been the themes of many twentieth-century writers, including Sylvia Celeste de Campos, who provided this text. After a performance of *Sêca* in São Paulo in April 1959, in which Mary Gazzy was soloist, Caldeira Filho wrote:

> A transcription of the poem permits, beyond an appreciation of its intrinsic beauty, an understanding of the musical structure in which the composer transposes into sound the aesthetic strength of each verse, commenting with vocal and instrumental resources on the plastic and emotive suggestions which each contains.
>
> The vocal soloist presents each of these verses; the unison chorus has the two final words of each. The last verse is sung entirely by the chorus. It results in a work of great expressive intensity, rigorous and simple in its plan, moderate in the means used, but rich in the performance of these means: a beauty of orchestral colors, the use of the timbres, and principally of the percussion which assumes a strength which is almost thematic.
>
> Few have been as powerful as Guarnieri in his suggestion of melancholy, of distance, and of the infinite. The concise manner of our own composer is present in this work, clear and dry—and why not with such a title? His control of expressive economy brings him the most beautiful results which he obtains in leading the emotive process, which culminates in a really grand finale where the chorus dominates and the human presence takes the place of nature. This conclusive grandeur is "effective" in the good sense, according to Mário de Andrade, and is obtained without breaking the high quality in which the whole piece moves.
>
> An authentic first work, and in itself of national significance, it is also an example of the approach to art for the public. Despite its modernism, it was immediately understood and appreciated.[10]

Guarnieri used solo woodwinds effectively in this work, particularly in the interludes. The entire texture has a suspended quality, with the absence of a strong foundational bass line. Persistent timpani beats add to the sense of drudgery and hardship. Sustained tones or brief ostinati also give the texture a sense of motionlessness. Only in the final *Maestoso* is there a continuity of the orchestral writing and a more martial character to express the hopeful challenge of the closing lines of the poem. The orchestral writing is generally dry in its own way. It has a dull dissonance and conjunct movement that suggests the difficulty of life, or even of breathing, in the intense heat and dryness of the land. Both triadic and quartal sonorities occur, usually in bitonal or cross-relationships.

The vocal writing, like that of the orchestra, is restrained and declamatory for the most part. It lies between low C♯ and touches a high G♯ once, though the tessitura is confined to the lower half of that range. It stays remarkably close to an E tonal center. *Sêca* was granted the "Best Symphonic Work of 1959 Award" by the Paulistan Association of Theater Critics.

Colóquio (Conversation).
Cantata for Voice, Unison Chorus *ad libitum,*
Wind Quintet, Piano, and Percussion.
1959. Manuscript

Ernesto Guerra de Cal used a free translation of a passage from Genesis as the text for this work: "In the beginning, only God spoke and His voice—without echo, without end, without beginning—rolled on the empty empire of the waters with enormous thunder of absolute words."

After a severe *Maestoso* introduction, the melody, which is a unison line throughout, begins in a declamatory style. Both accompaniment and vocal line tend toward a chant style throughout the entire first half, suggesting a *parlando* style of God's speech indicated by the text. Where the people speak, the setting becomes a little more active. The sudden change, "And God said nothing," is marked both times by only one sustained note. The score then picks up the tempo, moving into a lively *Andantino* in which the people finally take things into their own hands. It remains jubilant to the *fff* ending.

Colóquio has had two performances. Its premiere was on September 20, 1959. The work had been commissioned for the 1959 Fourth International Meeting of Luso-Brasilian Studies organized by the Federal University of Bahia. Olga Maria Shroeter was soloist, and Hans Joachim Koellreutter conducted. Carleton Sprague-Smith, to whom the piece was dedicated, was flutist in this performance. A second performance was at Carroll College in Waukesha, Wisconsin, on February 10, 1977.

Um Homen Só (Only a Man).
Lyric Tragedy in One Act.
1960. Manuscript

Guarnieri's second opera is not as nationalistic in its theme as *Pedro Malazarte,* although Eurico Nogueira França commented upon its importance in the development of Brazilian opera at its first performance in Rio in 1962:

> Brazilian opera, although hardly born, had indeed registered its birth in the two works of Camargo Guarnieri and is sure to provoke a series of disagreements when treated as comic opera. Those who frequent the Municipal Theater and who hear foreign operas without knowing the text will be scandalized to hear [in *Malazarte*] a mulatto and a Portuguese on stage. They will condemn the common dialect of our comic opera as in the case of *Pedro Malazarte* which placed on stage a Baiana and a German-Brazilian. This type of opera can nurture a great richness of folkloric forms and of a more Brazilian sentiment, which *Um Homen Só* does from beginning to end.[11]

The librettist, Gianfrancesco Guarnieri (no relation to the composer), presents the tragic character of José Pires de Assunção, who was "only a man," and a sick one at that. There are thirteen characters and a mixed chorus in the cast of this fifty-six-minute work. The format through which the story is unraveled is that of an extended Prologue, in which the various characters drone on, giving little bits of information about the man, endlessly repeating them as if they, too, were affected with José's mental maladies. The actual opera begins with and centers on José, his search for living responses from people amid his hallucinations, and his final demise. An Epilogue by the chorus repeats the bland facts concerning the impoverished personality as his body is carried to its grave.

The orchestral Prologue sets the stark musical mood with its dry, almost motionless fragments, with a preference for extreme high and low ranges. When the chorus finally enters with the Prologue text, it is as barren and motionless as the orchestra. Fragments move in harmonic conflict, but always with a stagnancy and starkness of death itself. The chorus serves the function of commentator and protagonist of José's conscience. A climax is reached at José's death near the end of the opera. An immediate continuation in the *Lento* Epilogue returns to the morose plodding established in the Prologue.

The premiere was given in Rio's Municipal Theater October 21, 1962, with Eduardo de Guarnieri, father of the librettist, conducting, and Paulo Fortes singing the role of José. Lia Salgado was the soprano in the role of Mariana. Ziembinski was the director, and Tatiana Leskova the choreographer. França's extended commentary placed the importance of the work in perspective:

> Guarnieri has written a new opera which should not cause his critics to mobilize against him because of its serious style; rather, the tragic element in this work constitutes an important advance over his first opera. This progress is neatly marked by the greater theatrical quality of *Um Homen Só*. All moves along together here in terms of good, modern, vigorous, advanced theater. We have arrived at a concept of Brazilian opera in which the theatrical dimensions confer upon it an irresistible legitimacy. The scenery, ballet, direction, soloists—all added to its success.
>
> Is not solitude, the impossibility of communication among us, one of the dominant themes of modern drama? To the degree that man advances his destiny, he communicates with his fantasies, his memories, interacting with his anguish more than with his living passions. There are neurotic situations in which an individual creates a whole world of fantasy around himself. But there are also situations in which, by a kind of collapse of the spirit, he builds imaginary walls around himself. Guarnieri's *O Homen Só* touches

the solitude of interior life. He believes that his loved ones—Mariana, his son, friend, dog, canary—have deserted him. Wandering lost through the city, he supposes that he is abandoned in the world. The scenes support this loneliness.

The musical construction of the dramatic work is fully valid in the palpitating lyricism of the music of Camargo Guarnieri; the diversity, adequacy, and economy of expressive accents in the score combine the chorus integrally with the orchestra and the dramatic interpreters, the solo voices. There are moments of solemnity in the music which honor the stylistic versatility of the composer, such as in the mystic, rapid church music which leads José to the threshold of the church, and the music of the internal chorus which comments and carries the action and which give the score a notable distinction.

Between the voices and the orchestra there is established a subtle, contrapuntal interaction which is really elegant; it has a strength which is so Brazilian, a naturalness of rhythmic invention which controls the polyphony, as noted in other works, and it becomes one of the most salient characteristics of the style of Camargo Guarnieri.[12]

O Guaná-bará. Cantata for Baritone, Mixed Chorus, Narrator, and Orchestra. 1965. Heliograph Copy. Manuscript

This full-length cantata on a text by Cecilia Meireles, composed in 1965, premiered in 1968 in Rio, an event which could well be forgotten. As recounted earlier, the State of Guanabara had instituted its first composition competition, which was open to composers from all over the country. What was not mentioned in the initial literature was that it was intended for young composers. Guarnieri, as well as several other older, established composers, entered scores. They not only did not receive favorable consideration from the jury, but their works were jeered at the performances by the young audience.

Before the performance of Guarnieri's cantata, fliers were distributed which ridiculed portions of the text, especially a phrase "let us lift up the city." Likewise, Rádames Gnatalli and Francisco Mignone were openly criticized, and their music was booed during performance. Ironically, six of Guarnieri's own students were among the top prize winners, the first prize going to Almeida Prado, one of his most gifted young students. Guarnieri took the happenings in stride.

The cantata glorifies the spirit which permeated the founding of the City of São Sebastian of the River of January, Rio de Janeiro's original full name, located in the then named state of Guanabara. It falls into four sections:

Part I: The land of early discovery is extolled—natural riches, sky, mountains, and sea; the first contacts with unfriendly Indians, a feast to celebrate the settling of Guanabara, the establishment of homes among the mountains in the city. "Levantaremos a cidade"—let us lift up the city to commemorate our hero, São Sebastian.

Part II: The narrator picks up the phrase "Let us lift up the city" and calls upon the "holy" Indians and Christians and the Jesuit Padre Anchieta to make a city in honor of São Sebastian, to build monasteries, churches, and schools—all as an example for future generations.

Part III: The narrator again opens with "Let us lift up the city." There is a passing reference to the royalty of Portugal who came and went, and then a call to all—Whites, Mamulucos, Blacks —to work together to build a city of arts and sciences where thousands of voices will sing the mass, operas, hymns, and in which the Blacks will be free.

Part IV: The affluence of the Republic is extolled in the short text, which is extended through repetition.

Harmonically the work is definitely Guarnieri's, with its dissonance resulting from conflicting lines and chord streams among the varied parts. Ostinatos are likewise present, in both the orchestral and the vocal parts.

O Caso do Vestido (A Case of a Gown).
Cantata for Soprano and Orchestra.
1970. Manuscript

For several years Guarnieri mulled over the dramatic poem of his contemporary Carlos Drummond Andrade before he decided to set it. This fourteen-and-one-half-minute work deals with the painful relationships in a dysfunctional family. In written program notes Guarnieri commented on the difficulties he faced in trying to find different expressive modes for the four characters in the poem—the wife, two daughters, husband—all to be sung by just one voice. He wrote:

> When the daughters ask the mother a question, they speak freely without determined pitch. When the mother answers them, she sings a melodic fragment that conforms to the expressive intensity of the specific passage. When she has a long narrative section, the mother's vocal tessitura is higher and the expressive melodic line much more anguished. The second woman, the lover, narrates her tragedy with a tessitura more central, and the melodic line is full of feeling. The father appears only once at the end of the work to say: "Woman, put another place at the table." This phrase is pronounced by the soloist in a deep, almost masculine tone of voice.[13]

Guarnieri used a full orchestra in this work, expanding the percussion to include timpani, xylophone, vibraphone, piatti, tam-tam, side drum without snares, and harp. As with other works, he emphasized the solo capacities of the instruments, creating a colorful backdrop for the soloist.

The moving text of *O Caso do Vestido,* so powerfully set, is probably one of Guarnieri's most successfully wrought dramatic works, along with *Sêca.* It is successful both by reason of the text—its realism and the limitation he had to exercise in developing it for solo voice—and in the complete mastery of harmonic, melodic, and contrapuntal materials and orchestral timbres that he brought to it.

The anguished text, with its extreme feelings of despondency and hopelessness, is intensified by the atonal texture, which at times is reflective and tense. At other times it bursts into angular, precipitous comments from the accompaniment. The orchestra never overpowers but always supports the soloist, frequently with single lines, adding strength to its activity when more support is needed.

Guarnieri's use of instruments with their expressive contrasts of attack, sustaining power, and nuance possibilities gives his orchestra the flexibility of a most supple voice. His eminent position among composers of the Brazilian song is not hidden as he combines orchestral timbres with the human voice. This sensitivity to vocal nuance, along with his complete mastery of the craft of composition—that can come only from the kind of personal and artistic discipline which are his—give him in this work the rare kind of complete freedom to deal with the powerful story.

O Caso do Vestido was premiered in São Paulo on September 10, 1971, with Edmar Ferretti, to whom it is dedicated, as soloist, with the São Paulo Municipal Symphony Orchestra under Felipe de Souza. Ferretti again performed it in Porto Alegre on May 14, 1974, with Henrique Morlenbaum and the Porto Alegre Symphony Orchestra. The *Diário do Povo* of that city carried the following review by Celso Loureiro Chaves a few days later:

> This cantata is extremely difficult for any soloist who might want to sing it, but Edmar Ferretti knew how to transform her interpretation into an unforgettable experience. Mr. Morlenbaum maintained complete control over the orchestra, directing simultaneously with security and flexibility. We believe that *O Caso do Vestido* will be counted among Camargo Guarnieri's most important works.[14]

Missa Diligite (Love One Another).
Mixed Chorus and Organ or String Orchestra.
1972. Manuscript

Other than fourteen *Ave Maria*'s and a *Psalm,* this is Guarnieri's only work in a liturgical vein. It was commissioned by his good friends Nenê and Luis

Medici to commemorate their fortieth wedding anniversary. It was recorded on that occasion, June 20, 1972, in the Church of Our Lady of Fatima in Sumaré, São Paulo. Angelo Camin was the organist, Edmar Ferretti the soloist, and Guarnieri himself the choral conductor.

Guarnieri appropriately turned to the modes and a medieval polyphonic style in writing this work. Neither were new to him, although his expressive conception here was new to his works. There are four sections: Kyrie, Gloria, Sanctus–Benedictus, and Agnus Dei. The Credo was not needed in the particular service and therefore not included. Guarnieri used the Latin text, even though Portuguese was in liturgical use at that time.

The Kyrie begins with a peaceful organ introduction of undulating lines, which lead directly into the soprano's entrance. There follow imitative entrances of the alto, tenor, and bass as each in turn states the same motive alternately on the tonic and dominant of the Dorian mode. The Christe is stated only once, rather than three times, by all four voices simultaneously. A short interlude leads to a restatement of the Kyrie, this time with the tenor leading, followed by alto, bass, and then soprano. The purely Dorian quality of this movement, its conjunct movement of lines, and the direct treatment of the text reflect, as Caldeira Filho wrote, "a solemn supplication which originates in the depths of the heart, submissive but not heroic."[15]

The organ part is continuous, most often quite independent of the vocal lines, thus creating a linear dissonance of mild intensity. The vocal lines themselves frequently pass through sevenths and ninths, creating their own plaintiveness as they rise and fall. This is noted particularly in the Christe.

The Gloria opens directly with an unaccompanied "Et in terra" sung by the basses. Again, the text moves directly without repetitions. The texture alternates between homophonic and linear passages. At times phrases are treated antiphonally or with imitative entrances of two or more voices. Cadences tend to lack a third in the chord, creating an open, medieval effect. The organ part is again independent of the voices through most of the movement, serving as obbligato through the entire latter portion of the movement. The absolute lack of accidentals and the continual return to A as a tonal center place this movement in the Aeolian mode.

Open, ringing chords mark the opening of the Sanctus as well as the Hosanna. Stately moving linear textures separate more homophonic sections. The Benedictus is given to a solo mezzo-soprano and serves, as Caldeira Filho notes, "as a brief meditation on the holy mysteries."[16]

Filho noted the popular spirit of the rising line of the Agnus Dei, which he considered "less modal but creating a clear and luminous atmosphere which will close the work."[17] He reflected on the work as a whole:

> This composition was completed with a perfect distinction between the technical and expressive functions of the voices and the organ without de-

tracting from the real unity of those elements which must be combined to achieve a common aesthetic result. Camargo Guarnieri—and this is typical of him as a composer—captured the expressive character of a specific epoch and not merely its technical or artistic qualities. While they are reflections of one culture, they passed with it. Here they are an expression of a human necessity, of something permanent. It is in this spirit that the sensibilities of the composer freely expanded to arrive at using a polyphony in which all of the voices really sang. The general impression of the work is energetic and robust, an incisive affirmation of faith.[18]

This Mass has had a number of performances. It was included in one of the three concerts in December 1977 which honored the composer on his seventieth birthday. Again in São Paulo in 1987, on his eightieth birthday, the Coral Camargo Guarnieri from Minas Gerais sang it with his own string orchestra from the University of São Paulo at a mass in his honor.

Auto de Todo Mundo e Ninguém
(Story of All in the World and None).
Cantata for Narrator, Tenor, Mixed Chorus, and Orchestra.
January 1–12, 1981. Manuscript

This is a poem which uses the eternal dialogue between Everyman and the Devil, a characterization in which selfish concerns drive the person. "Nobody" does the questioning, and the Devil has the last, intervening word. The text is by Carlos Drummond de Andrade, who based it on *Auto da Lusitânia* (Story of the *Lusitania*) of Gil Vincente.

Guarnieri has set the text for narrator (the Devil), tenor (Nobody), and an SATB chorus (Everyman). Instrumentation includes timpani, *xocalho, reco-reco,* triangle, *pratos,* tam-tam, and woodblock. He treats the text in a very straightforward manner with little repetition. Occasionally the chorus echoes portions of the solo text, but the story moves without interruption. The dissonant, unaccompanied choral lines make it a challenge for any group. Guarnieri noted in his score: "The Devil's part should be given to a deep bass voice. He must always speak very loudly in a free rhythm." The work's powerful statement is eternally appealing.

Canto de Amor aos Meus Irmãos do Mundo
(Song of Love for My Brotherhood of the World).
Cantata for Baritone, Mixed Chorus, and Orchestra.
(Dedicated "In Memory of Our Parents.")
December 1982. Manuscript

Dedicated to their parents and using a text by his brother Rossine, this work of two brothers is scored for baritone solo, SATB chorus, strings, harp, piano, vibraphone, and percussion. It was commissioned by the State Secretary of Culture of São Paulo. Rossine's moving poem and its musical setting both speak to the heart of the human struggle, particularly in Brazil, as well as to solidarity with the poor of the world. The text can be summarized: "We are poor, scrubby people whom the wind of death convulses and disperses. One day, united in love, we will march hand in hand to the frontiers of the world, and, with our souls shining, we will form the last obstacle to the hate which corrupts life, which corrupts the soul."

This is probably Guarnieri's most moving large choral work. He developed the text through repetition, which is not usual for him; usually his texts are dealt with in a very straightforward manner. This poem of universal sentiment is given a very feelingful setting, which uses the atonal language that has marked his music. He divided the text into three quasi movements that parallel the three sections of the poem:

1. *Lento:* The gentle opening of the high muted strings is suddenly dominated by the strong baritone voice. The chorus initially speaks some rhythmic phrases, then adds harmonic support. The resolve of the strong text is mirrored in the forceful musical writing.

2. *Contemplativo:* Gentle chromatic string writing introduces again the baritone solo and the fragmented comments of the chorus. The mixed voices end their contribution by spoken lines under the receding baritone line.

3. *Confiante:* *"Meu espiritu"* ushers in this third section. Defiance of being dominated colors the music with a strong opening, a four-voiced choral fugue in the middle, and full four-part harmonic writing for the close. The fugue treats the text which begins "I swear to you." These words also form the basis of the final, ringing measures of this powerful work.

Salmo 23 (Psalm 23). Psalm for
SATB and String Orchestra (or Organ).
November 1, 1982. Manuscript

This work was composed for the fiftieth wedding anniversary of Alda and Luciano de Campos. Guarnieri again returns to his very direct setting of text without much elaboration. It opens forcefully with the words, "The Lord is my shepherd; there is nothing I shall want!" The music is basically in the Aeolian mode with a few inflections. The texture is homophonic for this opening, but as each new line enters, it is treated distinctly, often with canonic imitation. Longer, connected passages develop in the course of the psalm. It closes again with a gentle recall of the opening line.

Cinquentenário da Universidade de São Paulo
(Sesquicentennial of the University of São Paulo.
Cantata for Narrator, Mixed Chorus, and String Orchestra.
1984. Manuscript

Commissioned by the dean of the University of São Paulo, Dr. Antônio Hélio Guerra Vieira, this cantata again uses a text by Guarnieri's brother Rossine. It was premiered in 1985 during the celebration of the university's fiftieth anniversary. Guarnieri conducted his String Orchestra in the Palácio dos Bandeirantes in São Paulo, and Jarbas Braga was narrator with the University Chorale. The piece also won the 1985 ACPA prize as the best vocal work: "Melhor obra vocal." Guarnieri cast it in three movements:

1. *Lento:* The strings provide a contrapuntal fabric against which a narrator reads three of the four verses of the poem, extolling the virtues of the true learning situation where the world is constructed. The voices then enter with a unison line, singing the word "Universidade" three times, each a step higher. A final statement in rhythmic augmentation closes the movement forcefully.

2. *Allegro Enérgico, Calmo, Tempo primo:* This movement is given almost entirely to the strings and is typical of Guarnieri in its energetic restlessness and angular thematic material. In the middle *Calmo,* the viola presents an *Espressivo* melody, which is then developed before a return of the opening material. The voices begin chanting "Universidade" in the last nine measures and, as in the first movement, close this movement singing it triumphantly.

3. *Maestoso:* Over a low pedal point in the string bass, the voices begin their "Universidade" chant, then mount it into a fugal exposition by each voice in turn on the fourth stanza of the poem. When the fugue has been exposed, they present a unison-version *Grandeoso* with full string and percussion support. The voices then spread into a six-part version of "Universidade" and repeat it for the closing *fff* measures to climax the work.

These final choral works of Camargo Guarnieri were written on commission, several of them using texts by his brother. The strong bond that bound these two men was more than filial affection. They were both very strong-minded and great-hearted individuals who had shared many things over the years: their love for their parents and family, concern for their country, and care for the human condition of the poor. Rossine never lacked for words or ideas, and these resonated strongly in Camargo. It was natural that he should turn to his younger brother for the words to express these final grand choral gestures. They are among his best choral compositions.

EIGHT

Music for Solo and Chamber Strings

Camargo Guarnieri's early study of the violin is evident in his writing for this instrument. There are five short pieces, seven sonatas, one sonatina, two concertos, and one *choro* with orchestra. He had also transcribed his Seventh Violin Sonata for piano trio. For viola there is one sonata and a *choro* with orchestra. The works for cello include three sonatas, two *cantilenas,* a *choro,* and *Ponteio e Dança,* which he later arranged for cello and string orchestra.

In addition to the pieces written specifically for solo violin, Guarnieri also transcribed a number of his other works for this medium, including *Canção Sertaneja* (1928), *Toada Triste* (1936), *Encantamento* (1941) (from violin and orchestra version), *Valsa* no. 1 in C Minor (1942), *Improviso* no. 3 (1973), and *Ponteios* nos. 36 and 38 (1957) (see Chapters 4 and 11.)

A great variety of styles is evident, particularly in the violin sonatas. The three cello sonatas likewise reflect the growth of the composer between 1931 and 1977, when the last was written. Two string trios, three quartets, and a single-movement piece complete his string ensemble works.

MUSIC FOR VIOLIN AND PIANO

The first three violin solos with piano are of early vintage, dating from 1930, 1931, and 1939. The fourth was written in 1953, and the fifth in 1978. All five share several characteristics: they give complete freedom to extended melodic lines of the solo instrument, utilize some type of ostinato accompaniment that is initially static but gradually expands in range and activity, and present fairly complex rhythmic fabrics in which the freely moving melody has a rhythm that is different from that of the accompaniment, which itself may contain cross-rhythms. The harmonic language is mildly chromatic, with dissonance resulting from the conflict of ostinatos and solo lines. The fourth piece is more atonal in effect than its predecessors. The two *Cantos* are through composed, while the two *Cantigas* contain brief extension-developments of their opening material with a restatement, suggesting Guarnieri's typical three-section design within a monothematic context. Tonal orientation tends to be ambiguous, although the pieces finally come to settle upon some tonal center. The first three were published under one cover by Associate Music Publishers, New York. The *Cantiga de Ninar* and *Canto I* were recorded on the Festa label together with the Third Sonata.

Cantiga lá de Longe
(Song from Afar), *Indolente, p.* 1930.
[AMP–1950; RB–1950]

The complex rhythms of the tightly knit piano ostinato differ from the rhythm of the solo violin, providing a high degree of inner rhythmic tension in the somberly moving lines. The shifting ostinato also provides some bitonality in the resulting harmony. The middle section of the piece is in a faster tempo and a more sprightly mood. The return of the first part has the two instruments separated by several octaves, the piano being an octave lower than in the opening section and the violin one octave higher. However, at the end of the piece they have crossed lines, leaving the piano in the upper register and the violin below it. The total effect is one of pensive, nostalgic, suspended emotion.

Cantiga de Ninar
(Cradle Song), *Balançando, pp.* 1931.
[AMP–1944; RB–1950]

Cantiga de Ninar is a Brazilian generic term for melodies of the lullaby or berceuse type. In this piece the piano ostinato establishes the required rocking movement between B minor and E minor. The tonally ambiguous melody moves with great rhythmic freedom and is restated in a final section one octave higher. The solo part is written in $\frac{2}{4}$ meter, the accompaniment in $\frac{6}{8}$. Guarnieri dedicated the piece to violinist Yehudi Menuhin.

Canto 1. 1939
[AMP–1943; RB–1950]

This first *Canto* is through composed. Its long melodic line is rhythmically free and independent of the accompanimental rhythm. More augmented harmonies are present than in the two preceding pieces, and the piano accompaniment is more of an equal partner in projecting the melody.

Canto II.
1953. Heliograph Copy

This piece, written for a friend, Paulo Guedes, is through composed with several varied restatements of a gentle theme. The piano ostinato begins in the middle register and gradually expands. The melody is more rhythmically unified and regular in its subtle inner syncopation than in the preceding pieces, creating a pensive, reflective quality. After a performance of the piece by Maria Vischnia and Guarnieri in October 1965, Caldeira Filho wrote in the *Estado de São Paulo:*

> This *Canto II* maintains itself on the level of simple and pure lyricism because it is really a song in which the melodic line is expanded with a largesse worthy of the expressive power of the principal motive. Its traditional form contrasts with the somewhat advanced sonorous masses of the piano; there are brief developments and an atmosphere which suggests a demanding situation. It is in the spirit of a Schubert *Lied,* a song which still has discrete national inflections sufficiently suggestive to be recognized as such.[1]

Seresta (Serenade).
1978. Manuscript

This is a one-movement work and represents Guarnieri's first piece with this title that does not have an orchestral accompaniment. It is a "serenade," but with piano accompaniment only. It is one of several pieces dedicated within the space of a few years to the composer's friend Dr. Max Feffer.

The piano begins a slow ascending arpeggio which culminates in the violin's entrance on a high E. The solo line gradually descends from this point, leading to a cadenza which serves as a development or middle section. The reexposition recalls the eight measure opening of the piece. Guarnieri then builds a climax before the energy recedes. The piece ends as it began, with the piano's ascending arpeggio.

Sonata no. 1 for Violin and Piano.
1930. Manuscript Lost

Guarnieri was twenty-three when he wrote this first violin sonata. It resembles more a study for piano with violin obbligato than a sonata for violin. The piano part contains very angular, dissonant, and generally complex writing. The violin part is not distinctly thematic, especially in the first and last movements. It is not the work of a composer who does not know how to write, but rather of one who is seeking the obscure rather than the obvious. It presages his atonal period in its strong linear dissonances. The result is that there is too much in the melodic line, which prevents it from having a distinctiveness of its own. The phrases are too rambling with too many rhythmic combinations that do not "jell" into anything memorable. The piano writing is continuous, with the violin joining it for some segments of the piece.

This work, which I examined in 1969, could not be found after the death of the composer, and he may well have destroyed it himself, something he did not usually do. All three movements are in ABA form: I, *Alegre Moderato, f;* II, *Saudoso com muito espressivo, p;* and III, *Depressa, mas bem ritmado.* In the last movement, polymeters are conscientiously indicated to acknowledge the conflicting groups of notes in both the solo and accompaniment.

Sonata no. 2 for Violin and Piano. 1933.
[Ponteio–New York, 2005]

This is the sonata which caused Mário de Andrade such irritation at first sight. Ironically, when it was premiered a few years later in Rio de Janeiro, Andrade was the first to come up to Guarnieri with a warm embrace and praise for the piece, forgetting his own original opposition. One can easily agree with Andrade that Guarnieri's music gives a visual impression that is often in striking contrast to its aural realization.

In the program notes for a compact disc which Tânia Guarnieri and Lais de Souza Brasil recorded of Sonatas 2, 3, and 4, Lais wrote:

> These works reveal some characteristic traits of the composer's style, mastery of balance and depth of meaning as in:
>
>> The confidential tone of the second movements, almost always summits of expression in which the composer exposes his most intimate and predominantly melancholic sensitivities;
>>
>> The ostinati, incessantly repeated rhythmic-melodic patterns, providing background while reinforcing the atmosphere surrounding the theme;
>>
>> The lovely dissonances so typically Guarnierian, which will keep turning up progressively more frequently in his later works, and of which the second movement of this Second Sonata is a sublime example;
>>
>> A touch of mystery.
>
> Besides these features, one finds the general elements of Guarnieri's style: a taste for polyphony, asymmetry within the measure's symmetry, the profound rendering of Brazilian roots.[2]

In this work the piano writing is continuous and virtuosic in many places, but it maintains a better dialogue with the soloist than it did in the First Sonata. The texture is contrapuntal with both performers sharing the material. There are tonal centers, but they are not adhered to in any functional way. The work is full of resounding sonorities and long flowing lines. The themes share a descending direction, for which reason Guarnieri considers the work to have a cyclic quality. The themes are somewhat more individualized than in the preceding work, although they are still a long way from the type of tune one could easily "whistle."

The three movements are: I, *Sem pressa e bem ritmado, f* in sonata-allegro form; II, a gentle, atmospheric *Profundamente terno, pp;* and III, a final *Impetuoso, molto ritmado, ff,* which moves forcefully to a final bravura ending.

Sonata no. 3 for Violin and Piano. 1950.
[Ponteio–New York, 2005]

Following the Second Sonata by seventeen years, this is a well-integrated work whose themes have a fairly strong linear tonality, but a rather bitonal harmonic language, resulting in a mild overall dissonance. The percussive approach of the piano writing in the two outer movements accentuates this. Harmonically the piano makes great use of open intervals—fourths and fifths—in the vigorous sections, although it becomes very linear in the more melodic sections. The pianist has a good share of the work, particularly in the last movement. The soloist has some sections of double notes, but the greater portion of the solo writing is in single notes. The general impression one receives from this piece is that it is vigorous but not harsh; the slow movement has the characteristically pensive quality, but perhaps with less *saudades* or longing than many of Guarnieri's other slow movements.

In the opening *Moderato espressivo* movement, themes are introduced by the piano and then imitated by the violin. Lais de Souza Brasil writes of the second, *Terno* movement:

> In the central movement, the two instruments speak in that confidential tone that is typical of Guarnieri in such moments. The soft energy only intensifies for brief instants and finally ends in a whisper. The conversation taking place between the violin and piano takes the form of a dialogue or counterpoint.[3]

The final *Decidido, sonoro* is in sonata-allegro form. The violin leads with the first theme with its flatted seventh degree in a soaring $\frac{5}{4}$ meter. A second theme, *Piu calmo,* is introduced by the piano. The coda utilizes both themes. Brasil notes, "The Guarnierian technique of developing thematic material is, from here on, transmitted through pseudo-canon, transpositions, reinforcements, diminutions, inversion, etc."[4] The movement ends vigorously.

Sonata no. 4 for Violin and Piano. 1956.
[BA–1957]

Probably his best known composition in this medium because of its early publication, the Sonata no. 4 is a colorful, energetic work with all three movements thematically related. Each movement retains a basic tonal orientation with dissonance serving an enriching, coloristic function. The harmonic language is basically extended tertian and quartal but within a modal framework. The first two movements do not strongly evidence the typical Latin syncopated rhythms, but the third has a bounding *samba* background throughout. The piano writing is integral to the entire fabric and is considerably more demanding in the final movement.

This piece was first performed at Carnegie Hall in New York in 1959 by Eva Kovach and David Garvey. After a 1960 performance in São Paulo, Caldeira Filho wrote:

> The Brazilian composer seems to have a demi-urge to make the violin, most often a secular voice, find in this work a miraculous renewal of its possibilities to express not only the feelings of modern music, but also the new music which really is actually shaping an expression which is both national and continental.[5]

Brasil notes that the theme of the first *Enérgico ma espressivo* movement "contains the cyclical cell which will punctuate the three movements' musical discourse. This cell is the insisting and disturbing element which introduces the turmoil of the predominantly affirmative atmosphere of the first movement."[6] It has a Phrygian quality, and its shape easily lends it to development.

The second movement, *Intimo,* has a supple, simple melody stated by the violin with minimal support from the piano. It is a transformed line derived from the first movement theme. Of it, Brasil writes, "A dialogue takes place between violin and piano in counterpoint, where both instruments expand in brief exaltations but, above all, exchange in lyrical love terms."[7] The piano part uses the Mode of the Northeast.

In the *Allegro appassionata,* the piano's robust *ff* theme is again derived from that of the first movement. A *samba* rhythm ensues, becoming more frenzied and with more extended lines and augmented harmonies in the agitated final movement. The piece ends *Grandioso.* Of this movement, Brasil wrote:

> The cyclical theme is transformed and opens the movement and runs through it uninterrupted, in a multifaceted array of colors that go from brilliant to somber. The music works in unison in both instruments as in the opening, but now the impulse is twice as imposing and majestic.[8]

Sonata no. 5 for Violin and Piano. 1961.
[Ponteio–New York, 2005]

The Sonata no. 5 represents a return to an almost purely modal writing in which all the themes are modally oriented and litany-like in construction. The harmonies that support them are likewise of greater simplicity than in the preceding works. The last movement has more dissonance, but it is subservient to the melodic structure. Frequently, as in the opening unharmonized line of the first movement, the general impression is one of openness of texture. All three movements are monothematic, but the third uses its material in a way to almost suggest rondo structure.

The first movement, *Comodo,* illustrates Guarnieri's typical ABA structure of exposition-development-reexposition. It uses the Dorian mode on A, changing meters which give it a sense of being freely rhythmic, and a litany-like structure, all enhanced by its austere modal harmonization. This second movement, *Terno, dolce,* originated as a recording by Daniel Ferreira of Guarnieri improvising without realizing he was being recorded. The final *Gingando* dances from beginning to end with a theme in two parts. After the theme has been exposed once, it continues to reappear, at times combining its two halves.

This work received its very successful first performance by Maria Vischnia (to whom it is dedicated) at a Sociedade Pro Música concert in São Paulo on November 30, 1963. Guarnieri was accompanist for this performance.

Sonata no. 6 for Violin and Piano. 1963.
[Ponteio–New York, 2005]

The Sonata no. 6 received its premiere in Rio de Janeiro at the Teatro Municipal on June 8, 1965; Carmela Saghy and Guarnieri were the performers. Eurico Nogueira França wrote of the piece at that time: "It is a work nourished by the melodic possibilities of the violin whose cantabile line opens and expands with wonderful harmonic support from the piano."[9] Guarnieri pursues here what might be termed an impressionistic atonalism. The harmonic structures, particularly of the first two movements which are gentle, almost become ends in themselves within the supple, slow-moving textures. There are more vertical concurrences of bitonally related chords within the piano accompaniment than are found in many of his earlier works. In this sense it is less linear. Triads and augmented chords are superimposed, creating cross-relations. The violin line is frequently pursuing an independent linear tonality over this already dissonant accompaniment.

Like the Fifth Sonata, the thematic material has a chantlike quality. Two principal motivic sources unify all three movements. One is a brief, ascending three-note fragment that appears inverted in the second and third movements. The second motif is actually drawn from the introduction but takes on its own independent character. It opens with a *Tranquillo ma espressivo, Allegro-Tranquillo.* The second movement, *Misterioso, dolce,* has a suspended, hovering quality. Seconds, ninths, and strongly bitonal chords maintain a high level of dissonance. The final *Grandeoso-Impetuoso-Grandeoso* is an exuberant development and restatement of fragments presented earlier. Both performers are kept busy in this bustling section, the piano commenting on the violin's more continuous line. The piano begins a toccata-like accompaniment, preparing for the *Poco meno.* A final *Grandeoso-Lento* closes the movement with strongly bitonal harmony.

The structural uniqueness of this final movement, and of the entire work for that matter, reveal Guarnieri's mastery of the traditional forms in that he can treat them plastically without losing a sense of continuity. It also reveals his growing tendency toward a kind of motivic development in which the movements seem to flower from within. This tendency continues, even into his atonal works which follow this particular sonata by a few years. His penchant for developing the small germ motive is particularly evident in this work.

Sonatina for Violin and Piano.
1974. Manuscript

Guarnieri's oldest daughter, Tânia, had barely begun to study the violin when he composed this sonatina for her: she was eleven at the time. He wrote it in anticipation of a contest she planned to enter. It is a very youthful, joyful work, which she premiered with pianist Joaquim Paulo do Espírito Santo on May 5, 1978, in the Museum of Art in São Paulo. Tânia subsequently performed it numerous times both in Brazil and in the United States, where she studied for two-and-one-half years in Milwaukee at the University of Wisconsin–Milwaukee's Chamber Music Institute. Its two outer movements in particular maintain an exuberance.

The first movement is *Com Alegria,* the second *Triste e Melancólico,* which sustains an ethereal mood throughout. It requires a good deal of maturity on the part of a young performer to sustain the intense, slow-moving line. The final *Festivo* movement is very rhythmic and percussive, an exciting challenge to both violinist and accompanist. It moves to a final, joyful ending.

Sonata no. 7 for Violin and Piano. 1978
[Ponteio–New York, 2003]

Guarnieri continued to travel for many years from São Paulo each month to teach in Goiânia and Uberlândia. This composition was completed on one such trip in Uberlândia. It has three movements and is an exceptionally energetic work. The dedicatees, Jerzy Milewski and Aleida Schweitzer, premiered the piece at the Federal University of Goiâs in 1978. This work, which was later transcribed as a piano trio in 1989, completes Guarnieri's cycle of violin sonatas.

The opening *Enérgico* is an explosion of energy. The gentler *Magoada* suggests a strong emotion, which is immediately evident as the piano sets the stage for the *Molto íntimo* violin line. Actually the melody feels very restless in places, as if expressing some smoldering feelings. This second movement fades into nothingness. Whether Guarnieri thought better of the depression which marked the second movement, or whether a change of scenery (Uberlândia) lifted his spirits, he imbued this last movement, *Com Alegria,* with a bristling, joyful energy. The violin has harmonic double notes over the piano's toccata-like figuration. A descending violin cadenza leads into a *Vivo* coda, where the piano intensifies its support of the violin.

MUSIC FOR VIOLA AND PIANO

Sonata for Viola and Piano. 1950.
[Ponteio–New York, 2004]

This sonata is an effectively written work. The solo instrument frequently soars in its high, brilliant register, giving the passages a particularly poignant expressiveness. The piece's three movements are thematically related, and there is a strong linear modality with supporting harmonies of both tertian and quartal structure. The piano writing is conceived with an uncluttered texture which uses the middle register, giving the viola support with ample sonorous flexibility. At times the piano is a conversant partner, while at other times it provides a strongly rhythmic and percussive basis for a more agitated solo writing. The soloist has long, soaring lines, a more rapid figuration, and double stops, particularly in the last movement. Through it all, the melodic strain is strong. As Dinorah de Carvalho noted in reference to another of Guarnieri's works, "Camargo Guarnieri is a congenital melodist and is spontaneous in all of his creative work.[10] The sonata was premiered in Caracas by Lazaro Sternic and Henrique Trigo in 1959. Peres Dworecki also performed the work on an American tour in 1969.

The *Tranquillo* indication is maintained almost throughout the melodically conceived first movement. The movement is monothematic and based, as Caldeira Filho wrote, "on a melodic-rhythmic figuration found among the Indians of Brazil."[11] Its reflective melody is stated two octaves apart by the piano and is then taken by the soloist and developed into a longer line. It is concise, calm, moving gently in the opening bars, but be-

Sonata
for Viola & Piano
1st movement

Sonata for Viola
and Piano
3rd movement

coming more agitated as the moods change. The viola states the theme in augmented note values as a coda, bringing the movement to a *ppp* close on E, which serves as a tonal center.

In contrast to the unusually gentle first movement, the second, *Scherzando, grazioso,* is more playful and light-hearted. It develops in a series of ideas which could be described as ABACAB, in which the brief C section recalls the first-movement theme.

The third movement, *Con entusiasmo,* rounds out the work. It is actually a series of variations on two themes. In the second appearance of this second theme, the viola has pseudo-Caipira thirds which are not really thirds, but rather a double-stop harmonization of the second theme. A final A section has several versions of the principal theme, which uses repeated notes and octaves in the solo part, adding to the excitement of the closing pages of the piece.

MUSIC FOR CELLO AND PIANO

Guarnieri composed six pieces for cello: *Ponteio e Dança,* three sonatas, one of which is a very early work, and two *cantilenas.* There is also a *choro* with orchestra.

Ponteio e Dança (Prelude and Dance)
for Violoncello and Piano. 1946.
[Ponteio–New York, 2004]

The *Ponteio e Dança* are a pair of contrasting pieces, both of which are in ABA form. The monothematic *Ponteio* evolves sustained, evocative, lengthy lines in E minor for the soloist with the piano providing continuous contrapuntal fragments in support of it. Paulo César Martins Rabelo, whose doctoral dissertation deals with these works for cello and piano, notes that the ascending opening line "corresponds exactly to the open strings of the guitar."[12] In the *Dança,* the key changes to G major as the spirited cello theme appears over a very rhythmic piano accompaniment. With its raised fourth and lowered seventh degrees, the melody is redolent of the Mode of the Northeast. An extension in double notes for the cello serves as a codetta.

Perez Dworecki, who transcribed the work for viola and piano, performed it at Ohio State University on October 14, 1969. Guarnieri transcribed it in 1982 for cello and string orchestra.

Two Cantilenas

The two *cantilenas* are well described by their title: intense, gentle expressions with melodies composed of phrases "chained" together. The first is particularly expressive, the second more animated. They were not written as a pair. The demands on the cellist are expressive rather than technical. They were premiered by Antônio Lauro del Claro and Maria de Lourdes Imenes in São Paulo in 1976 and 1984, respectively.

Dança
Cello & Piano

from *Ponteio e Dança* for Cello and Piano

Cantilena no. 1—Calmo e Triste. 1974
[Ponteio–New York, 2003]

The piano initiates the intense, nuanced movement and mood of this piece with gently undulating, chromatic lines in both melody and bass. The cello enters in the sixth measure with an emotional line marked by upward leaps, followed by descending intervals with sequences of this design rising and falling as the tension increases or subsides. A climax gives way almost immediately, as if apologetically. The cello returns with a restatement of its theme an octave higher, intensifying its already tense mood. Because of the shortness of the piece and its middle climax, Rabelo prefers to identify the form as AA' rather than ABA.[13]

Cantilena no. 2—Muito tranquillo. 1982.
[Ponteio–New York, 2003]

This is more developed than the first *Cantilena* with more activity for both instruments. Rabelo relates a story of the origin of this piece shared with him by its dedicatee, Lucia Valeska:

> Valeska's father, a renowned pianist in Brazil, received a visit from Guarnieri. During the visit Guarnieri said to Lucia, still a teenager at the time, that it was very easy to compose a musical piece, and asked her to choose three notes at random on the piano as the basis for a composition dedicated to her. Guarnieri made the sketches of the piece that night and completed the work the next day. The notes chosen were D, F, and E♭.[14]

Guarnieri wrote his own notes for this piece, his last for cello:

> The *Cantilena no. 2* written in 1982 follows an ABA form. The first *Muito tranquillo* theme has the character of a serenader and develops until a small cadence introduces the second theme, *Bem ritmado.* After a long development, the first theme returns, similar to its first statement, ending with a short coda. It is an effective piece for the cello within the spirit of the instrument.[15]

The piece ends with the cello disappearing gently into the upper register of the instrument.

THREE SONATAS FOR CELLO AND PIANO

Sonata no. 1 for Violoncello and Piano. 1930.
[Ponteio–New York, 2003]

Dedicated to Iberê Gomes Grôsso, the First Cello Sonata is an early work and bears a strong resemblance in its musical language to the First Piano

Concerto and the First Violin Sonata, which stem from the same period. It has a tenseness and restriction of material which does not very easily lend itself to expansion. Thematic imitation between soloist and accompanist is frequent. There is harsh bitonality in places and a general obtuseness of harmony. The themes do not seem unified in their rhythmic structure in that various rhythmic values follow each other without a sense of culmination, climax, or continuity. One senses in this work that Guarnieri was trying to avoid the obvious. Mário de Andrade gave this work an extensive, laudatory review before its premiere on April 27, 1935, by Calixto Corazza with Guarnieri at the piano in the Municipal Theatre of São Paulo. He hailed it as "one of the most significant works produced in contemporary Brazilian music. Rare are the composers who have systematized their polyphony the way Camargo Guarnieri has."[16]

In the first movement, *Tristonho,* the themes seem nonintegrated, uncharacteristic, and therefore more difficult to define in terms of the structure they create. Rabelo notes what he calls a third theme:

> Where one would expect the beginning of the recapitulation, the third theme enters with its cheerful character, tireless up and down scales, rapid modulations, and great virtuosity characteristic of the Brazilian *choro.* The African features of the *choro* can be noticed in the syncopated rhythms which permeate this theme.[17]

The piano opens the second, *Apaixonadamente,* movement with a somber ostinato over which the cello states its long, meandering line. A middle section, typical of Guarnieri, is a development of this material in a somewhat more syncopated texture. Mário de Andrade noted that this movement seems to have drawn its inspiration from the popular *modinha* and that, at times, the theme fulfills almost the function of a Wagnerian leitmotif.

The indication *Selvagem* for the third movement suggests its quality of wildness. In the review cited above, Andrade noted:

> It is savage in its harshness, its psychological character, but it has nothing that evokes the American "savages." It is a frenetic *batuque* of legitimate Negro character. Camargo Guarnieri achieved one of the most curious inventions in this sonata. When the second theme appears, the ostinato in the lower register of the piano changes and acquires an Amerindian character. After a few measures, this ostinato moves to the cello while the piano has the initial ostinato with the second theme in its high register with Caipira thirds. This second theme is a rural *batuque* inspired by the instrumental technique of the urban mulatto *choro.* The cello's Amerindian ostinato is four centuries old and imitates the song of the arara canide bird. This has a powerful sym-

bolism because it merges the urban mulatto *choro,* the Negro *batuque* from the grasslands, and Amerindian prairies.

Despite some brilliant moments, the sonata is somber. It frequently stays in the lower registers of the two instruments, and this is justified logically by its expression of pain, unspeakable evil, and force; the *maxixe* episode in the first movement notwithstanding, it is a sonata in purple. The second movement with its great beauty, its noble and expressive sadness, is one of the most beautiful pages of the composer, one of the most impressive lyric passages in contemporary music.[18]

The first hearing of the piece in Rio on July 8, 1935, seemed to have taken the critics by surprise. To Guarnieri's great benefit as a young composer, every critic in the city must have been at this premiere, granting him some much needed publicity in his young career. Ayres Andrade noted that it was his first exposure to the music of the young Paulistan, and he was favorably impressed.[19] João Itiberê da Cunha, who had railed at Guarnieri for the atonalism of his Second Piano Sonatina, had words of praise for the Cello Sonata, despite "revolutionary ideas and almost extreme substance."[20] Otávio Bevilacqua wrote that "his folklore in some cases is still not well enough subordinated and filtered by his temperament. The personal lyricism of the composer, nevertheless, oozed out in some brisk, youthful passages."[21] One of the reviews appears humorous in retrospect. Arthur Imbassai complained that he had not the patience to endure the entire, horrible concert. He wrote of this sonata:

> The sonata in its first hearing is a cacophonic orgy of disconnected sounds, in disregard of all the laws of aesthetics, sounds without continuity or agreement, irreconcilable with the exigencies of the educated ear and good taste. It brought us a cruel dismay, a pungent and eternal pain by the disappearance of the divine art of music which has been with us.[22]

Guarnieri programmed this piece a number of times after the 1935 concert. Among them was a performance in São Paulo at the Municipal Theater on March 29, 1938, in a program devoted completely to his works. Calixto Corazza was the cellist, and Guarnieri was at the piano. After this performance, Caldeira Filho wrote:

> The frequency of syncopation marked the earlier period of the composer, the phase in which this sonata was written. It seems to have been created under a lively flux of inspiration, and it has the merit of a great sincerity, not obscured by an intellectualism which might have damaged the noble enthusiasm and generous inspiration.[23]

Sonata no. 2 for Violoncello and Piano. 1955.
[Ponteio–New York, 2004]

This work is at an opposite pole of the preceding one in almost every way. The second has what the first lacked in maturity, unity, effectiveness, and appeal. The brief, germinal themes that mark so much of Guarnieri's output during the mid-1950s also are present in this Second Cello Sonata. Litany-like, the brief thematic material lends itself both to contrapuntal and fragmentary development and to transformation into ostinato-type accompanimental figures. All three of the movements are thematically related. Each movement can be considered monothematic, with relationships existing also among all three.

Harmonically, the linear fabric is frequently bitonal, particularly in the first movement. The second is principally extended tertian with some augmented and whole tone implications. The third movement uses the Caipira thirds reveling in cross-relations, adding a particularly colorful nuance to the playful theme. The soloist has a good share of double notes, mostly in the last movement, and they lie well for the instrument. The piano shares equally with the cello in thematic responsibility. The three movements are *Allegro moderato, Melancólico, molto espressivo,* and *Festivo, bem ritmado.*

The piece was first performed in Paris by Jean Reculart. It had its first performance in São Paulo in 1965 by Calixto Corazza and Guarnieri in the Paramount Theater. It was also presented in Rio in 1987 for the VII Bienal da Música Brasileira in which special homage was paid to Guarnieri because of his eightieth birthday. The performers were Antônio del Claro and Lais de Souza Brasil. Luiz Paulo Horta wrote of this performance and the sonata:

> This is a work only a master could create—with a security of touch and mature inspiration, which justifies every artistic movement. It is well beyond nationalism (though it is curious that, in his discussions, the Paulistan master insists at times on these older concepts). Only the third movement has a Brazilian atmosphere. The first two movements are pure music without any sense of being Brazilian, "ripe fruit falling in the tropical night" as Augusto Frederico Schmidt put it. The composer, who was present at the concert, bears living testimony to the fact the Brazilian music already has its own "classics," that is, works and artists who challenge the corrosion of time.[24]

Sonata no. 3 for Violoncello and Piano. 1977.
[FUNARTE–1986; Ponteio–New York, 2004]

This Third Cello Sonata was premiered by its dedicatees, Antônio Lauro del Claro and Maria de Lourdes Imenes, on December 4, 1978, in Rio's Funarte Salon. Cast in three movements, it is a serious work, opening with a deliberate, intense mood which is sustained until the more rapid coda of the first movement. The second is serene, and the third carries the spirit of a dance. The sections are marked *Sem Pressa, Sereno e Triste,* and *Com Alegria.* The final movement maintains an extremely high energy level throughout. The intensity increases into the final *Lento,* where the theme is stated once more in grandiose style, ending *fff.*

Rabelo analyzed this work in light of Guarnieri's development at the time of its composition. He noted that the works written in the 1970s were becoming more abstract and atonal:

> His nationalistic vein becomes less discernible and a movement toward a more international style is noticeable. The first movement of the sonata in question follows this path. It is not atonal (in the sense of denying tonality systematically) nor is it tonal (in the sense of functional tonality). It may be described as a nontonal work, nonetheless having tonal centers.[25]

Helena Freire, who studied Guarnieri's sonatinas and sonata for piano, wrote a very clear summary of his evolved harmonic language:

> Guarnieri's neo-tonality is synthetic; he went through a process of redefining his own limits as those of functional tonality. [His language] is firmly based on the use of chromatic and expressive dissonance and intense contrapuntal chromaticism. However, he never really abandoned functional tonal centers; they are somehow still operative in his attempt to turn back to classical principles and techniques, such as the sonata form.[26]

Ponteio Publishing Company in New York is making these works available, adding a wonderful body of works to the material accessible to American cellists.

STRING CHAMBER MUSIC

Guarnieri's string chamber music includes two trios, three quartets, and a single-movement work for string quartet which he entitled *Angústia.* A very early work for string orchestra, *Toada à Moda Paulista,* and his Concerto for Strings and Percussion will be considered in the next chapter. He had set his *Cinco Peças Infantis* as a first experiment in orchestration, and he arranged many pieces for the string orchestra that he conducted at the University of São Paulo in his later years. It is curious that he did not write a work which featured piano with strings.

Many consider Guarnieri's chamber music, in the broad sense, his best music. Whether this is due to the sheer number of compositions for solo instruments and voice or to their greater accessibility remains a question.

His propensity for smaller forms seems to be due to two things: his consummate craftsmanship and ear for detail, and his preference for traditional forms, both of which are revealed in his string quartets. He does not tend to overstate, but lets lines move with both poise and precision. Counterpoint enriches the lines with restraint and appropriateness, a characteristic which caused Eurico Nogueira França to call him "the most aristocratic of our composers." He further noted: "Guarnieri is especially a composer of the intimate forms, and those in which he succeeds best are the chamber works: quartets, songs, and music for piano. In my opinion he is a master of small forms, a miniaturist."[27]

França had written in 1947:

> Guarnieri has a magnificent equilibrium where idea and form are concerned. All the classic virtues of musical construction, the complexity of sound structures which contain in simple transparency of lines the power of thematic elaboration which confers on the music an intimate unity, a wonderful sense of proportion—all are found in his work.[28]

In record jacket notes Adhemar Nobrega wrote the following commentary, which further places Guarnieri in the forefront of the development of Brazilian chamber music:

> Chamber music represents the purest and most substantial flowering in the art of sound, a field where no disguises are accepted, only works of rich vigor, elaborated with mastery. This is why it is not always present in the first creative harvest periods of a country or the collection of an artist. Only with Villa-Lobos, when our music was already gaining its rightful international place, did chamber music productions open the vast chapters in the catalogs of our composers.
>
> One of these vast chapters we owe to Camargo Guarnieri. A chamber musician by temperament, a virtue also revealed in his orchestral works, his vigorous technical formations prepared him especially for the subtle manifestation of this refined music.[29]

Whereas Villa-Lobos and Mignone seemed to be more at home in the freer, fantasy type of piece redolent of folkloric material treated in a rhapsodic manner, Guarnieri's clear preference was for the more restrained, structured setting. Luiz Heitor de Azevedo noted in 1950 that it was precisely this "return to voluntary submission, to a worship of order, to a hierarchy of form,"[30] which distinguished him from preceding Brazilian composers. With his formal approach, Guarnieri was able to retain a sense of spontaneity, power, and expression.

The six pieces to be discussed here are all being published by Ponteio in New York. The first two quartets are both prize-winning pieces.

Trio for Violin, Viola, and Violoncello. 1931.
[Ponteio–New York, 2003]

This Trio comes from Guarnieri's early period of personal search for his own direction. He had achieved such early success in 1928 and 1929 with his *Dança Brasileira* and the Piano Sonatina no. 1 and was at a point of self-evaluation. The Constitutional Revolution had closed schools and businesses, giving him time to explore new ideas. This work, the First Piano Concerto, and his first sonatas for violin and cello all stem from this period and bear similarities. He seemed to not be satisfied with the free, spontaneous melodies which came so easily, as Mário de Andrade also noted, and so launched himself into this period of search for a more intense, concentrated musical language.

This piece is relatively short with three movements, none of which is extensively developed. The thematic material lies someplace between his carefully constructed lines and his more expansive style. Also, the structure does not seem clear, which is characteristic of some of his early works. There tends to be too much material with little delineation and strong characterization of ideas. For all its weaknesses, however, it indicates the potential of the young composer.

This Trio was premiered by Oscar Borgeth, Edmundo Blois, and Iberê Gomes Grosso in a program devoted entirely to Guarnieri's music on April 24, 1941, in Rio de Janeiro at the Escola Nacional de Música. After that performance Andrade Muricy wrote, "It sounded good and contains good and lively music."[31] It was also included in a program of his works in New York at the Museum of Modern Art on March 7, 1943. He received high praise from a critic for this many-faceted program:

> Many affirmative qualities in Mr. Guarnieri's art were summed up in the opening Trio for Strings. It had an impressive amount of lyric sensitivity, creative impulse and rhythmic impact. To Mr. Guarnieri's credit, there was little evidence of deference to current creative clichés or striving for effect in his music.[32]

Back home in Brazil, Guarnieri continued to program this work. Following a 1946 performance in São Paulo, one critic wrote:

> Guarnieri was little more than an adolescent when he wrote this score. Meanwhile, he has appreciably strengthened his security and dexterity in writing. It is a work of complex design and represents that aesthetic phase of development of the eminent Brazilian composer that has happily turned to that which is essential and transcendingly simple.[33]

Mozart Araujo also noted that "in the *Trio para Cordas,* we see him in search of a decisive orientation, a style in which he can affirm his vocation.[34]

Enérgico e Ritmado, Só rumbático, cantando, and *Com Alegria* character- ize the movements. The piece is tonal, rhythmic, and full of almost too many ideas that can be given enough temporal space to be heard. One senses that the young composer had not yet refined his art of selection and development.

Trio for Violin, Violoncello, and Piano. 1989.
[Transcribed from the 1978 Violin Sonata no. 7]
[Ponteio–New York, 2003]

Guarnieri transcribed this work for the Guarnieri Trio founded by his daughter Tânia, Robert Suetholz, and Jairo Teixeira Grossi, which pre- miered it at the VIII Bienal de Música Contemporânea in Rio de Janeiro in 1989. The three movements of this composition—*Enérgico, Magoada, Com Alegria*—are a recasting of Guarnieri's Seventh Violin Sonata. He es- sentially added a cello line to the existing piece.

String Quartet no. 1. 1932.
[Ponteio–New York, 2005]

Like the Trio of 1931, this First String Quartet reflects the period in which it was written. The fabric is taut and very contrapuntally conceived, and there is a successful effort to move away from tonality. The rhythmic struc- ture is also tense, with a constant syncopation and frequent cross-rhythmic groupings. The second movement uses polymeters to acknowledge this di- verse metrical organization. All movements end on C, although the chro- matic writing and linear dissonance obscure any definite tonal magnetism in the course of the movements. The ostinatos are again present and have a peculiar litany-like quality in this work. The themes are short and compact, in both range and movement, stressing the minor third. The last movement drives with hard hammered chords of syncopated accentuation. The piece has vitality and intensity.

The quartet was first performed in São Paulo in May 1935 by the Quartet Paulista. Mário de Andrade wrote after the performance:

> The four artists—Zacharias Autuori, Luiz Oliani, Enzo Soli, and Bruno Kunze—gave their best efforts to this work, which is very stringent. It is al- most perfect in architecture and construction. Here the composer has launched perhaps his richest, most elastic and logical ideas in polyphony. The fugue of the first movement is an exception: its subject is drawn from the sonata-allegro theme, but its development seems less logical to me, less

unified, giving it the character of a fughetto. With this exception, the rest of the quartet is magnificently well written.

Chromaticism is taken to its limits, however, giving a splendid composition an aridity which is beyond the reach of most people. Without any political references, the work is one of challenge; even the rhythm is atonal! I'm referring to the curious theme of the third movement where the composer, by using different accents, suggests that he is not within a determined dynamic form.[35]

The three movements are *Enérgico e Ritmado, Amarguardamente, muito espressivo,* and *Depressa.*

String Quartet no. 2. 1944.
[Ponteio–New York, 2003]

This Second String Quartet brought Guarnieri his second international prize, this one awarded jointly by RCA Victor and the Washington, D.C., Chamber Music Society. He had already received the 1942 Fleischer Prize for his Violin Concerto no. 1. This quartet was premiered by the String Quartet of Rio's Escola Nacional de Música on June 18, 1945. Following a 1948 performance in São Paulo by the Haydn Quartet, Caldeira Filho wrote:

> The artists gave a convincing performance of this work, placing in relief both general lines and details. Among them in the first movement were the alternation of unison lines and polyphonic sections, and the musical eloquence of the lines which came through so clearly because the whole texture of sound is organized without breaks. The wonderful effects were especially pleasing because of the Brazilian character of the themes. Especially in the second movement, their profound expression seemed to transcend the limits of their national character.[36]

Eurico Nogueira França also remarked on Guarnieri's national appeal:

> The music of Camargo Guarnieri has a musicality so natural to our people, as the material of a master painter is to his rustic model. Especially lovely is the second movement, *Lento,* whose two powerful themes [the second is from the Northeast: *Gurytatan do Coqueiro*] combine at the end. The delicate polyphony of Guarnieri's Second Quartet has an intimate and poetic richness.[37]

This work is well integrated with a vital rhythmic fabric which is not Latin in the narrow sense of the term. The first movement uses sonata-allegro form, the second ABA, and the third is a rondo. The work has a strong modal quality and within that framework uses both tertian and quartal chords as well as some bitonality. Instruments appear frequently in pairs.

The first movement in particular contains many unison thematic statements by all four instruments. These alternate with more independent lines. Its thematic unity, lively rhythmic fabric, and good distribution of activity among the instruments make it an effective, interesting composition.

Enérgico opens with a vigorous unison statement. *Nostalgico e espressivo* maintains a peaceful and gentle atmosphere, and *Allegro, sciolto* is a boisterous dance movement which opens immediately with a teasing theme stated in Caipira thirds in the two violins. This entire work retains a very carefree, joyful character, especially in its two outer movements. Its straightforward, clean writing reveals a deftness and mastery of technique in the developing composer. It comes from a period in which Guarnieri was doing a considerable amount of orchestral composition, and that seems to have benefited his chamber music writing as well.

String Quartet no. 3. 1962.
[Ponteio–New York, 2005]

This work was commissioned by the Elizabeth Coolidge Foundation in Washington, D.C., for the Third Inter-American Festival, which, after a postponement, took place in 1965. Guarnieri had completed the piece by September 23, 1962, and programmed it in São Paulo on October 24, 1963, in a concert sponsored by the Sociedade Pró Música Brasileira. After this performance Caldeira Filho wrote:

> This work marks the current position of Camargo Guarnieri. He continues [to be] faithful to thematic composition and to the necessary consequences of formal design; he proceeds in the use of seasoned sounds in intelligent freedom from harmonic tonalism, in a creative process rooted in high [cultural] concepts of nationalism, using a language that is not aggressive. The work is structured in the contrast of two basic principals: lyricism and drama, the dynamic source of his personality. And it is in this human font that, to our view, lies the reason for his universality.[38]

Its American premiere was in the Library of Congress in 1964. It was again performed for the 1965 Inter-American Music Festival in May. All of the critics who heard it were impressed. Donald McCorkle of the *Washington Evening Star* wrote:

> It is without doubt one of the best works heard in the Festival. It is a most ingratiating and grateful quartet, passionate, vigorous, and above all, imaginative. Clearly, Guarnieri is a man who has something to say and proceeds to say it with forthright felicity and exquisite lyricism. His contrasting three movements range from polytonal counterpoint with a touch of Bach and some Stravinskian motoric rhythms, to a gorgeous neo-impressionism. And

all in all, Guarnieri understands the quartet medium and exploits it fully. Though he is fairly traditional in his expression, with however a healthy dose of contemporary devices blended in, there is no question that his work is original.[39]

A *New York Times* critic wrote, "On the surface, more conservative—but inventive and imaginative beneath—the Guarnieri was eminently reachable music. The composer uses the simplest means to produce positive, joyful results."[40]

The frequent double notes of the middle instruments on repeated, accented chords also give the texture a fullness and aggressiveness which caused Charles Crowder of the *Washington Post* to note: "The Third Quartet of Guarnieri started and sustained that impression throughout."[41] Another Guarnieri characteristic is present here, the recall of themes from previous movements. His Caipira thirds in the second movement and a wild *frevo* in the last help to give the work a Brazilian quality which rises beyond mere "Latin rhythms." One senses in this work no searching for new sounds, but rather an inner contentment and playfulness in using a very familiar language that has been well mastered to say something meaningful.

In the opening *Violento,* Guarnieri used a fugal form for his development and ignored the second theme in his recapitulation, giving the movement an interesting design. The second, *Lento,* utilizes the style of the *moda Paulista* with its thirds, or in this case tenths. The final movement, *Vivo e Rítmado,* is a stylized version of the vigorous dance from of the Northeast, the *frevo.*

The good response to these works in the United States helped Guarnieri feel that he was more recognized there than in Brazil. One cannot attribute this merely to the novelty of his style to American ears. Crowder once again speaks of the substance of his work:

> This composer is steeped in the quartet sound of the past, as well as traditional forms. This quartet is excellent in its use of what sounds can come from four players. Above the materials used, there is a real sense that this composer has his techniques well enough in hand to continuously write music, not just notes.[42]

The Third Quartet received the Silver Medal in 1963 from the Paulistan Association of Music and Theater Critics as the best chamber work of the year.

Angústia (Anguish). 1976.
[Ponteio–New York, 2005]

This is a single-movement work for string quartet composed at a time when Guarnieri was experiencing some personal problems, and the entire tenor of the piece attests to his personal feelings. It was commissioned by Brazil's Ministry of Exterior Relations and was premiered by the String Quartet of the University of Brasilia in Washington, D.C., at the Festival of Inter-American Music and again in the Edifício Casa Thomas Jefferson Auditorium in Brasilia on August 26, 1977.

Guarnieri exploited the possibilities of what four instruments could possibly do to express his meaning: sustained high registers on single notes, tremolos, trills, downward slides, very close dissonant harmonies, and occasional percussive interruptions.

Caldeira Filho wrote of it after a performance in a 1977 three-concert festival of Guarnieri's music: "The exaltation of expressive power of sound was given in *Angústia,* an authentic poem in the form of a long sustained meditation."[43]

SIX PIECES FOR GUITAR

Though Guarnieri did not play the guitar, he wrote six pieces over the years for this instrument, two of them dedicated to his son Mário. They are all difficult and far from any simple diatonic arpeggiation found in guitar pieces of many other composers. He seems to be "pushing the envelope" of atonal language with very rare points of diatonic familiarity or expected melodic and harmonic resolution. American guitarist Peter Baime noted:

> In the 1950s and 1960s there was a strong movement to popularize the guitar in which many older works were revived and others transcribed for the guitar, a movement led primarily by Andre Segovia. On the other hand and almost in spite of the instrument, Guarnieri seemed to be pursuing a musical language new for its time, not necessarily music amenable to the guitar.[44]

Guarnieri completely avoided the natural temptation to succumb to any typical or identifiable Brazilian rhythms. These pieces challenge the listener and certainly any performer. All but the *Valsa Choro* no. 2 have been published.

Ponteio (Prelude). 1944.
[*Guitar Review*–1951]

A very angular, chromatic melody is marked by successive upward leaps of fourths. Guarnieri uses sequences to develop this and subsequent patterns. A *Grazioso* introduces wider leaps, which create even more chromatic dissonance. The flow of eighth notes is broken only a few times as the melody seems to pause on a high point. A middle B section has a series of repeated notes accompanying a brief melody, which continues to articulate the interval of a fourth. A retransition marked by descending and widely spaced dominant thirteenth chords leads to a return of the opening material. The repeated-note idea recurs, leading to an ending on an A-minor chord. The piece reveals a strong inclination toward atonality despite a few moments of more consonant sounds.

The piece was dedicated to Abel Carlevaro and published in the vol. 12 (1951) issue of the *Guitar Review,* New York. Ricordi Brasileira also published it in 1978.

Valsa Choro no. 1. 1954.
[RB–1978]

Guarnieri dedicated this piece in rondo form "To my son, Mário." It was published by Ricordi Brasileira in 1978 and in *São Paulo Musical* no. 32, ano VI, pp. 20–21.

As its title suggests, this *Valsa Choro* in minor is full of a feeling of *saudade* or longing, and its texture is of a melody with accompaniment. It opens in E minor with an eight-measure phrase, followed by a rising melody over an F$\sharp$7 chord and more active texture, then moves to a climax in measure 15. The opening melody returns with a slightly different harmonic setting. A first ending calls for a repeat of the entire first part of the piece.

Valsa Choro no. 2.
1986. Manuscript

Separated from the *Valsa Choro* no. 1 by thirty-two years, this is Guarnieri's last composition for the guitar. It is closer to the harmonic vintage of his third *Estudo* written four years earlier than to the first *Valsa Choro.* Guarnieri retains the $\frac{3}{4}$ waltz meter, but that is his "farewell" to tradition in this piece. Already in the opening bars cross-relations in close proximity and other unexpected chromatic alterations hint at what is to follow. It was dedicated to Jodacil Damasceno.

Três Estudos
(Three Studies) for Guitar

Guarnieri's three studies for guitar were written over a period of twenty-two years: the first in 1958, and the second and third in 1982. All three have been published by Ricordi Brasileira and Edizione Musicale Berben in Ancona, Italy.

Estudo no. 1—*Moderato, p.* 1958.
[RB, Berber]

The fifty-three measures of the piece continually change time signatures: $\frac{3}{2}$, $\frac{2}{2}$, $\frac{7}{4}$, $\frac{3}{4}$, $\frac{2}{4}$, $\frac{5}{4}$. A very chromatic angular line moves above the rising bass melody.

Developed in sections, a gentle climax is reached in measure 8, and a second one halfway through the piece in measure 24. The angular, atonal figuration continues and is softened only occasionally by extended tertian chords with diminished fifths. A *Piu Lento, Sonoro, ff* halts the forward movement momentarily. An *A Tempo* two measures later recalls the opening bars of the piece, leading to a striking ending on a final, pungent *ff* bitonal chord.

The work is dedicated to Isaías Savio. Manuel Barruecco has recorded it several times. In the cover notes to the last recording, Richard Freed wrote, "The first *Estudo* recorded here exudes an air of elegant craftsmanship."[45]

Estudo no. 2—Tranquillo, f. 1982.
[RB, Berber]

Also dedicated to his son Mário, the second study begins with a angular figuration similar to that of the first *Estudo*. This is an uninterrupted flow of rising and falling eighth notes following a quartal outline, initially patterned but becoming gradually less predictable in its outline of fourths, simple scale passages, or expanding harmonic intervals. The wandering line becomes more agitated in this middle section of the piece. As in the first *Estudo,* the changing meters are more apparent to the eye than the ear within the flow of notes.

Estudo no. 3—Sem pressa, p. 1982.
[RB, Berber]

The shortest in this set of three pieces, this one begins innocently enough but quickly reveals a texture which seems to seek the most dissonant relationships possible within the melodic line itself and its chordal support. It pursues an increasing density of texture to measure 23, where a climax is reached. An *A Tempo* recalls the first thirteen bars of the opening section. The two added final measures melt into a relatively consonant final chord. Guarnieri limited himself in this *Estudo* to $\frac{3}{2}$ and $\frac{2}{2}$ time signatures.

NINE

Music for Strings with Orchestra

There are five pieces in this category: two concertos and a *choro* for violin, and a *choro* each for viola and cello. None of these works have been published to date, but all have been performed and several recorded.

VIOLIN AND ORCHESTRA
Concerto no. 1 for Violin and Orchestra.
1940. Manuscript

This concerto is dated January 18, 1940, shortly after Guarnieri returned from his interrupted European studies in Paris. The material in the piece should have convinced anyone who may have feared that he might have been "Europeanized" that he came through the experience intact as a Brazilian composer. Although the last movement is full of syncopated patterns, the work does not possess a strong "Latin" flavor as such. Rather, it is a development of the stringent style the young composer imposed upon himself in the early 1930s, evidenced in such works as the Piano Concerto no. 1 of 1931, the Violin Sonata no. 1, Cello Sonata no. 1, and the First String Quartet.

The themes in this work are a little longer and slightly more developed. They are, however, still marked by a conciseness and tension that place the burden of development upon the orchestra, rather than the themes themselves. The first and last movements are related, and both use a sonata-allegro design. The middle movement is monothematic, and all three movements are connected to each other: I, *Heroic, ff;* II, *Com grande calma, p;* and III, *Allegro molto e ritmado, pp.* The heroic character of the work results from the open sounds of quartal chords. Linear dissonances and chord structures tend to weaken the tonal feeling of the piece.

This concerto won the Samuel Fels Prize in a 1940 international contest sponsored by the Fleischer Music Collection of the Philadelphia Library. Guarnieri received his prize money of $750 in person during his first trip to the United States, presented to him in a ceremony at the Pan American Union in Washington, D.C., on October 9, 1942. This was his first international recognition as a composer. The piece had been premiered on September 9, 1942, in Rio by Eunice de Conte with Guarnieri conducting the Brazilian Symphony Orchestra, just before he left for his six-month stay in the United States. The first U.S. performance of the piece was given in 1944 by Milton Wohl with the United States Marine Band.

Andrade Muricy wrote after the Rio premiere: "The first hearing struck me as if the work outlined a strange physiognomy, not so much virtuosic for the violinist, but rather as though it was a piece for a principal violin, not a solo violin."[1] Ayres de Andrade wrote:

> Of the three movements, the second seems to me to be the most happy and integral realization. The ideas are expressed with largeness and naturalness. The last movement is conceived with audacity and vivacity. If there is a moment in which the inventive fantasy of the author is revealed with a certain aggressiveness, there are others in which he engenders combinations of rhythms and instrumentation full of originality and taste.[2]

A third critic, Francisco Cavalcanti, reacted less favorably: "The concerto of Camargo Guarnieri presented here for the first time is a piece which lacks originality. Perhaps the word 'fantasia' would have been a better title."[3]

The concerto was performed again in São Paulo in 1943 after Guarnieri's return from the United States. Caldeira Filho, close friend and frequent observer of the composer, wrote:

> In musical language, it confirms a richness of orchestration, using to the maximum the orchestral timbres with a great simplicity of realization, avoiding the eloquence of the easy *tutti*, obtaining in consequence a greater instrumental strengthened purity of writing. It is original with the merit of not being extravagant or mundane. On the contrary, it is felt to attain an adequate expression of his feeling, a proof of sincerity, always well done, at times even a little sad, but meanwhile constant despite the numerous possibilities of evasion offered by orchestral virtuosity.
>
> In the view of Brazilian music, he is a creator, not one who cites folkloric themes. His themes are his own creations, making use of some specific melodic-rhythmic-harmonic processes of our music in building his structures.
>
> But it is not only this which makes it Brazilian, which makes it seem like our own. It is such themes, as well as the entire piece, the general impression of the music which reflects that expression that is ours, indefinable but without doubt. From this point of view, it appears to us that he has been particularly successful in the slow, expressive movements which we have noted in

earlier works. As a modern composer, living fully in this moment, Camargo Guarnieri can permit himself greater freedom of expression. Meanwhile, this concerto marks a moment in his evolution. We feel a certain sobriety, a control and self-criticism, a probable consequence of his stay in Europe which was unhappily interrupted by the war.[4]

Choro for Violin and Orchestra.
1951. Heliograph copy

This *Choro* for Violin and Orchestra is perhaps the most rhapsodic of Guarnieri's *choros* for solo instruments and orchestra. As this composer uses the term *choro,* it is actually a concerto with distinctly national qualities. This particular piece partakes to a greater degree than his others of this title in the improvisational style so common in the streets of Rio and São Paulo some decades earlier. Its three movements—I, *Andante, ppp;* II, *Calmo, dolcissimo, pp;* and III, *Alegre e ritmado, mf*—are joined together, and the first and third are thematically related. The very first appearance of the solo violin is an improvisatory passage. The fabric is basically contrapuntal, with the orchestral part well integrated with that of the solo violin. The slower tempo of the piece and its gentle character, with the exception of the last movement, permit the dissonance to function, not as harshness, but rather as an intensification of the nostalgic expressiveness of the piece. All of the dissonance lies within a strong modal framework.

The close relationship of thematic material, stemming from its germinal development, becomes more and more common in Guarnieri's music, particularly in his later works. Elements of previously heard themes, the use of percussion instruments, and the insistent rhythmic reiteration of the orchestral material bring the work to a triumphant close on C♯.

This *Choro* was composed in the same year as the Third Symphony, 1952. The next year saw a return to a more stringent musical language, as will be seen in the Second Violin Concerto. The *Choro* received its premiere performance in Paris under the direction of Eugenio Bigot with Mariuccia Iacovino as soloist.

Concerto no. 2 for Violin and Orchestra.
1953. Manuscript

This Second Violin Concerto follows the *Choro* by one year. It is definitely Guarnieri's music, and yet, like the *Variations on a Northeast Theme* for piano and orchestra which dates from this same year, it has some very different qualities, particularly in the way in which the harmonic material and the texture are integrated. The quartal, tertian, and some quintal structures are prominent. The chords and melodic fragments, however, succeed each other and overlap in relationships which are frequently bitonal. One gets the impression of rapidly changing tonal centers, cross-relations, bitonality, and stringent vertical structures.

Technically the work is a virtuosic challenge for the performer, opening with a cadenza that leads into the first movement's plentiful double stops and passages of three-note chords. The orchestra is definitely accompanimental with the greater burden of the material allotted to the soloist. The three movements are I, *Lento, Allegro Enérgico, f;* II, *Triste, ppp;* and III, *Allegro Giocoso, ff.* The eruptive quality of the opening theme lends itself to the aggressive treatment it receives. An active percussion section of the orchestra reinforces its character.

The middle movement has mostly extended tertian harmony with shifting chords that do not follow a functional harmony pattern. The last movement serves to summarize some of the previously heard themes, as well as to introduce two new ones. The rhythmic role of the orchestra is immediately evident. Orchestral sonorities in the closing measures are open quartal and quintal, and they come to rest finally on a unison D.

Although this concerto was composed in 1953 for the competition "Music of the Twentieth Century," it was first performed in March of 1956 with Guarnieri directing the São Paulo Municipal Symphony Orchestra. It was dedicated to Henryk Szeryng, even though Anselmo Zlatopolsky was the soloist for the premiere. At that time Caldeira Filho particularly noted the unusual placement of the cadenza at the opening of the first movement:

> This cadenza contains thematic elements of the second and third movements by which it signifies a species of aesthetic anticipation. It is clothed in a writing so rich and complex that it does not damage the function of the passage, which is its traditional virtuosity. In the entire work there is evident another kind of virtuosity: that with which the composer writes for the violin. There are abundant problems of execution in the score, but they are always subdued to the expressive intent, never surrendering the means for the end, and this corresponds to the style of Camargo Guarnieri: profoundly significant content in the themes, expositional conciseness, and structural economy.[5]

VIOLA AND ORCHESTRA

Choro for Viola and Orchestra.
1975. Manuscript

This *Choro* for Viola and Orchestra also carries Guarnieri's meaning of a concerto with national roots rather than that of a small serenading group that played in the streets. It was premiered in the United States by Raphael Hillyer, its dedicatee, and conductor Lukas Foss.

Guarnieri takes more than normal freedom with his own brand of ABA form in the first movement, *Enérgico*. He explained his unusual procedure in his comments on the work. He noted an Introduction and three sections, each one preceded by a little refrain. After the last section, the viola plays a very brilliant cadenza that serves as a bridge between the last section and the reexposition. Brasses add strength to the final bars as the movement ends firmly.

The rather long, lovely meditative movement, *Tristamente,* belongs to the soloist with only sparse comments from the orchestra. The movement fades away gently as the vibraphone recalls the theme once more at the end.

Percussion instruments start the final *Bem Ritmado* movement softly, setting the stage for the viola's *embolada*-like tune. After a very active development and second theme, the piece ends with an *ff* unison E, which is sustained, in contrast to so many of Guarnieri's later works in which the final notes are short and percussive.

CELLO AND ORCHESTRA

Choro for Violoncello and Orchestra.
1961. Manuscript

The *Choro* for Cello and Orchestra is a virtuoso piece, with the greater burden of the work falling to the soloist. The orchestral writing is actually thin, with ample room being given to the cello for announcing and carrying the thematic material. The solo line is somewhat atonal, although each movement retains a pivotal tonal orientation.

The orchestral texture looks tertian enough, but in combination with the cello line the effect becomes more stringent and tense. All three movements are monothematic. The middle movement exploits the upper register of the instrument in its extended thematic lines. The last movement is like a "catch me if you can" race through the repeated-note theme with a combustible rhythmic drive. The three movements are: I, *Decidido e Apaixonada, f;* II, *Calmo e Triste, ppp;* and III, *Com alegria, ff.*

This *Choro* was commissioned by Aldo Parisot, to whom it was dedicated and who premiered it in New York in 1963 under Richard Korn. It was recorded by the Vienna State Opera Orchestra in 1976.

The *Ponteio e Dança* was written for cello with piano accompaniment in 1946. Guarnieri transcribed it in 1982 for cello and string orchestra accompaniment (see page 186).

TEN

Music for Wind Instruments

Within his total catalog of works, Camargo Guarnieri wrote relatively little music featuring solo wind instruments. He had studied flute briefly with his father when he was young, and he subsequently demonstrated a facile writing for all the wind instruments within his orchestral scores. Most of his pieces within this category feature the flute. There are *Three Improvisations* for solo flute, an *Estudo* for piccolo of 1953, a sonatina for flute and piano dedicated to his good friend Carleton Sprague Smith, a *choro* for flute and orchestra completed in 1972, an *Improvisação* for flute and string orchestra of 1987, and a duo for two flutes from 1989. There is an *Estudo* for solo trumpet and another for solo French horn, both published by Rongwen in the United States. The clarinet is favored with a *choro,* dating from 1956.

In addition to these pieces, the 1928 piano solo *Canção Sertaneja* has been transcribed for both clarinet and oboe solo. Both of these versions have been published by Cundy-Bettoney of Boston. Guarnieri's last work for woodwinds was a *choro* for bassoon and string orchestra with harp and percussion, written in 1991.

Three Improvisations for Flute.
1941–49. [Rongwen]

These three unaccompanied pieces for solo flute were written in 1941, 1942, and 1949, respectively. They reflect Guarnieri's gift for melodic development, particularly evident in these pieces without accompaniment. One finds quartal outlines, figures that expand intervallically from seconds to an octave or that contract inward, a free rhythmic structure within phrases, and finally, a rather imprecise tonal orientation.

No. 1—*Tristamente.* 1949

This first piece has a delicate, lacey texture featuring grace notes and a quasi cadenza in the middle of its ABA form. Dedicated to Moacyr Liserra, it was premiered by Hans Joachim Koellreutter in São Paulo in 1941 and was given an extensive review by Caldeira Filho, music critic of the *Estado de São Paulo:*

> With this work Camargo Guarnieri reveals a significant moment in his evolution, and it is curious that he has done so within the limitation and relative lack of resources of the instrument, unaccompanied by either harmonic or polyphonic support. The first thing to notice in the *Improviso* is the harmonic condensation implied in the solo melodic line. It consists of an exposition of the theme, a development, and a recapitulation. The use of this form in a piece of music that could be free is another element to note, as well as the substratum's popular quality—perhaps a waltz or a serenade felt in the large, soaring theme, understood as a development or expressive synthesis of melodies of this genre.
>
> All this reveals a spirit of conciseness and equilibrium, the intervention of an intellect that at the same time values and disciplines the initial emotion, and a constructive sense that simply does not dispose the elements as in a game, but attributes to them their maximum significance, precisely because they are condensed in a single melodic line.
>
> These qualities are not revealed here for the first time in Camargo Guarnieri. On the contrary, they are here reinforced more intensely, reaffirming the definitive manner of his creative personality. And we think it significant that the work, which was written this year [1941], denotes an independence and resistance of the author in relation to the influences he could have endured in his stay in Europe.
>
> Even admitting that the equilibrium and finesse might be French, his manner of feeling is a Brazilian thing, or it might be an evolution which he imposed on the waltz to transform it into the theme of the *Improviso*. It is one of those rare anticipations of the formation of a Brazilian spirit superimposed on folklore and regionalism.[1]

No. 2—*Ritmico.* 1942

Irregularity of meter is especially prominent in the long measures of this piece in ABACA form. It has many large melodic intervals and a rapid alternation of legato and staccato groups of notes. It was dedicated to Carleton Sprague Smith.

No. 3—*Lamentoso.* 1949

This ABA piece is the most sustained in character of the three *Improvisos*. It frequently uses long note values, although the phrases tend to be shorter. It is dedicated to Alferio Mignone, the father of Guarnieri's fellow composer Francisco Mignone.

Sonatina for Flute and Piano. 1947.
[Music Press/Mercury, N.Y.–1947;
Irmãos Vitale–1997]

This sonatina is a playful work in three movements composed in New York in January and February 1947. Dedicated to Carleton Sprague Smith, it has been recorded many times. Its dissonance results from the independence of linear elements, which, in context, create a humorous effect. The first movement, *Allegro,* calls for strong legato in its conjunct melodic lines. The piano begins with a melody over a walking ostinato bass line of rather independent tonal orientation. The flute repeats the idea, but the texture then becomes more fragmented. Canonic treatment of the theme leads to a coda in which the final staccato line ascends in the flute through nearly three octaves to a pianissimo disappearance on high C.

Sonatina
for Flute & Piano
1st movement

The slow *Melancólic* movement will not cause problems for a performer. Tension is achieved through the harmonic independence of the parts. The last movement, *Saltitante,* has a constant flow of rapid staccato notes, which give little time for such necessities as breathing. The music gives a sense of bubbling or perking. The lighthearted crispness of the work makes it very appealing.

Eurico Nogueira Franca wrote a lengthy article after the publication of this work which read in part:

As to the Sonatina for Flute and Piano, it is a work which is beginning to take its place among the literature of the instrument, proving again the mas-

Sonatina
for Flute & Piano
3rd movement

tery and freedom with which this composer moves among the classic forms. In the three movements of diverse expression—*Allegro, Melancolico,* and *Saltitante*—is shown a constant richness of invention and a transparent logic of structure. The expressive possibilities of the flute are strongly challenged by the author, based on the relationship of the flute with our popular music.[2]

Duo para Flautas (Due for Two Flutes).
1989. Manuscript

This is a brief, forty-five-measure, cheerful little *Scherzando* for two flutes that begins with the second flute imitating the first for two measures, then going its own teasing way, sometimes in mirror writing, sometimes independently. There is a brief climax and pause in measure 16, after which the second flute takes the lead and makes its way to a climactic close. Barbara and Frank Suetholz, to whom it was dedicated, characterized the piece as "exciting, very demanding, a whirlwind of a piece that is over almost before it begins, requiring challenging embouchure work on the descending octave leaps near the end of the piece."[3] They premiered it in Milwaukee.

Choro for Flute and Orchestra.
1972. Heliograph Manuscript

The *Choro* is scored for solo flute with oboe, English horn, clarinet, three horns in F, timpani, drum without snares (ad libitum), harp, harpsichord, and strings. Guarnieri again uses the term *choro* to denote a concerto with national content. The piece's three sections are played without pause, with the solo flute carrying the major responsibility with continuous interaction by the orchestra. The work reflects the atonal language of this period of his life to express a mood that is neither stern nor completely playful. It is rather a distilled, balanced expression proper to "absolute" music.

The first movement, *Calmo,* opens with a six-note line stated by the English horn. This line appears in retrograde in the oboe part and in harmonic intervals in the bassoon. The second, *Scherzando-Brincando,* opens playfully with punctuating strings in rapid tempo, and the addition of percussion instruments. The third is again a *Calmo,* which recalls first movement material. It progresses through a gradual but continual acceleration into the final climax of the piece, a fortissimo ending.

It was premiered in 1981 by Antônio Carrasqueira, flutist, and Alceu Bocchino conducting the Brazilian National Symphony Orchestra.

Improvisação for Flute and String Orchestra.
1987. Manuscript

This was one of Guarnieri's last compositions. It was commissioned in observance of an auspicious year by the Orquestra da Câmara de Blumenau and flutist/conductor Norton Morozowicz: In 1987 were celebrated the one hundredth birthday of Villa-Lobos, the ninetieth birthdays of Francisco Mignone and Lorenzo Fernandez, and the eightieth birthdays of Guarnieri and José Siqueira.

The strings unfold a linear introduction, which grows in intensity until the flute enters. The linear dissonance increases slightly, and the flute becomes more prominent. After an initial climax, the undulating lines continue to build a series of small points of intensity. A brief string interlude prepares for the reentry of the flute. The piece fades gently with a sense of peace.

Estudo for Trumpet in C. 1953.
[Rongwen–1958]

The study for trumpet stresses precision in articulation and rhythms. Phrases are developed sequentially, and the opening line recurs in a modi-

212 | CAMARGO GUARNIERI, BRAZILIAN COMPOSER

fied form throughout this monothematic piece, giving the impression of being through composed.

Estudo for French Horn. 1953.
[Rongwen–1958]

This work is basically a study in legato. The monothematic piece has some staccato passages and an ad libitum glissando near the end. Varied rhythmic groups are used, although actual syncopated figures are scarce.

Choro for Clarinet and Orchestra.
1956. Manuscript

The *Choro* for Clarinet and Orchestra was written in the same year as was the *Choro* for Piano and Orchestra, which it resembles in some ways. This *Choro* is conceived in only two connected movements. It uses the Mode of the Northeast and maintains a thematic relationship between the two movements. An interesting orchestral timbre is achieved in several places where a horn doubles the melody two octaves lower. The piece has a continuity and fullness of texture which is more reflective than aggressive. It has a feeling of being almost meterless, giving the sonorities full freedom to expand and contract under the poignant clarinet solo, which has an almost improvisatory character in places.

The last movement is rather unique in that its scintillating rhythmic effects are achieved not so much by its syncopated patterns as by the implied syncopation of a relatively sparse texture. It demands flexibility and rhythmic precision as the theme becomes transformed into a lively, brilliant tune.

The piece was commissioned in 1956 for the First Latin American Festival held in Washington, D. C. It was performed there during the April 1957 Festival, with Harold Wright as soloist with the National Symphony Orchestra under the direction of Howard Mitchell. Caldeira Filho wrote after a March 1959 performance of the work in São Paulo:

> In this piece the composer seems to dwell on making the orchestra perform in a way and manner expressively neutral so that, not withstanding the finesse of the compositional work, it still results in an of insufficiency of work for the solo clarinet and in some monotony, broken only by the rhythmic interest of the theme. It is a relatively long work, dealing more with details than long lines.[4]

The piece was explored in great detail in the doctoral dissertation of Maurício Alves Loureiro, completed in 1991 at the University of Iowa.[5]

Choro for Bassoon and Chamber Orchestra.
1991. Heliograph Copy

This was the composer's final work, but he did not live to hear it performed. Afonso Venturieri premiered it at the 25th Winter Festival of Campos do Jordão in Curitiba on July 17, 1994, with the Chamber Orchestra of the City of Curitiba directed by Lutero Rodrigues. The piece had been commissioned by the State of São Paulo Secretary of Culture. The original manuscript was lost, but a barely legible copy remains.

There are three connected sections: *Improvisando, Calmo,* and *Allegro.* The *Improvisando* is essentially a bassoon solo improvisation with occasional punctuation by the woodwinds and percussion. There is a gradual *ritard* into the *Calmo,* where an immediate change of mood is realized as the strings begin a gentle, though contrapuntal, web of supporting sound under the bassoon's soaring line. The texture waxes and wanes in intensity with a *Piu Lento* finally initiating a gentle descent into a *pp* resting point. The final *Allegro* is again energetic, drawing in the jubilant bassoon. It is a very challenging movement for the soloist.

ELEVEN

Music for Orchestra

The orchestral compositions of Camargo Guarnieri add an entirely new dimension to the understanding of his style. Their contrapuntal conception, the fragmentation and litany-like treatment of thematic material, the ostinatos and the rhythmic vitality—all are given new possibilities when the sheer numbers of possible instrumental combinations and unlimited timbre options are added as leaven to his textures.

Guarnieri had a way of treating each instrument as if it were his favorite. This is partly a result of the contrapuntal nature of his writing, but also because of the way he handled his textures. He had a propensity for fragmenting themes or distilling longer lines from simple fragments. He used the solo winds particularly effectively. Likewise, his doubling at the unison or several octaves apart created distinctive timbres. Frequently the strings were entrusted with an explosively syncopated accompaniment, functioning as one huge guitar, reinforced by an array of Brazilian rhythm instruments such as the *xocalho, reco-reco, cuica, maracá, agôgo,* and *cavaquinho.* His use of brass instruments as a chorus is sparse and is confined to finales or climaxes. Often these are paired on melodic fragments, as are the woodwinds.

Lower-placed melodies come through clearly and precisely due to their rhythmic nature and the choice he makes of instruments. In many of the orchestral movements, particularly the slow ones, Guarnieri achieves a suppleness or suspended quality by completely eliminating any lower line that would suggest a functional root movement of chords. Instead, the sense of movement is projected by the rhythmic fabric of the texture itself, which supports the melody. If a melody does occur in a lower register, the thinner texture and doublings permit it to project clearly. In many of the fast movements, the lower instruments function almost as part of the rhythm section, often providing a precision-perfect ostinato accompaniment.

As with his other works, Guarnieri often uses modal themes and shows a preference for the Lydian and Mixolydian modes and the Mode of the

Northeast, which combines the qualities of the other two (raised fourth and lowered seventh degrees). His melodies often rise through the scale degrees 1–3–5–♭7–6–5. He frequently uses double reeds, with their poignant evocative power, on plaintive themes

Guarnieri can alternate intensely touching melodic moments with full, soaring passages, or he can move from a *tutti* to thinner textures without losing the continuity or creating a vacuum of perception. The slow, suspended line never seems to lag because of the undulating rhythmic structure and the support it gives. More importantly, the listener never knows what is going to happen next. Lines are not obvious, movement never predictable. The music possesses an inner life that is completely under control: energetic but not brutal, tender but seldom morose or sentimental, although his later works seem to reflect accurately the increasing tensions of his life. In a very real sense, his music reveals both the personality and the ability of a creator who is in complete technical command of his materials, who has something to say that may be humorous, extremely gentle and tender, festive, pleasantly reflective, firm and energetic, or perhaps demanding. And he knows how to say it in purely musical terms with great finesse.

Guarnieri's melodies draw their living breath from the Brazilian forms: the *modinha* with its plaintive, supplicating rise and fall of phrase, and the *toada,* a simpler form which often uses the Paulistan or Caipira thirds. It is interesting to see the growing freedom with which he treats the thirds, adhering to a diatonic setting in the early *Toada à Moda Paulista* and later introducing the subtle little chromatic nuances and alterations to fourths, fifths, and sixths in his Piano Concertino. The slow lines have a peaceful character and, in a sense, have a quality of timelessness in their suspended, almost motionless breathing. Normally they have a strong linear tonality with a more or less tonally oriented accompaniment.

Guarnieri tends to become more monothematic in his longer works. His own peculiar brand of ABA design is frequently used in which the B material is merely a development of the A section. This growing inclination was the natural preparation for serialization—a more developed form of monothematic maneuvering. Many of his later works also have an interrelationship between the themes, either by using one as a common source, or by recalling one from a previous movement. Often several themes are so closely related that they thwart the function of contrast and serve rather as variations or development of the principal material. In longer movements this makes formal classification risky at times. When he uses the sonata-allegro form, he does not bind himself to the expected key relationships or sequences of themes. His approach to form, therefore, is more of a development of the inner logic of his musical ideas.

If there is one characteristic that marks all of Guarnieri's music, it is that of his contrapuntal mastery. In all of his work, however, there is only one actual fugue, and that is paired with the *Prologo*. The *Ricercare* of his *Sequência, Coral e Ricercare* is also developed in the fugal form. Many of his works contain fugal expositions within their developments. He freely used Baroque techniques of combined themes and of augmentation and diminution of rhythmic values.

Chronologically the orchestral works reflect vast differences. One piece may be completely accessible by any listener's standards, while the next may be a sheaf of serious business for the astute ear. For example, the cheery *Suite Brasiliana* falls between the more rugged *Prologo e Fuga* and the Third Symphony. Likewise, the genial *Homenagem a Villa-Lobos* was composed in the same year as the much more stringent *Sequência, Coral e Ricercare*.

A little familiarity with these larger works raises the question as to why Eurico Nogueira França referred to Guarnieri as a "miniaturist." Although this is one person's opinion, it is from someone who knew and followed Guarnieri's career closely. Perhaps it is due to his relatively larger number of shorter pieces, such as the songs and piano compositions. Or could it be that Guarnieri's brand of craftsmanship is so evident in the shorter works? He brings, however, the same skills and care to the larger works. His manner of delineation of line, complexity of fabric, and independence of phrases results in increasingly complicated textures in these larger orchestral compositions. Yet to examine some of his scores, one notices the many "open" places and the clarity of the sound.

This chapter will deal with all of Guarnieri's chamber and full orchestra efforts, two of which are written primarily for strings: the *Toada à Moda Paulista* and Concerto for Strings and Percussion. It is important to see all of these pieces in their chronological order. There are also transcriptions of works written originally for piano: the *Toada, Toada Triste,* three *Dances,* and a good number of *Ponteio* transcriptions: nos. 5, 31, 33, and 48 for strings, and nos. 1, 2, 7, 15, 20, and 45 for full orchestra. Excluding transcriptions, there are twenty-six major works for orchestra. His *Estudo para Instrumentos de Percussão* is also included here for want of a better category in which to place it.

Suite Infantil (Children's Suite). 1929.
[AMP–1944]

This seven-minute piece was Guarnieri's first attempt at writing for orchestra under the direction of Maestro Baldi. He scored it for piccolo, two flutes, oboes, clarinets, bassoons, trumpets, and trombones, tuba, celesta, harp, xylophone, *xocalho, reco-reco,* and strings. The textures are simple with cautious doublings of instruments on melodies. The modes, ostinatos, rhythmic vitality—all are here, somewhat less obviously than they will be in later works. There are four short movements, two of which were performed on April 5, 1929, by Lamberto Baldi and the orchestra of the Sociedade de Concertos Sinfônica de São Paulo. Guarnieri later transcribed this set for piano solo, but it is not available in that form. The movements are: I, *Acalanto;* II, *Requebrando;* III, *Ponteio, muito espressivo;* IV, *Maxixando, depressa.*

After the first two movements were performed in São Paulo in 1929, Mário de Andrade wrote:

> Musically speaking, I appreciated especially the *Requebrando* with its humorous ideas, so well constructed and with some polytonal excursions. The *Acalanto* suited the orchestra better and achieved a delightful effect in the first entrance of the strings. It is clear that the timidity of this first orchestral effort did not permit Camargo Guarnieri to give the *Suite Infantil* the beautiful force that his Sonatina had, but the pages left evidence of the extraordinary talent of the composer.[1]

Five years later, the entire Suite was performed in São Paulo by the same orchestra under Ernst Mehlich on January 30, 1934. Andrade again had the opportunity to review it:

> Despite the fact that this is the first orchestral work of this young man, the Suite lacks nothing in strength or freshness. He has kept the song quality in the first three movements. One can already see the great, bold efforts of Camargo Guarnieri. They are gracious pieces, perhaps too full of combinations of instruments, polyphony and new harmonics for their size and conception.
>
> The *Acalanto* has a really lovely melodic line with a rhythmic background stated by the winds—a legitimate idea. Also in the *ponteio*-like third movement, there rise lines of a *caipira* character, inspired by the Paulistan *modas* so simple, beautiful, and melancholic. I hesitate to say which of the first three movements I prefer.
>
> The fourth, a *Maxixe,* was completely sacrificed in its performance. Of great difficulty and demanding enormous security in attacks, it surely needs more preparation to actually show what it is. Some pieces came off, others did not. The themes here seemed more diffuse to me, more pleasing to the eye, perhaps in their polyphonic arrangement, than to the ear.[2]

Thus, this first attempt had ample press coverage. Guarnieri chose to have the first, third, and fourth movements of this early work performed by the CBS Symphony Orchestra during his first visit to the United States in 1943.

Toada. 1929

Written as a piano solo in 1929, Guarnieri transcribed the piece in July of the same year for full orchestra. (See page 83.)

Curuça.
1930. Manuscript

Guarnieri subtitled this twelve-minute piece *Choro para Orquestra* no. 5. He decided to withdraw the first four pieces in this series from his catalog, although the first two are still in existence as very brief sketches. The first exists in two versions with slightly different instrumentation, which clearly suggests his intent of writing in the serenade style of the *choro.* The third had several performances before it was withdrawn. It was premiered under the direction of Heitor Villa-Lobos in São Paulo on January 6, 1930.

The title *Curuça* is a reference to the composer's hometown of Tietê, which is circled on three sides by the River Tietê. A cross erected on one of the hills is called the Curuça. Guarnieri used this as a pseudonym when he entered his First Symphony in a contest sponsored in 1943 in São Paulo. The woman to whom the piece is dedicated, Olivia Guedes Penteado, was a wealthy music patron in São Paulo in whose home some of Guarnieri's first works were heard.

The *Curuça* is both interesting and important in the development of the young composer. Written when he was twenty-three, it follows his first orchestration of the *Suite Infantil* by one year and gives evidence of growing courage and facility in writing for full orchestra. The texture is already more contrapuntal and complex, and the orchestration which requires some *divisi* scoring is also more dense.

Dança Brasileira
(Brazilian Dance). 1931.
[AMP–1949]

Guarnieri made the orchestral transcription for full orchestra plus rhythm instruments from the 1928 piano solo. (See page 83.) Because it was published and recorded many times in the United States, it has been the principal piece by which the composer has been known here. It is an audience pleaser. In light of all that he subsequently wrote, it is a pity that one of his earliest pieces became his calling card. Guarnieri conducted its orchestral premiere in 1949.

Judith Cabette wrote program notes for a concert featuring the orchestral version of his three dances: "In the *Dança Brasileira* is found a game between various elements so characteristic of Brazilian music: the descending phrases, the repeated notes, our rhythms and the lowered seventh degree of the scale—all without actually citing directly any popular musical sources."[3] The piece has a spontaneity and exuberance that are infectious.

Dança Selvagem
(Jungle Dance). 1931.
[AMP–1949]

As with the *Dança Brasileira,* Guarnieri transcribed this 1931 piano solo for full orchestra plus rhythm instruments. Mário de Andrade had high praise for the piece in its original version for piano. (See page 83.) Of the piece, Guarnieri wrote, "It is constructed in an ABA form. The first theme has a primitive Indian quality, and the second is based on the spirit of the ciran-das."[4] It has been recorded along with the *Dança Brasileira.* Its premiere was conducted by the composer with the Orquestra Sinfônica Brasileira.

Em Memória dos Que Morreram por São Paulo
(In Memory of Those Who Died for São Paulo).
1932. Manuscript

This very short piece is one of two that were politically motivated by the Constitutional Revolution of 1932, begun on July 9 by the Paulistans against the dictator Getúlio Vargas. Counting on the support of *gaúcho* Flores da Cunha, Borges de Medeiros, and General Bertoldo Klinger, who was commander of Mato Grosso, the plan of the revolutionaries was to mount an attack against the federal capital. Rio Grande do Sul decided to change sides, and Klinger was able to recruit only a few men to help fight. Despite the inequality of the forces, the conflict was bloody and lasted three months. When the threat of occupation became real, the Paulistans surren-dered and lost men. Guarnieri had served in the Civil Guard of the city and related his feelings as Vargas's troops entered the city:

> On the day that São Paulo lost the revolution, I was profoundly affected. Everyone here had really taken part in this constitutional revolution in 1932. When the soldiers of Getúlio Vargas entered the city, it was as if the whole world died. There was silence, absolute silence. That is when I wrote the piece *Em Memoriam* for those who had died for São Paulo. It is a very short piece, very intimate, full of suffering.[5]

The piece conveys the sense of a gentle dirge. A viola maintains an F# major pedal point throughout with a few alternations a third higher. Against this, other instruments weave phrases in tonal conflict with each other. The result is an intense fabric with comparatively thin instrumenta-tion. Its very shortness speaks for its intensity and an emotion which seems unable to sustain itself any longer.

Toada à Moda Paulista
(*Toada* in Paulistan Thirds).
1935. Manuscript

This brief piece in ABABA form is as unassuming as it is short, and it demonstrates the pure simplicity of the Paulistan thirds. Harmonically, it is basically tertian and diatonic. All strings are directed to play with mutes.

The piece had an interesting origin. Guarnieri was asked to improvise something so an acquaintance could try out some new recording equipment. The composer liked what he heard, and subsequently he arranged the piece for strings, either a quintet or string orchestra. It is a genial piece, and although it has never been published, it has had periodic performances, in Porto Alegre in November 1940, and in the United States at the Alverno College Festival of Brazilian Music in December 1970. After the Porto Alegre performance, a reviewer wrote, "Guarnieri's inspired *Toada à Moda Paulista,* which he interpreted for us, made us experience a certain longing which at times breaks forth in our souls, almost to remind us of the great race which is ours."[6]

Toada Triste
(Sad *Toada*). 1936

This is another transcribed piano piece. Guarnieri arranged it not only for full orchestra but also for strings, a version premiered by his string orchestra at the University of São Paulo on November 26, 1977, and for violin and piano. Caldeira Filho wrote of this orchestral performance, "The *Toada* has features of the *modinha* or *caipira* singer and was well situated in an expressive setting, the kind to which Camargo Guarnieri has given so much of his creativity.[7]

A Flor de Tremembé
(Flower of Tremembé).
1937. Manuscript

This work was composed for fifteen solo instruments. Subtitled *Choro,* it is dedicated to Anita Queiroz de Almeida e Silva, his second wife. Written as a continuous piece, it falls into three sections with four themes. Guarnieri intended this work to be a concerto for solo wind instruments, which accounts for the solo quality of each instrument, although the strings function as an ensemble. Such writing lends itself to a contrapuntal treatment of the solo winds, a technique in which Guarnieri continued to grow in his mastery. After a 1940 performance in Rio, Luiz Heitor wrote:

It is a short work, not lasting ten minutes. The theme is deliberately treated polyphonically, revealing the principal preoccupation of the composer. It is divided into three short parts with no breaks. The first theme appears in the bassoon and is calm and moderate. The second shows a certain exoticism and appears to have Amerindian qualities. The last theme is typical of the gentle *choro* of Rio de Janeiro with a virtuoso flute giving it character and ending the piece in a magnificent counterpoint of all elements.

The use of some popular instruments is worthy of note. The *cavaquinho* [ukulele] adds some pleasant moments and impresses its character on the work. Camargo Guarnieri is a complete musician who lives of and for music. His works mark one of the most original and strongest forces in the history of contemporary Brazilian music.[8]

This followed a May 27, 1940, all-Guarnieri program, sponsored by the Escola Nacional de Música. It was reviewed by Andrade Muricy, who had this to say:

This work was played twice on the occasion of its premiere. That fact is significant. It is "characteristic music." Camargo Guarnieri did not present here a *choro* in the universal meaning of the term that was extended by Villa-Lobos. The *Flor de Tremembé* is really a Brazilian genre *choro* corresponding to the "night music" of the great classical composers, Handel, Haydn, and Mozart. Like night music, the *choro* is exclusively instrumental. Usually the instrumentation is limited to five instruments. Camargo Guarnieri used fifteen instrumental soloists. The *choro* is a free composition, usually with an improvisatory section, the music "bossa" in popular terms. This *choro* of Guarnieri begins with a short but determined *fughetto*. It tries to use even here the improvisatory practices of jazz. Near the end, we hear the eternal qualities of the *toada*. It ends like a *batuque* with its strummed instrumental style.[9]

Guarnieri derived the name of this piece, *Tremembé,* from a small town in the state of São Paulo. He submitted it in 1937 to the São Paulo Municipal Department of Culture and was awarded first prize. It was probably premiered at the Escola Nacional in Rio on May 27, 1940, and it also had a United States performance at the Fleischer Collection of the Free Library in Philadelphia. The German-Brazilian composer Hans Joachim Koellreutter, with whom Guarnieri had musical disputes over the years after his 1950 *Open Letter,* wrote of this piece in 1943:

I do not think I exaggerate when I say that *Flor de Tremembé* represents one of the most important Brazilian works of music, and perhaps of music of this continent. Deliberately polyphonic, a *choro* with typically national elements, it reveals a composer to whom the area of technique and problems of musical construction no longer constitute an obstacle.[10]

Encantamento (Enchantment). 1941.
[AMP–1941, RB]

Encantamento was composed on commission from the Division of Music of the Pan American Union in Washington, D.C. It was actually transcribed from a version for violin and piano. This orchestral version was conducted by Guarnieri in its first hearing in São Paulo in 1942 and again in 1947. Judith Cabette described the piece after a São Paulo performance in 1964:

> The piece is in ABA form. An undulating movement creates an atmosphere for the development of the theme stated first by an English horn. The second part begins with a very soft theme which has a character of the Northeast, and this reaches a great climax with the added trumpet. All strings sing fully at the height of the climax, and the winds offer counterpoint. In the repetition of the first part, the oboe has the theme with gradual help from the strings until the coda begins. The coda uses the second theme in the flute and violin, thus ending the piece.[11]

In this expression of "enchantment," Guarnieri achieved the undulation noted above in his typical way of setting the rhythms and melodic phrases, especially visible in the second violins as the work opens. The easily moving melody of conjunct motion retains the gentleness implied in the title, and its slow tempo and syncopation give it a nostalgic quality. A second theme receives canonic treatment. After a *Tempo primo,* the coda, *Lentemente,* as noted by Judith Cabette, uses the second theme to close the movement.

During Guarnieri's visit to the United States in 1943, he had the opportunity to conduct the Eastman Rochester Symphony Orchestra in this piece.

Abertura Concertante
(Concert Overture). 1942

When Guarnieri left São Paulo for his studies in Paris, he also left behind his teaching position at the Conservatory of Music and Drama, his private students, and the directorship of the Coral Paulistano, which he had founded three years previously. With his return late in 1939 due to the outbreak of World War II in Europe, he found himself without employment in São Paulo. An invitation to teach at the University of Panama raised complaints from various quarters suggesting that a composer of his stature should be able to be supported in his own country. An alternate solution arose when Guarnieri received an invitation from the Pan American Union to spend six months in the United States studying its musical institutions, participating in seminars, and having some of his works performed. He wanted to accept the invitation, which amounted to international recognition, but he had no money. He appealed to the Sociedade de Cultura Artistica, a group of wealthy Paulistan women headed by Esther Mesquita. He asked if they could perhaps sponsor a concert of his music to raise money for the trip. He heard, "Call me tomorrow." The morrow brought a commission with a stipend to write a new piece, the *Abertura Concertante*.

He dedicated the piece to Aaron Copland, whom he had met on his 1942 trip to the United States and with whom he enjoyed a warm friendship. The São Paulo Orquestra de Sociedade de Cultura performed the work on June 2, 1942, in the Municipal Theater under João de Souza Lima. One review was restrained:

> The work is advanced, very personal, and it was impossible in only one hearing to appreciate it fully. We note in a general way the originality of the first theme, predominantly rhythmic and full of life, rich in content and at the same time, more than could be handled by the group for whom it was written.
>
> The middle section reveals the lyricism of the composer. The general impression is that the Overture is a piece in which the composer leaves much to the feelings of his audience. It is full of suggestions of Brazil and is exciting both to the sensibilities and to the imagination.[12]

On the trip which followed, Guarnieri had the pleasure of twice conducting the Boston Symphony Orchestra in performances of this piece in March 1943, and it was very well received. The Brazilian consul, Ildefonso Falcão, and the vice consul, A. Silva Gomes, were both present. Guarnieri was applauded vigorously with a standing ovation by both the audience and the orchestra. A review described the piece: "The principal piece of the program was the *Abertura Concertante* in the classic form of an overture, reflecting all the heat, color, and limpidity of Brazilian life in the intense rhythms which rose from the initial motive."[13] The *Christian Science Monitor* noted that "Mr. Guarnieri's overture proved to be an amiable, ingratiating piece, well designed to cultivate good will between good neighbors."[14] Warren Smith of the *Boston Post* wrote:

> New to Boston was Mr. Guarnieri's *Abertura Concertante* and the immediate impression was that here is a composer who will bear investigating. To be sure, there is nothing conspicuously racial or especially personal about yesterday's *Overture* which is in fact one more example of the prevalent neoclassicism. But the music has both vigor and charm and it is plainly the work of an expert hand.[15]

Another critic, noting that Guarnieri also conducted the work, wrote at greater length:

> Making his debut in Boston both as conductor and composer, Mr. Guarnieri proved to be particularly interesting in the latter capacity. There was more in his music than he drew from it, for he was slightly tentative with the orchestra (as well he might be!). The composition, reflecting only in a secondary way the rhythmic turbulence we have come to feel as "Brazilian," made its way from beginning to end with its quiet lyricism, its constant counterpoint and its genuine flavor of inspiration. Well made, it is not put together brick by brick as most contemporary compositions are, and while it perhaps is not the most important work Mr. Guarnieri has done or will do, it is wholly grateful music. Mr. Guarnieri was also most cordially received.[16]

It is a vigorous piece, replete with Paulistan thirds and their chromatic nuances. It falls into three large parts which the ear could variously distinguish as a large ABA form, or a sonata-allegro design. The program notes from a June 2, 1942, performance of the work in São Paulo state that it is a large ABA design with each section having its own exposition-development-reexposition. Guarnieri treats the strings and winds as two large antiphonal choruses in much of the work. The full orchestra proceeds in a grand manner in the final pages.

When Camargo Guarnieri returned from the United States after the rich and enriching experiences he had enjoyed, he seemed ready to launch into a period of major orchestral writing. It is natural that he would dedicate this his First Symphony to Serge Koussevitsky, with whom he had worked in Boston. As though all preceding compositions had been an overture to this new phase in his creative life, Guarnieri began to reveal a new maturity and craftsmanship.

Symphony no. 1.
1943–44. Manuscript

When the State of São Paulo Council for Artistic Orientation announced a competition for composers, Guarnieri submitted this First Symphony under the pseudonym "a Paulistan from Curuça," which was a reference to his native Tietê. From among six entries, on July 6, 1944, he was awarded the Luiz Alberto Penteado de Rezende prize of 10,000 cruzeiros. A panel of four judges had chosen his piece, based on the requirements of its being of Brazilian and modern expression, a theme of free invention of the composer, and without using themes taken directly from folklore. That would have seemed to fit Guarnieri perfectly, and it did. Caldeira Filho wrote after its premiere in March 1945, "The entire piece is developed in an intense, very real modern atmosphere. No means or recourse of expression escapes the sensitivities of Camargo Guarnieri."[17] Guarnieri himself conducted the São Paulo Municipal Symphony Orchestra on this occasion.

In 1947 he had the opportunity to return to the United States, where he conducted this work with the Boston Symphony Orchestra. He recalled that one critic of the *Christian Science Monitor* wrote after this performance that the First Symphony was well written and well orchestrated, but he didn't like it. Guarnieri's response was that he was an honest critic.

This First Symphony is a very energetic work. It falls into three movements and possesses an air of excitement and energy because of the dialogical way in which fragments of themes are constantly shifted among the instruments. The material of all three movements tends to emphasize a minor third. Themes tend to be restricted in range, depending more upon rhythmic vitality of the fabric and fragmentary development of an inner driving force than upon expansiveness of soaring lines. Harmonically, there is a certain linear tonality to the themes, although the contrapuntal writing is much less tonal in effect. There is less use of ostinato in this work and more of fugal treatment and fragmentation of ideas.

I, *Rude, ff.* Sonata-Allegro Form

The movement has the customary two themes. Caldeira Filho wrote of this movement after its premiere:

> There are thematic fragments that continue in the air, at times as expressive echoes of the themes, and at other times as decorative elements, necessary, however, to the equilibrium of the development. The rhythmic richness, and agile game of timbres, does not hide the melodic ideas. The three themes, neatly differentiated, do not offer contrast or opposition in the Beethovenian manner. Freeing himself from this conception, and in accord with the form of the passage, the themes arise with an impulse and dynamism of a solitary, complex idea, really all as elements of the same theme.[18]

Guarnieri preferred to call the recapitulation a "reexposition," which makes sense.

II, *Profundo, pp.* ABA Form

Caldeira Filho gave this movement strong praise:

> It is the best moment of the symphony in my opinion. It is the best Camargo Guarnieri, or at least it is here, as in other slow movements of his where we sense the most complete style of the composer, his sensitivity and identification with the Brazilian soul. The charm of the themes is very special as are the timbres in which they are set.[19]

The minor third is again prominent in this movement. The texture becomes more complex as the theme is given a fugal development. There is a gradual diminuendo to a return of the *Tempo primo,* but only the second half of the A theme recurs. The ending is gentle.

III, *Radioso, f.* Sonata-Allegro Form

Caldeira Filho summarized the spirit of this final movement: "If *Rude* is a moment of action, *Profundo* one of meditation, then the final *Radioso* must be described as the apotheosis of light and color."[20] He also noted the "reaffirmation of the spirit" of the first movement in this third section. As with the first, this movement has fragmentary dialogue between the various sections of the orchestra.

Guarnieri's first major symphonic work in which he used a classic form was not lost on the perceptive Caldeira Filho. Guarnieri's First Sonatina in 1928 had been a successful excursion, but a symphonic work spoke even more loudly of the gradual synthesis of native elements and the great forms. Filho wrote:

> The constancy of his production in the ternary and sonata forms of classic conception makes one suppose that Camargo Guarnieri is a reflective, logical, and musical spirit (an exact feeling and expression which does not exclude, but rather strengthens, emotion). And since the artist is in constant evolution, we see his earlier phases as an affirmation of this spirit but also his gradual freeing from the immediate, sensory, and associative. For this reason, his works represent a culture and not a curiosity.[21]

Symphony no. 2 "Uirapuru."
1945. [AMP]

The Second Symphony followed close on the heels of the first. Submitted in 1947 to the Detroit-based International Contest for a "Symphony of the Americas," Guarnieri won the Reichold prize from among eight hundred entries, among which were works by both Villa-Lobos and Oscar Lorenzo Fernandez. He received $5,000, plus increased stature among the inter-American community of composers.

It was not until March 8, 1950, that the work was premiered in São Paulo, with Guarnieri himself conducting the State Orchestra of São Paulo. Eleazar de Carvalho conducted it two years later in Cleveland in its American premiere. In 1953 Carvalho conducted the work in Paris with the Orchestre Nationale de la Radio Diffusion Française. After the 1950 performance in São Paulo, Caldeira Filho wrote:

> Again we have seen in this work the most representative qualities of Guarnieri's writing. One of these is the economy of means by which he knows how

to extract the maximum return, and which he proportions for the serious-ness and unity of a work. We also note in his orchestration the treatment of mass sounds, distinct by timbre, always neatly shaped, through which they gratefully attain a sensitive outline.[22]

In addition to its expanded instrumentation, this Second Symphony is quite different from the First in its structural character. The themes are much longer and are more tonally oriented, requiring a kind of develop-ment different from the fragmented activity so prominent in the preceding work. The development of the first movement is full of sonorous and soar-ing lines and orchestral amplitude as well as more gentle solo phrases. The flatted seventh of the Mixolydian mode marks the first movement themes, and the last movement uses the Mode of the Northeast.

I, *Energico, ff.* Sonata-Allegro Form

The strings intone a long, germinal theme which is strongly oriented to C minor. This material is developed in dialogue by the entire orchestra. The horns enter with theme 2, which is in rhythmic conflict with the continu-ing first theme material. The development utilizes both themes. Caldeira Filho summarized his reactions to this movement:

> The first movement is well constructed and has as a sequence to its initial theme a second idea in which the author shows the diverse ways of exposing a melody, now sung intensely by the strings, then almost *parlando* style in the more energetic metal horns. One of the most beautiful moments in the first movement is the development of the second theme.[23]

II, *Terno, molto espressivo, p.* Monothematic ABA Form

An English horn states the long line which constitutes the principal the-matic material of this pensive, tender movement. Flavia Toni noted that, at some point, Guarnieri made a considerable cut in this movement, but the measures were restored for a 2002 recording by the São Paulo Symphony Orchestra.[24]

III, *Festivo, f.* Expanded Sonata-Allegro Form

The first of its three themes is stated by the brasses. It is strongly synco-pated, punctuated by percussion instruments. The English horn presents the second theme, which utilizes the Mode of the Northeast over a very rhythmic accompaniment provided by the strings. In the midst of the de-velopment, the cello suddenly states the third theme, *Un poco meno, molto espressivo,* which Flavia Toni says is a "clear homage to the memory of Villa-Lobos,"[25] who had just died on February 25th of that year. The reexposi-tion bursts in at a *Tempo primo.*

Caldeira Filho observed that in this work, "Camargo Guarnieri reveals that he is in full possession of his artistic means, clear in his intentions, and exact in the realization of them."[26] Luiz Heitor de Azevedo had similar observations: "Hearing them one has the impression that the composer has passed through his formative stage of nationalism in which many of his predecessors were caught. The transformation of national elements is absolute and touches a high level of refinement, very conscious, completely submissive to the thinking and technique of the composer."[27] Vasco Mariz concluded, "When Camargo Guarnieri arrived in the path already opened by Villa-Lobos, he entered resolutely with his symphonies in this new phase of spiritualization of Brazilian music, which will be a guaranty of his universality."[28] Despite the liberty with which Guarnieri treats forms, one does not sense that he is being led by them or giving in to any sense of fantasy or rhapsody. They proceed with an unvarying logic, which is one of the outstanding marks of Guarnieri's structural gifts.

After the U.S. premiere in Cleveland in 1952, Eleazar de Carvalho wrote to Guarnieri that he was called to the stage five times to acknowledge the applause. He then shared part of the critique of Herbert Elwell of the *Cleveland Plain Dealer:*

> The first execution here of the Second Symphony of Camargo Guarnieri was heard with great interest. It is music in which we find abundantly a rhythmic vitality, lyricism, and form. It forced the public to like it. The first movement is dynamic, the second genuinely poetic, and in the third festive movement there is a generous explosion of song.[29]

Following the Paris performance in February, 1953, critic Marc Pincherle observed:

> The specialists in Brazilian music materials are unanimous in placing Camargo Guarnieri in line after Villa-Lobos. His Second Symphony came from the hands of an architect, able to manage the grand forms and, what is more rare, he gives them a musicality, turning them into living realities. I did not recognize this at first.
>
> The opening movement, *Energico,* began with a unison whose angular design led me to believe that we would hear the thousandth imitation of Roussel. And because 999 others have been content to use a perfectly sterile mode of writing and separate themselves from the harmonic system of feeling and thinking, with those who form the group around Roussel, I didn't think anything good could possibly happen. But then suddenly there was a happy surprise: almost immediately a theme arose above this, and then a second idea, almost "Franckish."
>
> The slow movement is all melody. An English horn is heard alone, a moaning bassoon repeats in counterpoint. (The wonder here is that Camargo Guarnieri has made marvelous use of the bassoon.)

Camargo Guarnieri has given, in any case, a new proof of his freedom of spirit. He is not constrained by any school or creed, nor suffers any superstition regarding such hallowed formal schemes. His Symphony was a spontaneous success. The National Orchestra triumphed brilliantly over the difficulties which he presented and wrote so well for the instruments.[30]

The success of this work on three continents catapulted the forty-six-year-old composer into international recognition and confirmed his growing recognition as a principal spokesman for Brazilian music and culture.

Prologo e Fuga. 1947.
[AMP–1951]

This eight-minute piece represents one of the comparatively few examples in which Guarnieri's great contrapuntal skill flowers into an actual fugue. It is a dramatic and vigorous work in which the Brazilian elements are more internalized than in many previous works. Program notes by an unidentified author from a May 9, 1969, concert in São Paulo point out the "rhythmic and percussive effects of a high nationalistic inspiration." It is a complex and demanding texture, as noted after its premiere in Rio de Janeiro. Eurico Nogueira França wrote that it was poorly performed there because the orchestra had not mastered the polyphonic fabric and rhythmic complexity.[31] The same author wrote after a 1969 performance in São Paulo, noting particularly its synthesis of Brazilian elements:

> To transform such elements into a work of art, an understanding of the essence is needed and a precise, severe aesthetic style. Thanks to the universality of these essential strengths, the composer has become the representative of the epoch, really of a Brazilian national school in which he counters the luxuriant sonorous conceptions of Villa-Lobos which soared with recreation and emotion rather than impact or surprise.[32]

As the title suggests, there are two sections, a prelude and a fugue, which are thematically related, as were their Baroque counterparts.

Prologo, Vigoroso

The first theme serves as a dominating motif throughout the A-B-Dev-A form of this work. It is an ascending quartal idea, stated first by the woodwinds and trumpets, then repeated and extended with interspersed, punctuated commentary from the trombones and timpani. The second theme is developed extensively before the first theme reappears in the English horn. A *Grandeoso* introduces the coda, in which the motive has been augmented into whole notes. Percussion instruments help create a sense of climax up to the final *fff* chord. The *Fuga* follows the *Prologo* immediately.

Fuga, Deciso

The demanding six-measure theme is drawn from the opening motives of the *Prologo.* The entire movement consists of five sections, each with its exposition of the subject. The final exposition reaches its intensified climax through the introduction of the subject in its original eighth notes in the high strings and, simultaneously, in augmented quarter notes in the lower instruments. In addition to this, the brasses blast out the ascending motive in half notes. The augmented version of the subject ends with sustained chords, which continue until the end of the movement.

Dança Negra (Black Dance).
1947. [AMP]

This is one of three dances originally for piano solo. (See page 88.) It is in a double period stated four times. Resulting from Guarnieri's presence at a Bahian *condomblé* ceremony, its ostinatos and dark foreboding are given ample resonance through his setting for full orchestra. The *Dança Negra* rounds out the composer's set of three *Brazilian Dances,* all published in the orchestral version by Associated Music Publishers in New York.

Guarnieri wrote a few comments for program notes for a 1951 performance of the three dances:

> The *Dança Negra* was written in 1946. The composer wanted to invoke in this work the nostalgic sentiment of universal Black music, without those secondary characteristics acquired after they settled in different parts of the Americas. It is meant to be an evocation of Black music in its origin on the vast continent of Africa.[33]

Improviso no. 1.
1948. Manuscript

This *Improviso* is a transcription for orchestra. Guarnieri seems to have had a few years in which he wrote no new major works for orchestra. At such times he seemed to nourish his own soul with the gentle *modinha* type of piece, such as this. It was the first of a set of ten *Improvisos* for piano that would come into being over the next almost forty years, intimate little reflections of a very personal nature.

Suite Brasiliana
(Brazilian Suite). 1950. [RA]

The *Suite Brasiliana,* composed in 1950 and commissioned by the Natalie Koussevitsky Foundation of Washington, D.C., is quite different from the other works of this same year in its straightforward, genuinely playful spirit and complete accessibility. It is a charming twelve-minute work of three movements, lighthearted, fairly bursting with vital inner syncopation. Premiered in 1951 with Guarnieri conducting the São Paulo Municipal Symphony Orchestra, it was used for a ballet presented in Rio on April 5, 1952, in the Municipal Theater with choreography by Vaslav Veltchek and scenery by Carybê.

The orchestral writing is effectively top-heavy with the lower instruments serving melodic and rhythmic purposes. This enables the tunes to hold full sway above the actual or implied rhythmic pulsing. This set of pieces again breathes the Brazilian spirit with unabashed candor. It has had various performances including one by the Tulsa Symphony in a "Tribute to the Brazilian People" in early 1970, directed by F. Autori. The movements are: I, *Entrada, Incisivo e ritmado, ff;* II, *Moda, Terna, dolcissimo, p;* III, *Dansa, Moderato, scherzando, mf.*

Some unsigned 1956 program notes had this to say about the work:

> His *Brasiliana* is one of those moments in which Guarnieri's poetic clarity separates the picturesque and creates pure music with popular themes, a refinement of his processes, an originality of counterpoint, an aesthetic seriousness which places him among the most authentic of contemporary musicians.[34]

Symphony no. 3.
1954. Manuscript

The city of São Paulo was founded on the feast of St. Paul, January 25, 1554, by the Jesuit Padre Anchieta. In commemoration of the four hundredth anniversary of this event in 1954, São Paulo's Municipal Department of Culture sponsored a contest for new symphonic works. Guarnieri submitted this Third Symphony and won first place, the Prêmio Carlos Gomes. According to Vera Silvia, the composer's wife, Guarnieri lost the score of this work in a Paris taxi cab, spent several days trying to locate it, and ended up having to completely rewrite it, resulting in a totally new work. Caldeira Filho commented on Guarnieri's selection of the type of work he would submit to the competition:

> Avoiding the descriptive character of a symphonic poem, a form suggested by the circumstances and the moment in which the Carlos Gomes prize was instituted, Camargo Guarnieri preferred the form of a symphony, attributing to it nevertheless a symbolic significance, representing the presence of the three races which have become the Brazilian nation as is seen in the thematic superposition which ends the work. The indigenous element appears in the *O Teirú* theme, a melody of the Indians found in Roquette Pinto's Rondônia, and two other themes created by the author.[35]

The *O Teirú* theme is actually a very short fragment stated in the opening measures of the symphony. Ricardo Tacuchian noted the unusualness of Guarnieri's use of an actual folkloric theme, not just in its original form "but profoundly manipulated and redesigned."[36] The interval of a third which characterizes it ties it to all but one of the themes of the entire work, which is somewhat programmatic in origin. It seems to have a more active, fragmented texture than its predecessor. There are sections of soft, reiterated chords with syncopated accents, but in general, the full orchestra is used with discretion in climactic moments.

This work had its premiere in São Paulo with the Orquestra Sinfônica Brasileira under Eleazar de Carvalho on September 27, 1954, just four years after Guarnieri had written his famous *Open Letter*, which started a storm of controversy over nationalism in music. He dedicated the thirty-minute work to his teacher Lamberto Baldi. The critics were ready and listening.

I, *Lento, Energico e Violento, Lento.*
Sonata-Allegro Arch Form

The first movement was conceived by the composer as semidescriptive of the foundation and growth of the city. The slow, soft introduction symbolizes the gradualness with which the new settlement began to take root on the inland high, rolling plain. The exposition, development, and reexposition that follow are marked *Energico e violento*, suggesting the construction era and the hardships the people suffered. The coda is actually an expanded restatement of the introduction, forming an arch-form structure of the material. The second theme recalls the infancy of the composer—an evocation of a bird call from his native town, Tietê.

II, *Serenamente, pp.* ABA Form

Thematically marked again by the presence of the thirds of *O Teirú,* this movement has a vibrant scherzo placed between its two slower sections. The oboe begins a reflective Lydian melody. The entire orchestra takes part in the development of this section, including the percussion instruments. At the *Tempo primo,* a flute states the melancholy principal theme. The movement gradually draws to a *ppp* close. Caldeira Filho wrote:

> The most beautiful movement is the following *Serenamente* in which with much originality is inserted a scherzo. We note here an expressive economy which is characteristic of the author. It is enough to cite one example: on the return of the *Serenamente* after the scherzo, with only one note of special timbre, he creates the desired expressive atmosphere that represents to us a singular capacity of the power of sound as an emotional vehicle, a fact whose importance is accentuated by the power of emotional sonorities in the aesthetics of Camargo Guarnieri.[37]

III, *Decido.* Sonata-Allegro Form

The wind instruments immediately introduce the vibrant, Mixolydian theme: It ends with the familiar little fragment that marked the *Teirú* and *Serenamente* themes. Judith Cabette described the structure of this closing section:

> In the reexposition of the third movement, the second theme moves directly to the coda in which the trumpets and trombones state the first Mixolydian theme of this movement in "chorale" style with augmented note values, and simultaneously the upper strings introduce the second theme in diminished values and the woodwinds present the indigenous *Teirú* theme. The themes are superimposed, amalgamated in a powerful polyphonic texture, suggesting the formation of Brazilian nationalism, constructed of the elements of the three predominant races: indigenous Indian, Negro (Mixolydian), and White. The symphony ends when the violins in the final bars present the first theme of the first movement in a crashing fortissimo.[38]

The happy marriage of indigenous elements and traditional forms is not easy to achieve. Guarnieri seems to have mastered the feat as well as any, with theme elements always being subdued to his formal processes. One writer, however, wrote at length on Guarnieri's failure to achieve a synthesis. The curious thing is that this particular author, Koellreutter, had in previous years given very constructive, even complimentary, reviews to Guarnieri's music. His remembrance of criticisms of the *Open Letter* may have influenced his review:

> Each time Camargo Guarnieri avoids assimilating new elements and integrating them into his contemporary thinking. Even such a composer whose importance in relation to national music nobody can deny, in the international panorama takes the conscious position of a conservative, and even of a reactionary.
>
> In the Third Symphony Guarnieri uses a popular theme, served by a technique which recalls the Impressionists and Stravinsky. I do not believe that this species of synthesis can bear a truly national language. One can feel in the symphony the conflict that arises between a deliberately national theme and a technique which originated in the musical thinking, a fact which cannot be hidden—in the inevitable ostinato. The form of the work is primary, and the musical discourse lacks continuity.
>
> Certain clichés which are incompatible with content and form are observed in the symphony. Lacking a brilliant score and orchestral color, the instrumentation is routine and insignificant. The Third Symphony of Camargo Guarnieri is one more proof of the problem which affects our music.[39]

Eurico Nogueira França had also responded with a review of a 1956 performance of the piece, and he was generally supportive. Several years later he wrote an extensive article specifically on this piece, reflecting on the marriage of native material with the classic forms:

> The characteristics of the Third Symphony of Camargo Guarnieri led me to recall some things I had said previously when I spoke of the composer as an example of the last fruits of our musical creation with national roots, in the sense of qualifying him as a representative of excellence in neoclassicism, in opposition to the powerful neo-Romanticism, rich in the genial inspirations of Villa-Lobos.
>
> I am convinced that historically the pendulum swings between two poles of creation, classic and romantic, and in the face of such a clear example as Camargo Guarnieri, especially after Villa-Lobos, he does not follow this. In terms of the creation of a national music, a certain evolutionary process seems certain. Villa-Lobos is said to be the greatest Brazilian composer. And with all his formidable exuberance as a composer, he plunged into folklore as into a rapture. Camargo Guarnieri, however, assumes a purer attitude, comparable to that of de Falla after Albéniz. In his Third Symphony he uses an anonymous theme that is not folkloric but rather ethnic—*O Teirú*, Indian —which gives his score a cyclic unity, and all other themes are of his own making. There is absolutely no reason to consider as ideal a compromise between form and native sentiment. But it is ideal, given a master of such endowment and high skill as Camargo Guarnieri.[40]

One might wonder if those three little notes of the *O Teirú* could possibly have really carried such ethnic weight. Or was it the total musical language of a good composer who found in them a tiny, but potentially expansive, vehicle for his own intensely Brazilian message? One must admit the expressive power of this work in Guarnieri's growing catalog. A final word from Vasco Mariz: "I consider this the highest point in Guarnieri's orchestral music. It is great music from an author in full possession of his means of writing. He has arrived at full artistic maturity."[41]

Suite IV Centenário
(400th Anniversary Suite). 1954.
[RA–1957]

This work was commissioned and has been recorded by the Louisville Symphony Orchestra. Composed the same year as the Third Symphony, it also commemorates the four hundredth anniversary of the founding of the city of São Paulo. In contrast to the transformed formalized materials of the preceding work, this thirteen-minute suite of five movements features obviously Brazilian folk forms in each. Caldeira Filho wrote after its May 19, 1955, premiere in São Paulo:

In this work, we see Camargo Guarnieri less preoccupied with the exterior problem of form, technique, and themes than with an internal searching. It appears to be an exploration, more intense than broad, of his own lyricism, of a Brazilian depth which for him constitutes an aesthetic ambiance. The variety of orchestral effects, his own technique of orchestration, all appear here to lead to an effective unity: integral expression of a very Brazilian sentiment, a particular feeling which manifests the personality of our well known composer, neatly characterized, but never constrained by the limitations of folklore. On the contrary, he opens the feelings to large vistas—of personal sensitivity, of life, of creative force, and of communication to the listeners of human feelings by which we assign to the work an immediate universality.[42]

The five movements are: I, *Introdução, Lento;* II, *Toada, nostalgico, p;* III, *Interludio, scherzando;* IV, *Acalanto, terno, pp;* and V, *Baião, gingando, p.*

Suite Vila Rica. 1958.
[RB–1959]

Vila Rica is a historic town in the interior of Brazil. Now called Ouro Preto, it is a treasure house of colonial art, particularly that of the crippled mulatto, Alejedinho. Formerly the capital of the state of Minas Gerais, it was the scene of an 1789 rebellion which constitutes the narrative material of the 1957 film *Rebelião em Vila Rica.* This unassuming little suite of ten pieces is actually an orchestral concert version of music written for the film, transcribed the following year. Guarnieri dedicated it to his eminent friend Professor Clovis Salgado.

Guarnieri seems to have rediscovered the suite form as a vehicle for small national expressions. The functional origin of this suite gives it a quality very different from that of his other works. The phrase structures are fairly square, and the individual movements are not developed. Despite these rather obvious second-purpose signs, it is an interesting orchestral suite and is quite easy to perform, making it a suitable work for young ensembles. Caldeira Filho noted, "The interest that Camargo Guarnieri maintains in these little pieces is notable since they are unassuming and were destined as the soundtrack of a film. Heard in concert, they acquire personality and autonomy and surprise us by their integral symphonic validity."[43] Judith Cabette, too, justified the concert versions: "The sections taken from the film, despite their diverse character, present a great stylistic unity and a versatility in the use of the orchestra where there predominates a clarity and transparency which immediately identifies the author."[44]

The suite is scored for full orchestra with several additional Brazilian rhythm instruments added to the percussion section. All the thematic material is original with the exception of the fifth movement, in which a folk tune from Minas Gerais is prominent. The ten movements are given only tempo indications, not titles: *Maestoso, Andantino-dolce, Misterioso, Scherzando, Agitado, Alegre, Valsa-moderato, Saudoso, Humorístico,* and *Baião-gingando.*

Vasco Mariz commented on this suite after the premiere in Rio on April 10, 1958, with Guarnieri conducting the Orquestra Sinfônica Brasileira:

> The success of the first Festival in Ouro Preto, and the enthusiasm which filled the Cecilia Meireles Hall for the history of the city led him [Guarnieri] to accept the responsibility, with the participation of Lia Salgado and the Coral Paulistano. Perhaps because I had a part in this festival, I had a special predilection for this score, which clearly has the signature of the composer without any special novelty.[45]

After this suite of 1958, there was a five-year period in which Guarnieri did not write any major works for orchestra alone, although there were two major choral works, a sonata for violin and piano, and the Piano Concertino. In 1958–59 he transcribed the *Ponteio* no. 45 for full orchestra and no. 46 for strings only.

Symphony no. 4 "Brasilia." 1963.
[AMP–1966]

Despite its dedication to Leonard Bernstein, there is no evidence that the American conductor-composer ever conducted the piece. It was premiered in Lisbon, Portugal, by the Orquestra Sinfônica Nacional de Lisboa under Guarnieri's direction on June 29, 1964. It had received the Medalha da Prata (Silver Medal) from the Associação Paulista de Críticos Teatrais as "best symphonic work" in 1964. It was also performed in Rio de Janeiro and São Paulo in 1965, and in the United States by the Portland (Maine) Symphony Orchestra under Paul Vermel on December 5, 1967. The *Portland Press Herald* said in a review: "The 4th Symphony of Guarnieri which was given its first hearing here can be considered among the most important scores to come from Brazil in years. Guarnieri writes magnificently for the winds and strings. A dazzled and great crowd gave him warm applause at the end."[46]

This Fourth Symphony is subtitled "Brasilia" because Guarnieri wrote it to commemorate the first anniversary in 1958 of the groundbreaking of the vibrant new "Camelot" of the southern continent. He was president of a jury which was to have selected an award piece from among those submitted in a contest sponsored by the Ministry of Education and Culture in Brazil, directed by Guarnieri's good friend Clovis Salgado. In his official position, Guarnieri was not himself permitted to submit an entry. He was so inspired, however, by what he saw in Brasilia that he sketched the complete thematic outline of a symphony during his stay there, then slipped his sketches into a book he happened to be reading—*Viagem em Terra Brasil* (Trip to Brazil)—by a sixteenth-century writer, Jean Lery. Guarnieri forgot about the sketches until he happened to pick up the book in 1963 and found what he had written. He completed the symphony in New York, where he had gone to serve on the Mitropoulos jury for selecting young conductors in March 1963. He subsequently dedicated the piece to Bernstein.

Brasilia is a stunning achievement and must be experienced to be believed. It is understandable that the mammoth construction underway in 1958 would have fired the composer's imagination, and it is this aspect—the machines, energy, enthusiasm for the new creation—which is expressed in the first movement. The second movement attempts to give an impression of the endless panorama of the high plain where one can spin around quickly with an eye on the horizon and not appreciably raise or lower one's focus, so flat is the table-like terrain of the *planalto*. The final movement is a synthesis of various regional elements, drawing all into the new focus of the living, newborn capital city.

The outer movements in general are extremely agitated and restless. Each of the three movements uses melodic material of the utmost stringency. The restricted ranges and the litany-like quality of the themes and the equally frugal and rather static harmonic spectrum result in a taut fabric of great concentration. The rhythmic life and fragmented orchestral treatment add to the intensity and inner agitation which it conveys. In fact, in the presence of melodic and harmonic restrictions, the rhythm, dynamics, and textural inventiveness become more effective and important as a communicative medium. A first-movement fragment returns in the last movement and serves as a unifying element. The long-drawn-out melodic line of the second movement is a complete contrast, and the use of trumpets for fanfare-like quartal chords in the final movement is an element not found in Guarnieri's preceding works. Augmentation of themes also adds to the sense of climax.

I, *Allegro Enérgico, f.* Sonata-Allegro Form

The first bars set up an immediate conflict with a dizzying, machine-like $\frac{3}{4}$ pattern of hammered chords within a $\frac{2}{2}$ meter. The quarter note maintains its basic emphatic percussiveness throughout the movement. Over this harmonically static accompaniment of cluster chords in the brass and strings, the winds state in the high register a strident theme from which will be drawn the subsequent material. The last four measures of this theme, which expand outward from a third to an octave, appear in various forms throughout the work. Closely related is the second theme stated by horns. Another fragment found in the trombone takes on added importance in the final movement. These three themes continue to intermingle in the precipitous movement.

A sudden *espressivo* version of the first theme in the viola is the only relief, but this is temporary. A climax of the frenetic surge dissolves into a restatement of the material, somewhat shorter and modified. The strings pick up the reiterated chord pattern, which they carry to the end of the movement—a final crescendoing shriek of machine-like energy.

II, *Lento e tragico, ppp.* Monothematic Arch Form

The expansiveness of the flat horizon, its seeming endlessness and uniformity, are portrayed by one long, somber line stated by the violins which expresses the sadness and anguish that isolation in such a place of wilderness can produce. Other string instruments join in but maintain a unison line, which reaches a climax in sharply dotted notes, as if drawing the rest of the orchestra into the dialogue of brief alternating phrases. This line wanders as if in search of some gravitational point.

A more agitated middle section fragments the line, distributing phrases among solo or groups of instruments. The dotted rhythmic motive which led to the full orchestra entrance again prepares for its exit, leaving the strings to guide the line to its conclusion. The violins bring the melody in unison to a pianissimo close.

III, *Enérgico Triunfante, ff.* Monothematic

Brazil's northeastern region is strongly portrayed throughout the symphony but particularly in this final movement, in both the modal melodies and the syncopated dance character of the rhythms. Percussion instruments assist the rhythmic and percussive use of the orchestra, and the piano and harp add their own brittle contribution to the crisp texture. Because of the conciseness of the melodic material, it is easily transformed into flexible fragments and ostinatos. The principal Mixolydian-mode theme is an energetic joyful thrust of sound which recurs in many forms and versions. Toward the end of the movement it becomes an ostinato.

The whole texture is highly rhythmic and fragmented. The brief, rising principal theme is given a fugal exposition in the strings with interwoven fragments of the trombone theme. A brief *Piu Lento* uses fragments of the principal theme in augmentation. In a reexposition, both themes are combined in augmentation leading to the final close, all of which adds intensity to the climax of this relatively short movement.

Because this work was published in 1966 by Associated Music Publishers in New York, it has had performances in the United States, including one by the Milwaukee Symphony Orchestra in 1971 under Kenneth Schermerhorn.

Homenagem a Villa-Lobos
for Wind Symphony. 1966

Dedicated to the American Wind Symphony Orchestra, *Homenagem* is another of those pieces through which Guarnieri speaks simply and openly in a strongly national language. Having followed his Symphony no. 4, which is more stringent, and the Piano Sonatina no. 6, which was completed just weeks before this work, it would seem that the *Homenagem* is a retreat from his compositional directions set in these preceding works. However, in reality it reveals the composer's ability to use the proper language for the particular message. This piece is a tribute to Villa-Lobos, a genius of nationalistic expression. A musical eulogy could only realistically use material which was evocative of the sentiments one feels at the absence of a respected friend.

The first and last movements have an interior rhythmic life that continues to saunter along without a strong basic beat in many passages. In the first movement the timpani provides the only bass, with the entire texture bobbing untethered above it. The endings of the second and third movements have a more prominent lower register bass line, usually an ostinato. Distribution of parts gives the piece a characteristic suppleness and easygoing feel. Orchestrally, Guarnieri selects his instruments to maximize individual color display, saving the full ensemble for the final bars. The three movements are: I, *Tempo de Côco, f;* II, *Tempo de Toada, Dolce;* and III, *Tempo do Baião, p.*

Regarding this composition, Caldeira Filho noted:

> The significant thing with his Brazilian themes is that they relate to the aesthetics and method of Camargo Guarnieri. He plays with the emotions, of which his themes are his indispensable sonorous vehicles. But he has his feet on the ground and his ears on traditional sounds. He is rooted fundamentally in his native land and in a musical essence which, on the other hand, gives his hearers the impression of security, intelligibility, and aesthetic form. This *Homenagem* is a page of longing. It marks the real music of Camargo Guarnieri. In it he has made, perhaps intentionally, a stylistic regression to find a point at which he actually no longer is.[47]

Sequência, Coral e Ricercare
(Sequence, Chorale, and Ricercare).
1966. Manuscript

This work for chamber orchestra was commissioned by the Calouste Gulbenkian Foundation of Portugal, by whom it was premiered on June 3, 1967, under Adrian Sunshine in Lisbon. Its first Brazilian performance was in São Paulo the following November 9 with the Orquestra Filharmônica of São Paulo under Simon Bleck. It was performed again in Tatuí, São Paulo, with Guarnieri conducting.

The piece solidifies and confirms a manner of writing that is in complete contrast to the *Homenagem a Villa-Lobos* of the same year. It is rather in the same vein as the Fourth Symphony of 1963 and the Piano Sonatina no. 6 and *Seresta* for piano and orchestra, both from 1965. The harmonic language has now achieved much more of an internal atonality than was present in his earlier works, one which permeates the entire fabric and not just the chord structures which happen to support a more tonally oriented line. It marks the arrival at a point in his compositional life similar to that reached in some of the last Beethoven works where the material and message are beyond the realm of personal feelings or easy accessibility.

Caldeira Filho, who followed the development of Guarnieri through most of his creative life, wrote a rather extensive and very penetrating evaluation of this piece. His search for words is understandable when one hears the abstract quality of the composition. Filho wrote:

> In this moment of his evolution, Camargo Guarnieri seems to compose using material which almost transcends sound or the vibrations which cause it. The counterpart is to slight the importance of volume, intensity, timbre, and duration, using them in a more general and diluted way in everything (as seen in the orchestration of the *Coral*). His material is very minimized, and he moves more toward running the risk of abandoning traditional sound and falling into "musica concrete e electronic"—God save us!!—strengthening to the utmost the work of composition properly speaking (remember the first and third movements) in which the interplay of relationships among the integral parts is subtle but more solid in a cohesion which constitutes the unity of the work.
>
> The music of Camargo Guarnieri fires an appreciation, called spontaneous, in which the reaction of the listener is principally the play of associations of ideas, of remembrances, a reliving of emotional experiences accumulated by the senses. It demands more: the capture of themes in their relations so integral to the creation, of a living thing on the stage where intelligence conditions emotions, and sense perception is filtered and freed by accidental attributes. And it could be said that that is the reason why, in the *Sequência,* some portions seem cold. Camargo Guarnieri is beyond the call of qualities of sound and a striving for that which is common among so many arts and superior manifestations of the human spirit. It is dangerous, but is it not the way to universalism? [48]

In response to Filho's comment concerning Guarnieri's lapse into sounding like electronic or *musique concrète,* the composer responded by letter: "Before closing, I want you to be at peace, for I am full of concretism and electronicism! I sincerely believe that music is a purely emotional message." [49]

Sequência

As indicated in the title, the piece has three distinct sections, and there is a complete cadence ending each section. Regarding the first, *Sequência,* Guarnieri explained: "The first movement is constructed on one theme of rhythmic character and another more melodic. There is the exposition in which both themes are developed to a point at which they lead into a reexposition."[50] It moves at a ferocious tempo without any respite.

Coral, Contemplatívo, p

Of the second movement, *Coral,* Caldeira Filho wrote:

> An unsurpassable master of the slow movement, Camargo Guarnieri has succeeded in creating, in the *Coral,* the most rarified atmosphere in which the sounds (themes and motives) appear in the utmost clarity. An impression of calm results, not from recalling the plains, the long horizons, and immense expanses at times suggested in his music with a kind of horizontal development which suggests the invisible *sertão,* but in the treatment of the specific musical element, the sonorous colors, sustained and gradually dissipated almost to the limit of colorlessness. His orchestral mastery is really superior here, calming the sonorous vibrations almost to the point of giving an impression of light in repose.[51]

This *Coral* gives the impression of being fairly suspended in midair, fearing to breathe. Structurally it is written in an arch form. Guarnieri has written of this seven-minute movement:

> The *Coral,* constituted with one theme of sad character and confided to the strings, is tonally imprecise. Given the aesthetic atmosphere of its harmonic expression, it is felt as a force which gradually grows little by little until it reaches the tragic. From the middle to the end of the *Coral,* all the elements which were part of the development are now presented in retrograde.[52]

Ricercare, Risoluto, sonoro, f

Guarnieri's contrapuntal writing reaches a peak in the *Ricercare.* He describes its structure as having "four thematic expositions with a development in the first only."[53] He uses the Baroque techniques of development —augmentation, diminution, inversion—within his contrapuntal writing. He brings other themes back so that all three movements participate in this final closing section of the *Ricercare.* Caldeira Filho remarked that its theme could well be dodecaphonic:

> To express decision and energy, he rejects the habitual suggestion of rhythm and adopts a short, pointed line of large intervals with incisive differences of

frequency within a few notes. This passage can be considered a synthesis of the technical and expressive process of previous scores, using the polyphonic spirit which is preferred by the composer.[54]

Coming near the end of the list of orchestral works, this piece reveals a composer who has developed an extremely powerful musical language and who has refined and distilled a style which is both expressive and potent. In this particular work these characteristics are verified in the paring down of the instrumentation to the essentials. Guarnieri was fifty-nine at the time he wrote this piece, at the peak of his career but with almost twenty more years ahead of him. There would be a five-year interim between this piece and his next large orchestral work, the *Abertura Festiva*. However, he arranged several piano works for orchestra in the interim: in 1969 his first piano *Ponteio* for orchestra and, the following year, his fourth *Improviso*.

Abertura Festiva (Festival Overture).
1971. Manuscript

This work was commissioned by the Orquestra Filharmônica de São Paulo and was premiered at the opening concert of the 1971 season under the direction of Simon Blech, on April 20. It was recorded by Brazil's National Symphony Orchestra under Carlos Eduardo Prates in 1988. Guarnieri noted in the score that he used three themes of different character in this work. Each of the three themes dominates one of the principal sections.

Improviso no. 3.
Transcribed for String Orchestra in 1972
from 1970 Piano Solo

This is one of the loveliest of Guarnieri's ten *Improvisos* with its plaintive descending two-note figure, wonderful climax, and gentle recession once again to a peaceful end. In addition to the 1972 transcription for string orchestra, he transcribed the piece for violin and piano the following year. It was included in a series of three concerts observing his seventieth birthday in 1977, performed by his String Orchestra of the University of São Paulo. Caldeira Filho wrote:

> The *Improviso* no. 3 reaffirmed not only the originality of the composer in whatever he writes, but also the artistic quality of the string ensemble from OSUSP. The interpretation followed the splendid development of the expressive power of the motive based on the interval of a descending half step which is fundamental to the piece.[55]

It is curious to note that the descending second which marks the thematic content of this piece, as noted previously, consists of the same two notes Chopin had used in his *Prélude,* Op. 28, no. 4: C–B. Cradled within Guarnieri's sensitive harmonic and rhythmic fluctuations, these notes breathe the Brazilian soul in ways both similar and different from the equally sensitive composition by Chopin. Each is an expression of its own time and culture.

Concerto para Cordas e Percussão
(Concerto for Strings and Percussion). 1972.
[Broude, N.Y.–1975]

Scored for strings and three percussionists, this work was commissioned by the Orquestra Armorial de Câmara of Pernambuco. The piece was also featured at a concert honoring Guarnieri at the Cleveland Institute of Music, where he served as head of the Robert Casadesus International Piano Jury in 1981.

This kind of scoring is a special challenge to a composer, particularly one like Guarnieri who thrives on precision of rhythms and contrapuntal textures. The lack of wind instruments could have been a serious handicap, but he rose to the challenge. Caldeira Filho noted in regard to this after its 1976 premiere:

> Guarnieri is a friend of clear figurations, translucence, not losing any of its transparency even when it is needed to preserve the mystery he is developing. The neat image and the vague projection are balanced to free the listener's imagination without losing any of the intricate concept which is his goal.[56]

I, *Vigoroso.* ABA Form

An energetic rhythmic theme stressing sevenths and ninths opens the movement. A canon constitutes the middle section, stated first by the high strings and closing the movement with the theme in retrograde in the lower strings. The reexposition is essentially a repetition of the first part. A small bridge binds it to the second movement. Filho observed that the *Vigoroso* has a playful feel to it.

II, *Saudoso.* ABA Form

Grieving the death of his mother, to whom he was very close, the choral-like texture of this movement dedicated to her reveals these feelings. Violins carry the opening section, and the cellos the middle section. The movement ends peacefully. After the premiere, Filho wrote: "It is very expressive and soars as an echo of dark remembrances. There is scarcely any rhythmic insinuation in the melody, and it has such deep significance and such lyric force that one has the illusion that we are hearing a voice of longing with its emotional connotations."[57]

III, *Jocoso.* ABA Form

This movement has the character of a *cocô* and uses the Mode of the Northeast. Unlike Guarnieri's previous works, this movement includes an aleatoric section for the performers. Both the A and B themes are playful and lighthearted. At the end of the B section, the orchestra stops, and the percussion instruments softly begin to improvise on any patterns they have already played. After about a minute, following a pianissimo ending, a violin intones a brief cadenza, and the reexposition begins. The texture again gains in force, and in the coda the strings function as one great rhythmic guitar. Filho had this to say at its premiere: "The third movement *Jocoso* is full of lively movement. The rhythm runs like quick silver among the meandering figurations, always alert, fusing sonorous elements, creating a dense fabric, especially with its game of durations, with the melodic web not quite losing its lightness or its hold."[58]

Carlos Vergueiro wrote a review of the recording which appeared in 1984 to honor the tenth anniversary of the orchestra at the University of São Paulo:

> The pieces are of superior quality, especially the Concerto for Strings and Percussion of Camargo Guarnieri, a composer who must be called both national and international. He has used his Brazilian ideas, with rhythms and *toadas* not only from São Paulo but from all over Brazil, treating them in a form which is of interest not only to us but to the entire world which can value music which is well written and inspired, which springs from such a strong sensitivity.[59]

Caldeira Filho gets the final comment: "Guarnieri continues faithful to his aesthetic conviction, which is: 'Music is emotion.'"[60]

Improviso no. 6. 1974.
Transcribed for Chamber Orchestra
from 1974 Piano Solo

This is another of Guarnieri's gentler musical expressions which he felt the need to transcribe for chamber orchestra. It originated as a piano improvisation at the house of a friend. The orchestral version was premiered July 4, 1975, in São Paulo. (See page 118.)

Symphony no. 5.
1977. Manuscript

This twenty-minute work breaks more new ground for Guarnieri. A chorus is featured in its third movement on a text of Guarnieri's brother Rossine. It hails the Tietê River, which flows, not to the sea, but northward through

Tietê. Both Rossine and Camargo, who were born in Tietê, look to this "stubborn river" as a living symbol of the life struggle. The symphony was commissioned in April 1977 by the Department of Culture, Science, and Technology of the University of São Paulo as requested by Dr. Max Feffer. It had its premiere on July 30, 1977, in Campos do Jordão. It was performed again in São Paulo on August 8 of that same year with the Orquestra Sinfônica Estadual of São Paulo under the direction of Eleazar de Carvalho. The twenty-minute work is scored for full orchestra, SATB chorus, and expanded percussion section, piano, and harp.

The text:

> RIO TEIMOSO (Stubborn River)
>
> Tiê, Tiê, Tietê. . . .
>
> BRAVO ANHEMBI
>
> Rio de Pássaros, (River of birds)
>
> Que nasce na serra, (born in the hills)
>
> ex foge do mar, (from the fire of the sea)
>
> para voltarão coração da terra. (to return to the heart of the earth.)
>
> Volteia! Volteia! (Return, return!)
>
>> Arco da aliança (Circling form)
>>
>> Desenho no chão do Brasil! (cut into the ground of Brazil!)
>>
>> Semente da união (Seeding union)
>>
>> Caminho da paz . . . (way of peace . . .)

Guarnieri had hesitated to write his Fifth Symphony, feeling some intimidation from the great Beethoven. It took him fourteen years after his Fourth to produce this Fifth. In trying to describe his music, particularly a work like this with such obvious devotion to his own rootedness in Brazil, it is difficult not to use terms of human experience and emotion, such as tenderness, anguish, anger, gentleness. Guarnieri's increasing use of percussive chords within his syncopated rhythmic fabrics often seems to shout a defiant "No! No!" to the more melodic material. These spaced, percussive chords are also frequently used to end movements in a highly dramatic, definitive way.

His "musical themes" are no longer just melodic lines, but more often they are an expression of a less tangible mood or feeling in dialogue with a contrasting feeling or mood. Guarnieri's musical language has definitely become more atonal in these later works, and he depends heavily upon quartal harmony and melodic fragments. These not only contribute to the angularity of his short motives, but also affect the required technique of the performers. Thus, in this work the three movements are all tightly woven thematically. The chorus enters only in the latter half of the final movement. In addition to this innovation for him, the first movement is constructed in an arch form.

I, *Lento, Allegro Impetuoso, Meno mosso,*
Tempo Primo, Lento. ABCBA Form

The themes of this ABCBA arch form are all closely related. In the *Lento* a rising four-note figure begins in the basses as a single line and grows with the addition of other strings into a full-textured *fff* statement. The entire orchestra is gradually drawn in, and the section ends with a series of percussive chords, heralding the arrival of the main section. The principal *Allegro Impetuoso* motive, which is actually an inversion of the opening *Lento,* takes off with a lilt and a jolt in the strings. It dominates the entire section in various fragmented and augmented forms.

The middle section, *Meno mosso,* is gentler version of the second theme and appears in a fughetto carried by the clarinets, a bass clarinet, and a flute. The strings reassert themselves and seem to become one huge guitar with an ostinato that underlies the growing crescendo as the theme returns in augmentation.

The *tempo primo* is reintroduced but with an exchange of instruments. The texture continues to gain intensity through greater fragmentation of material and recurrence of the percussive chords. These help to build the final climax, where they finally, with the timpani, call a halt to the movement. A measure of silence clears the air before a recall of the opening *Lento.* Woodwinds restate the string theme gently, but the calm is short-lived before moving to a climax. The percussive chords, supported by timpani, finally bring the movement to an end on a resounding unison.

II, *Lento Nostalgico.* ABA Form

Guarnieri has again succeeded in creating one of his suspended atmospheres in this movement through his use of pedal points and ostinati which seem to hold the listener transfixed at a basic awareness level while fragments of melodies drift in and out as indistinct images. These melodic fragments move within restricted compasses in widely spaced thirds and with conflicting tonalities, thus increasing the sense of mystery and suspension.

III, *Allegro.* Two-Part Form

A six-measure introduction states a short theme for which the instruments seem to jostle for control. Strings and winds struggle with the brasses momentarily. A longer idea then emerges which is a development of the opening notes.

Several times as this movement develops, the texture thins out to reveal a few measures of *samba*-like accompaniment. The lower strings sustain an E while the remainder of the strings become one large guitar accompaniment, preparing for the entry of the female voices of the chorus with the poetic text. In a quasi development of the musical material, counterpoint increases the density of the texture; Guarnieri then creates virtually a musical game of ping-pong, challenging the listener to hear the fragments of themes tossed back and forth among the instruments. Throughout the interspersed vocal sections, the orchestral texture wonderfully supports but does not overpower the voices. All forces join together in the final climax, a ringing unison on the word *paz*. It is a forceful call for peace.

Symphony no. 6.
January 31–March 1, 1981. Manuscript

This work is dedicated to Filipe de Souza and was commissioned by the Secretaria Municipal da Cultura de São Paulo for the seventieth anniversary of the inauguration of the Teatro Municipal of São Paulo. Scored for full orchestra with expanded percussion, it had its premiere in 1981 with Guarnieri conducting the Orquesta Sinfônica Municipal of São Paulo. It was also featured in Campo do Jordão, in Rio de Janeiro on October 1, 1984, under Henrique Morlebaum with the Orquestra Municipal do Teatro, and again in São Paulo on September 27, 1985, under Guarnieri and the Sinfônica Municipal in the new Sala Cidade de São Paulo.

There are some structural similarities between this and the Symphony no. 5. Guarnieri again uses an arch form for both the first and third movements. The opening section in both movements begins with a short introductory section; the third movement is anything but gentle. Ricardo Tucuchian wrote of Guarnieri's mastery of symphonic writing here:

> The 6th Symphony, with its cyclic form and excellence of thematic material, is a crowning work of symphonic writing by Guarnieri. It is his "Jupiter Symphony." This symphony is revealed, not through the rigor of its formal structure, but through the paradoxical duality of the synthesis and expansion of ideas, of the richness of writing and an economy of the means used, of a unity of form and at the same time the conflict or contrast of its structural parts. If in its contents Guarnieri pursues here the quintessence of Brazilian music, he also achieves the quintessence of the symphonic form in a sense more broad than even he intended.[61]

I, *Enérgico e Rítmado*. Introduction–ABA–Coda Form

This opening movement explodes into action as the strings and lower woodwinds state an attention-getting angular outburst, punctuated by timpani, flute, and oboes. Within a few measures the main theme of this section evolves from the opening bars.

A harp introduces a *Calmo* section with a glissando, a mere ten-measure respite from the driving energy. Timpani, *agogô*, and wood block intensify the material as it develops, then connect it to the returning theme. A brief coda recalls all thematic fragments, building with timpani and percussive chords to a final explosion of sound on a unison *fff.*

II, *Triste.* Monothematic ABA Form.
Completed March 17, 1981

This movement bears an unusual degree of restraint with longer, more sustained lines than in many of Guarnieri's recent works. Nothing happens quickly, and everything bears the signs of the heaviness indicated by *triste.* It is one of the more consistently sustained movements of Guarnieri's later years. This movement begins and ends softly with only strings, appearing from out of seeming silence, and that is where it returns. The longer lines, deliberate rhythms and tempos, and controlled dynamics help to give it an intensity that is impossible to miss.

III, *Solene.* ABCBA Form

Guarnieri revised the opening of this movement after its premiere. He utilizes three distinct elements here, none of them sad or introspective: a majestic processional theme (*Solene*), a playful angular tune with light-hearted rhythm, and a third *Calmo* with a longer line and an intense sense of well-being. These three make a good combination as material for this new arch form.

The *Calmo* middle section is a long, expressive line, introduced by a flute which radiates a sense of well-being. The return of the B theme is given a canonic treatment which enhances its playful character. Brasses restate the B theme again under trills and tremolos, which crescendo mightily into the final *Grandeoso.* All the orchestral forces move toward the final *fff* chord. This final chord is short and definite, as though the composer has made his point and refuses to dwell on it.

Symphony no. 7.
1985. Manuscript

This last large symphonic work was written on commission for Dr. Max Feffer for the seventieth wedding anniversary of his parents, Antonietta and Leon Feffer. Completed on December 22, 1985, it was premiered in May 1987 by the Orquestra Sinfônica of São Paulo. It was performed again by the Orquestra Sinfônica Brasileira in Rio de Janeiro under Isaac Karabitchewsky on August 12, 1987. It is scored for very full orchestra with expanded percussion and "Voz ad libitum" (voice ad libitum). Ricardo Tacuchian offers some lovely imagery to describe this work:

> While the Symphony no. 6 is a leafy *manguiera,* the Symphony no. 7 is a delicate orchid. Almost five years separate the two works. The intimacy of

the Seventh distinguished it among Guarnieri's symphonic works, especially from those explosions of such expressive impact, denouncing the old wars rising here and there. These eruptions are here restrained by a kind of philosophic and evocative reflection rising from a solitary and passionate soul. Here the master does not compose, he plays with sounds, he weeps and dreams with them.[62]

Guarnieri again uses monothematic development in the first movement and an arch form in the second. One might think he has concretized his approach in these last three symphonic works. However, the similarities end there. He launches into more new than old concepts in this Seventh Symphony. There are only two movements, lines are longer and less agitated, there is virtually no mood change in the first movement, and an ad libitum voice is indicated in the second movement, which follows a chantlike course with no accidentals, a real departure from the composer's then-current instrumental language. Perhaps it was the occasion, a wedding anniversary, that suggested this semi-liturgical reference.

I, Calmo e Triste. 82 Measures in $\frac{4}{4}$

One is immediately aware that Guarnieri sets a very different atmosphere as this movement opens. The strings set an almost mesmerizing, gentle rhythmic ostinato which permeates the movement with its pastoral quality, heightened by parallel harmonic movement in places. There are no meter or tempo changes, or rhythmic interruptions, just one dynamic high point. Calmness is maintained throughout. Over the string ostinato, a clarinet initiates the first and only thematic material. A secondary idea is an ascending line which first occurs in the oboe and recurs periodically. A flute recalls the opening motive of the French horn, but the sounds fade into nothingness to end the movement.

II, Lento, Allegro, Calmo, Allegro,
Grandeoso, Piu Vivo. Arch Form.

The most obvious thing about this movement is its monothematic construction and the arch form which gives it meaning. All material is derived from the opening bars of the *Lento,* which is an old Hebrew melody which Dona Antonieta Feffer recalled from her youth. The form can be identified as ABCBA.

A solo clarinet intones the Hebrew *Lento* melody, imitated by a lone oboe over descending thirds in the violas. The texture of sound increases until the entrance of the *Allegro.* The second section is more animated, but the middle section is a *Calmo* in which strings set a sustaining, gentle background for an unusual theme. It is almost chantlike in its rhythm and its pandiatonic tonality. It is stated by alto flute and vibraphone with an indication "Vox ad libitum," with no indication of vowel or hum sound to be used. The *Allegro* bursts back in after a gentle timpani roll, but gradually gives way to a rapid crescendo leads into the final *Grandeoso.* All orchestral forces seem to break free of the restraint that has marked most of this composition. Fragmented lines and percussion all build into the hammered chords which hail the final *fff* unison C. Thus ends a major contribution to orchestral literature by one of the creative lights in the twentieth-century musical world.

Estudo for Percussion Instruments.
1974. [Broude, N.Y.]

This 1953 piece requires four performers who play triangle/tambourine/ *réco-réco,* snare drum/military drum, cymbals/bass drum, and timpani. Exploiting various combinations of rhythms, it begins pianissimo and ends in a huge crescendo.

Miscellaneous Works

Guarnieri's work with his String Orchestra at the University of São Paulo prompted his arrangements of pieces for that ensemble. Among his own original works are the *Ponteio e Dança* for cello and strings, and several more *Ponteios.* His *Improviso* for flute and strings, discussed on page 211, was also written for this group.

Early on Mário de Andrade had warned Guarnieri: "You will suffer much in life because your music is not 'love at first sight.'"[63] His music challenged listeners, and not all responded positively at first. As one reflects upon his pieces for orchestra, they reveal a very progressive development. One does not get the sense, however, that his *Dança Brasileira* or the more folkloric inspired pieces are less valuable than are this Third or Fourth Symphonies, or that the *Homenagem a Villa-Lobos* which followed the Fourth Symphony represents any kind of nostalgia for the simple melodic line, a whimpering return to the "easy music." Nor is there any suggestion that his last three symphonies are the work of a tired, old composer. Rather, each of the orchestral pieces possesses an integrity of its own. It is, as Virgil Thompson remarked in 1943 after hearing a concert of Guarnieri's chamber music: "No one piece has it all. Indeed, he is too sound a musician to ask of [the instruments] what they cannot do or to neglect their characteristic possibilities."[64]

His monothematic tendency moved with naturalness into atonality and, in his later works, almost into serialism. Conductor Lutero Rodrigues wrote, "The innovations which occurred in his work, especially those after 1960, were born of the necessity of expression and not from some intent to be innovative."[65] Guarnieri indeed created sounds that at times sounded as if they were electronically produced, something which could only have come from within his own need to express his thought and feeling.

Lifelong student and friend of Guarnieri Osvaldo Costa de Lacerda wrote in 1991, "Camargo Guarnieri is recognized and respected as one of the greatest contemporary composers."[66] Time will surely prove him correct. As seen in these final symphonies, Guarnieri had not exhausted his creativity by his seventy-fifth birthday. He continued to hone the power of his unique musical voice, exploring new ways to express the fire that burned inside of his musical soul, refining and simplifying the means, adapting to the circumstances and occasions. In and through it all, one recognizes Guarnieri and a music which is identifiably his: unique, colorful, intense, well crafted, sensitive, expressive, and deeply moving. What more could be asked of any composer?

Fame during one's lifetime is unduly dependent upon conditions which are frequently peripheral, such as being fortunate enough to have one's works published and promulgated by respectable publishers, performed, and recorded. Every composer is also subjected to the distorted view which his own times and peers can occasionally put forth. More difficult is the frequent interference of personalities and the "glares" which prevent the public from seeing beyond certain qualities which either attract or repulse. Performers may or may not do justice to a work in performance, thus jeopardizing critics' reflections. And some critics feel a personal need to "be hard" on musicians.

In the history of erudite music, the music of those composers who have "made it" often is accepted without critical distinction between their uncontested masterpieces and some lesser works which probably should never have gotten into print, much less recorded or aired.

Camargo Guarnieri has not been exempt from such limited perspective. Because his music is not easy to read, many performers have given up before giving the music a fair chance. Guarnieri's strong temperament and determination often worked against him. The term "nationalistic composer" has been applied to him until it has come to sound like a condemnation.

With the passage of time, perhaps very little time, history may well be able to place the works of this man, one of Brazil's greatest composers, into a clearer perspective, removed from the personality issues and stylistic preferences of individuals. Two large volumes on his life and works, published in Brazil, are a beginning. This current volume is another effort. Publication of his scores and several existing and other planned series of recordings of his music will further ensure his continuing musical presence.

When a well-constructed piece of music that clearly communicates a strong message is discovered, it makes little difference whether it was written ten years earlier or later than some moment in music history. It is the power inherent in the work of art that will communicate to those who are willing to listen. All else is secondary, as history testifies.

APPENDIX:
CATALOG OF WORKS

ABBREVIATIONS:

ce = cello
gu = guitar
fl = flute
pi = piano
va = viola
vi = violin
vo = voice
arr. = arrangement
trans. = transcription

Vocal	Instrumental	Chamber & Orchestral
1928		
As Flores Amarelas dos Ipês	Canção Sertaneja—pi	Trovas de Amor + vo (trans.)
Cantinga Noturna	Canção Sertaneja—vi (trans.)	
Lembranças do Losango Cáqui	Dança Brasileira—pi	
Manchas de Esfuminho	Sonatina no. 1—pi	
Prelúdio no. 2		
Toada do Pai do Mato		
Trovas de Amor		
1929		
Canção das Iaras	Suite Infantil—pi	Choros nos. 1, 2, 3
Cantiga Contraditório	Toada—pi	Noturno (trans.)
Cantiga Sentimental		Prelúdio e Fuga
Ciúme		Suite Infantil
De Você		Toada (trans.)
Despeito		Três Danças + vo (trans.)
Minha Viola		
Noturno		
Ser Feliz		
Sofia		
Três Danças		

Vocal	Instrumental	Chamber & Orchestral
1930		
Brinquedo	Cantiga lá de Longe—vi & pi	Cantiga da Porteira (trans.)
Canção—SATB	Choro Torturado—pi	Curuça
Cantiga da Porteira	Sonata no. 1—vi & pi	
Minha Terra		
O Impossível Carinho		
Oração a Santa Teresinha		
do Menino Jesus		
Oração no Saco de Mangaratiba		
Tetêia		
Três Brinquedos com a Lua		
1931		
Cabedelo	Cantiga de Ninar—vi & pi	Concerto no. 1—pi
Duas Irmãs	Dança Selvagem—pi	Dança Brasileira (trans.)
Irene no Céu	Polca—pi	Dança Selvagem (trans.)
Macumba do Pia Zuzé	Ponteios nos. 1–4—pi	Quatro Poemas da Macunaíma
Madrigal Tão Engraçadinho	Sonata no. 1—ce & pi	Ponteio no. 1 (trans.)
Prece Lírica		Ponteio no. 2 (trans.)
Quatro Poemas de Macunaíma		Trio para Cordas—vi, va, & ce
(+ trans.)		
Quatro Trovas		
Sinhô Lau		
1932		
A Glória de São Paulo—	Lundu—pi-	En Memória dos Que Morreram
unison men's chorus	O Cavalinho de Perna Quebrada—pi	por São Paulo
A Morte do Aviador—cantata	Piratininga—pi	Quarteto de Cordas no. 1
Carícia	Ponteios nos. 5, 6—pi	
Chiquinha—children's chorus		
Den-Báu		
Doze Canções Populares Infantis		
Lembranças de um Sonho		
Mestre Carlus—TTB		
Mofiladofê		
Pedro Malazarte—opera		
Prenda Minha—SATB		
Tenho um Cachorrinho—		
children's chorus		
1933		
E uma Pena, Doce Amiga	Chriança Triste—pi	Choro no. 5—wind quintet
Gosto de Estar a Teu Lado	Cinco Peças Infantis—pi	
João Corta Pau	Criança Adormece—pi	
Nas Ondas da Praia—chorus	Estudando Piano—pi	
of 4 equal voices	Ponteios nos. 7, 8—pi	
Plumas	Sonata no. 2—vi & pi	
Solidão		
Vocé e Tão Suave		
1934		
Acuti-paru	Ponteio no. 9—pi	—
Modinha Triste	Sonatina no. 2—pi	
Não Sei por que Espirito Antigo	Valsa no. 1—pi	
Quando		

Vocal	Instrumental	Chamber & Orchestral
1935		
Constância	Ponteio no. 10—pi	Toada à Moda Paulista
Dona Janaína	Tocata—pi	
Olhando para Teus Olhos	Valsa no. 2—pi	
1936		
Acalanto do Amor Feliz	Toada Triste—pi, vi & pi	4 trans. of other composers
Canção do Passado		Se Você Compreendesse + vo (trans.)
Egbê-gi—SATB		
Enlouvor do Silêncio		
Milagre		
Ninguém Mais		
Se Você Compreendesse		
Tempo Perdido		
Você		
1937		
Ave Maria—SATB	Sonatina no. 3—pi	Flor de Tremembé
Canção Tímida	Valsa no. 3—pi	Desesperança—vo (trans.)
Cantiga da Tua Lembrança		Flor de Tremembé—15 solo instruments
Coisas deste Brasil—SATB		4 trans. of other composers
Desesperança		
Por quê?		
Segue-me		
Talvez		
Treze Canções de Amor		
Você Nasceu		
1938		
—	—	—
1939		
Cantiga Triste	Canto no. 1—vi & pi	Três Poemas—vo (trans.)
Dois Poemas	Ficarás Sozinha—pi	
Modinha		
Quebra o Coco, Menina		
Três Poemas		
Vai, Azulão		
1940		
Prenda Minha (arr.)	—	Concerto no. 1—vi
1941		
A Culpa de Perder o Teu Afeto	Encantamento—vi + trans.	A Culpa de Perder o Teu Afeto + vo (trans.)
A Serra do Rola-Moça	Improviso no. 1—fl	A Serra do Rola-Moça + vo
Não Faça Assim		Cinco Peças Infantis (trans.)
Para que o Céu Não Me Tanteie		Encantamento + vi (trans.)
Pousa a Mão na Minha Testa		Tostão de Chuva + vo (trans.)
Tostão de Chuva		
1942		
Canção	Improviso no. 2—fl	Abertura Concertante
Cantiga de Quem Te Quer	Valsa no. 1—vi (trans.)	Quebra o Coco, Menina + vo (trans.)
Dois Poemas		Trovas de Amor + vo (trans.)
Já Hoje que Aqui Me Vistes		Vai, Azulão + vo (trans.)
Madrigal		
Porque Estás Sempre Comigo		
Prelúdio no. 2 (trans.)		

Vocal	Instrumental	Chamber & Orchestral
1943		
Es a Totalmente Amada	Valsa no. 4—pi	Canção Sertaneja (trans.)
Te Dei um Vidro de Cheiro		Desafio + vo
1944		
Coco do Major—tenor, bass, & SATB	Maria Lucia—pi	Quarteto de Cordas no. 2
Duas Miniaturas	Ponteio—gu	Sinfonia no. 1
Louvação ao Senhor—SATB		
Louvação do Amor Êtê		
Se Desses ao Fundo		
1945		
Foi Vento . . . Foi a Vida		Sinfonia no. 2, Uirapuru
1946		
Declaração	Dança Negra—pi	Concerto no. 2—pi
Viola Quebrada (arr.)	Ponteio e Dança—ce & pi	
1947		
Cadê Minha Pomba Rola	Ponteio no. 11—pi	Dança Negra (trans.)
	Sonatina—fl & pi	Prologo e Fuga
1948		
Dois Cantos Espirituais Norte- Americanos—children's chorus	Dança Negra—2 pi arr. Improviso no. 1—pi	Improviso no. 1 (trans.) Quando Embolada + vo (trans.)
Esse Vazio que Nada Enche	Ponteios nos. 13, 16, 17—pi	
Nove cantos populares infantis —children's chorus	Valsa no. 5—pi	
Quando Embolada (trans.)		
Três Canções Brasileiras		
Vou m'Embora		
1949		
A Cantiga da Mutuca	Estudos nos. 1–3—pi	Por Qué? + vo (trans.)
Dois Cantos Populares Infantis	Improviso no. 3—fl	Rondó do Eco e do Descorajado + vo (trans.)
Duas Canções	Ponteios nos. 12, 14, 15, 18–20—pi	Saudade Indefinida + vo (trans.)
Duas Quadras	Valsa no. 6—pi	
Maria—SSA		
Mineiro Pau—SSA		
Rondó do Eco e do Descorajado		
Saracutinga—SA		
Saudade Indefinida		
Só Vivo as Horas que Passo		
Três Cantos Populares Infantis		
1950		
Pensei em Ti com Doçura	Estudo no. 5—pi	Suite Brasiliana
	Sonata—va & pi	
	Sonata no. 3—vi & pi	

Vocal	Instrumental	Chamber & Orchestral
1951		
Aceitei Tua Amizade	—	Porque Estás Sempre Comigo + vo (trans.)
As Vezes, Meu Amor		
Eu Gosto de Você		
Oito Canções		
Olha-me Tão-Somente		
Quero Dizer Baixhinho		
1952		
Espera	Acalanto—pi	Choro—vi
Não Fale por Favor (+ trans.)	Aria—vi (arr.)	Sinfonia no. 3
O Saci Pulou no Meio—SATB		
1953		
—	Canto no. 2—vi & pi	Concerto no. 2—vi
	Estudo—French horn	Estudo para Instrumentos de Percussão
	Estudo—piccolo	Variações Sôbre uma Tema Nordestino—pi
	Estudo—trumpet	
	Géssia—pi (trans.)	
	Suite Mirim—pi	
1954		
Cinco Poemas de Alice	Estudo no. 4—pi	Suite IV Centenário
	Ponteios nos. 21–24, 28—pi	
	Valsa Choro no. 1—gu	
	Valsas nos. 7–8—pi	
1955		
Agora	Ponteios nos. 25–30—pi	Aria + vo (trans.)
Cantiga	Sonata no. 2—ce & pi	Lamentação da Hora Perdida + vo (trans.)
Duas Canções de Celso Brant		Três Poemas Afro-Brasilieros + vo (trans.)
Isto é Você!		Eu Gosto de Você + vo (+ trans.)
Lamentação da Hora Perdida		
Três Poemas Afro-Brasilieros		
1956		
Adoração	Ponteios nos. 31, 33, 34—pi	Choro—clarinet
Ave Maria—contralto & organ	Sonata no. 4—vi & pi	Choro—pi
Castigo		Ponteio no. 31 (trans.)
Duas Canções		
Não sei . . .		
Quatro Cantigas		
Vamos Dar a Despedida		
1957		
Duas Cantigas de Amor	Ponteios nos. 32, 35–40—pi	Ponteios nos. 36, 38 (trans.)
Es Mais Bela	Valsa no. 9—pi	Rebelião em Vila Rica—film score
Libera Me—soprano, chorus, & organ		
Madrigal Muito Fácil (+ trans.)		
Não Adianta Dizer Nada		
Ondas de um Mar Crescente		
Sai, Aruê (+ trans.)		
Teus Olhos Verdes		

Vocal	Instrumental	Chamber & Orchestral
1958		
Ai¡ Meu Bem (arr.)	Estudo no. 1—gu	Suite Vila Rica
Amo-te Muito (arr.)	Ponteios nos. 41, 42—pi	
Aribu (arr.)	Sonatina no. 4—pi	
Duas Canções de Silvia Celeste de Campos		
Duas Canções de Susana de Campos		
Elvira Escuta (arr.)		
Perpétua (arr.)		
Roda Morena (arr.)		
Sêca—cantata + orch		
Sereno da Madrugada (arr.)		
Tim, Tim Oi Lá La (arr.)		
1959		
Amo-te, Sim	Ponteios nos. 43–50—pi	Ponteios nos. 45, 46, 48 (trans.)
Ave Maria—contralto & organ	Valsa no. 10—pi	
Canção Ingênua		
Colóquio—cantata + instruments		
Nada de Mágoas		
O Amor de Agora		
Onde Andará		
Seca (trans.)		
1960		
Um Homen Só—lyric tragedy + orch	Brincando—pi	—
	Improviso no. 2—pi	
1961		
Eu Sinto Dentro Do Peito	Baião—pi	Choro-ce
	Sonata no. 5—vi & pi	Concertino—pi
	Valsa—pi	
1962		
Ave Maria—SATB a cappella or with organ	Estudos nos. 6–9—pi	Quarteto de Cordas no. 3
	Sonatina no. 5—pi	
1963		
		Cinco Poems de Alice + string quartet
	Sonata no. 6—vi & pi	Ponteio no. 33 (trans.)
		Sinfonia no. 4
		Meus Pecados (trans.) + strings
1964		
O Flor Do Meu Coração	Estudo no. 10—pi	Concerto no. 3—pi
Toada		
1965		
O Guaná-bará—cantata SATB	Sonatina no. 6—pi	Guana-bará—SATB
	Tanguinho—pi	Seresta—pi
	Valsinha pretencios—pi	

Vocal	Instrumental	Chamber & Orchestral
1966		
—	—	Homenagem a Villa-Lobos—winds Seqüência, Coral e Ricercare— chamber orchestra
1967		
Duas Canções de Renata Triptico de Iêda	—	—
1968		
Biborá da Cru—children's chorus Escravos de Job—children's chorus Música e Letra de Modinha Não Sei se Estou Vivo Quartro Cantigas Três Epigrammas	Estudos nos. 11, 12—pi Interlúdio—pi	Concerto no. 4—pi
1969		
Ave Maria—contralto & organ Cuziribâmbo Súplica	Danca da Pulga—pi Estudos nos. 13, 14—pi Flavinha—pi	Ponteio no. 45 (trans.)
1970		
Caso do Vestido—cantata (trans.) Não é Joe, Não é Joana—SATB Rosalina—SATB	Estudo no. 15—pi Improvisos nos. 3, 4, 8—pi	Caso do Vestido—cantata + instruments Concerto no. 5—pi Improviso 3 & 4 (trans.)
1971		
E Mô Kanceó Que Nunca Pude Ser	As Três Graças—pi Sonatina no. 7—pi Toada para Daniel Paulo—pi Valsinha—pi	Abertua Festiva
1972		
Duas Canções de Menotti del Picchia Madrigal do Amor—SATB Missa Diligite—SATB & organ Seria tão Fácil	Em Memória de um Amigo—pi Improviso no. 1—pi Sonata—pi	Choro—fl & chamber orchestra Concerto para Cordas e Percussão— strings & percussion Improvisos nos. 3, 4 (trans.) Missa Diligite—SATB & strings
1973		
Ave Maria—contralto & organ Ave Maria—contralto & organ Cantiga de Ausência Em Memória do Meu Pai—SATB Intermezzo	Fraternidade—pi Improviso no. 3—vi & pi (trans.)	Cantiga de Ausência + strings (trans.)
1974		
Ave Maria—2 vo & organ or string quartet Deslumbramento Estou com Medo Lá Longe no Sul Não Sei Porque os Tetéus	Cantilena no. 1—ce & pi Improviso no. 6—pi Sonatina—vi & pi	Ave Maria—2 vo & strings (trans.) Estudo—percussion (trans.) Improviso no. 6—chamber orchestra (trans.)

Vocal	Instrumental	Chamber & Orchestral
1975		
Ai Momentos de Físico Amor	Improviso no. 9—pi	Choro—va
Es na Minha Vida		
Hea o Mutisomo Exaltado dos Astros		
Lembrança Boa		
Na Zona da Mata		
Nega em Teu Ser Primário		
1976		
Amor Mesquinho	—	Angústia—string quartet
Migalhas		
1977		
Ave Maria—SATB & organ	Acalanto para Barbara—pi	Sinfonia no. 5 + chorus
Oferta	Série dos Curumins—pi	Toada Triste—strings (trans.)
Poema Interior	Sonata no. 3—ce & pi	
Vocalise		
1978		
Depedida Sentimental	Improviso no. 7—pi	Improviso no. 7—strings (trans.)
E Fico a Pensar	Saracoteio—pi	
O Que Podia Ter Sido	Seresta—vi & pi	
	Sonata no. 7—vi & pi	
1979		
—	—	Arioso-Bach—strings (trans.)
1980		
Ave Maria—SATB & organ	Improviso no. 8—pi	Ave Maria—SATB & strings (trans.)
Ave Maria—SATB & organ		Fuga em sol menor–Frescobaldi—strings (trans.)
Que Pena		Improviso no. 8—strings (trans.)
		Que Pena—vo & strings (trans.)
		Seis Prelúdios Organisticos sobre Corais–Buxtehude—strings (trans.)
		Você Nasceu—vo & strings (trans.)
		Você—vo & strings (trans.)
1981		
Auto de Todo Mundo e Ninquem—SATB & orchestra	Estudo no. 19—pi	Sinfonia no. 6
	Improviso no. 10—pi	
1982		
Canto de Amor aos Meus Irnãos do Mundo—SATB & orchestra	Cantilena no. 2—ce & pi	Improviso no. 6—strings (trans.)
Desejo	Estudo no. 20—pi	Momento no. 2—strings (trans.)
Eu Te Encontrei	Estudos nos. 2, 3—gu	Ponteio e Dança—ce & strings (trans.)
Salmo 23—SATB & strings (+ trans.)	Momentos nos. 1–4—pi	
	Sonatina no. 8—pi	
	Toada Sentimental—pi	
1983		
Miniatura	—	—

Vocal	Instrumental	Chamber & Orchestral
1984		
—	Estudo no. 16—pi Momento no. 5—pi	Cinquentenário da Universidade São Paulo —narrator, SATB, & orchestra Dança Brasileira—strings (trans.) Sarabanda–Debussy—strings (trans.) Toada no. 4–Viana—strings (trans.)
1985		
Ave Maria—contralto & organ or string orchestra	Estudo no. 17—pi Momentos nos. 6, 7—pi	Ave Maria + strings (trans.) Ave Maria + strings Sinfonia no. 7 Xácara-Nepumoceno—strings (trans.)
1986		
Ave Maria—contralto, organ, & string orchestra (+ trans.)	Momento no. 8—pi Valsa Choro no. 2—gu	Ave Maria + strings (trans.) Fuga en lá menor–Bach—strings (trans.) Homenagem a Fructuoso Viana
1987		

—	Momento no. 9—pi	Concerto no. 6–"Sarati"—pi, strings &
		   percussion
		Improviso—fl & strings (trans.)
		Valsa de Esquina, nos. 5, 8–Mignone—
		   strings (trans.)

1988		
—	Estudo no. 18—pi Momento no. 10—pi	Dançarinas de Delfos–Debussy—strings (trans.)
1989		
Acalanto para Luisa	Duo para Flautas—2 fl	Ponteio no. 43—strings (trans.) Trio—vi, ce, & pi (trans. of Violin Sonata no. 7)
1990		
—	—	—
1991		
—	—	Choro—bassoon, harp, percussion, & string orchestra
1992		
—	Improvisando—pi	—

NOTES

1. THE MAN

1. Heleno Godoy, "Mario Segunda Guarnieri," *Folha de Goias* (Goiânia), May 3, 1970.

2. Camargo Guarnieri, interview with author, São Paulo, November 24, 1969.

3. Ibid.

4. Ibid.

5. Ibid.

6. Ibid.

7. Ibid.

8. Antônio Sá Pereira, "Mozart Camargo Guarnieri: Uma Esplendida Afirmação de Música 'Brasileira,'" *Diário de São Paulo*, September 8, 1929.

9. Vasco Mariz, "Camargo Guarnieri aos 80 Anos," *O Estado de São Paulo*, January 31, 1987.

10. Godoy, "Mario Segunda Guarnieri."

11. Eurico Nogueira França, *Música do Brasil* (Rio de Janeiro: Edições de Ouro, 1968), 124.

12. Guarnieri, interview, November 1969.

13. Maria Abreu, "O Homen e Episódios que Caracterizam Sua Personalidade," in Flávio Silva, ed., *Camargo Guarnieri: O Tempo e a Música* (Rio de Janeiro: Funarte, 2001), 9.

14. Godoy, "Mario Segunda Guarnieri."

15. Silva, ed., *O Tempo e a Música*, 75.

16. Mário de Andrade, "Compositores Paulistas," *Diário Nacional* (São Paulo), September 7, 1930.

17. Guarnieri, interview, November 1969.

18. Flávio Silva, "Uma Sonata, Alguns Enigmas," *Revista Brasiliana* (Rio de Janeiro), 2003, 14–21.

19. Guarnieri, interview, November 1969.

20. Mário de Andrade, "Uma Sonata de Camargo Guarnieri," *O Jornal* (São Paulo), n.d. (circa May 1935).

21. Mário de Andrade, "Música: Camargo Guarnieri," *Diário de São Paulo*, May 28, 1935.

22. Ayres de Andrade, "Academie Brasileira de Música: Obras de Camargo Guarnieri," *Diário Carioca* (Rio de Janeiro), July 16, 1935.

23. Artur Imbassai, "Instituto Nacional de Música: Camargo Guarnieri," *Jornal do Brasil* (Rio de Janeiro), July 12, 1935.

24. Otávio Bevilacqua, "Música," *O Globo* (Rio de Janeiro), July 11, 1935.

25. Andrade Muricy, "Camargo Guarnieri." *Festa* (Rio de Janeiro), August 1935, 21.

26. Fernando Mendes de Almeida, "Música: Camargo Guarnieri," *Diário de Notícias* (São Paulo), August 14, 1936.

27. Silva, ed., *O Tempo e a Música*, 75.

28. Abreu, "O Homen," 41.

29. Guarnieri, interview, November 1969.

30. Camargo Guarnieri, as quoted in "Maestro Camargo Guarnieri," *O Estado de São Paulo,* December 29, 1939.

31. Mário de Andrade, "Camargo Guarnieri," *O Estado de São Paulo,* January 28, 1940.

32. Mário de Andrade, "Camargo Guarnieri," *Chronicle Musical,* 1940.

33. João Itiberê de Cunha, "Composições de Camargo Guarnieri," *Correio da Manhã* (Rio de Janeiro), April 26, 1941.

34. Andrade Muricy, "Pelo Mundo da Música: Obras de Camargo Guarnieri em 1° Audição," *Jornal do Comercio* (Rio de Janeiro), April 30, 1942.

35. D'Or [Ondina Dantes], "Música: Camargo Guarnieri," *Diário de Notícias* (São Paulo), April 17, 1942.

36. João Itiberê de Cunha, "Música," *Correio da Manhã* (Rio de Janeiro), April 16, 1942.

37. Editorial, *Folha de Noite* (São Paulo), April 10, 1942.

38. R.C.B., "Guarnieri Honored by Composers," *New York World Telegram,* March 8, 1943.

39. Virgil Thompson, "Excellence from Brazil," *New York Herald Tribune,* March 8, 1943.

40. Sergio Vasconcellos Correa, *Music in Brasil: Now* (Brasilia: Ministério das Relações Exteriores, Departamento Cultura, Educação e Cultura, 1974), 27–28.

41. Camargo Guarnieri in Silva, ed., *O Tempo e a Música,* 62–63.

42. *São Paulo Gazette,* October 28, in Silva, ed., *O Tempo e a Música,* 62.

43. Osvaldo Costa de Lacerda, "Meu Professor Camargo Guarnieri," in Silva, ed., *O Tempo e a Música,* 62.

44. Kilza Setti in Silva, ed., *O Tempo e a Música,* 66.

45. Camargo Guarnieri, interview with author, São Paulo, December 20, 1969.

46. Camargo Guarnieri, "Sob a Regência de Camargo Guarnieri, Inaugurado Orquestra Sinfônica da USP," *Nossa Folha* (Tietê), December 20, 1975.

47. Silveira Peixoto, "Un Encontro com Camargo Guarnieri," n.p., n.d (circa October 1978).

48. Mauricio Ielo, "Camargo Guarnieri, 75 Anos e os Planos de um Compositor Polêmico," *O Estado de São Paulo,* February 10, 1982.

49. Mariz, "Guarnieri aos 80 Anos."

2. EVOLVING A NATIONAL MUSIC

1. Mário de Andrade, *Pequena História de Música,* 8th ed. (São Paulo: Martins, 1968), 171.

2. Fernando de Azevedo, *Brazilian Culture,* trans. William Rex Crawford (New York: Macmillan, 1950), 91.

3. França, *Música do Brasil,* 26.

4. Oneyda Alvarenga, *Música Popular Brasileira* (São Paulo: Livraria Duas Cidadas, 1982).

5. Azevedo, *Brazilian Culture,* 91.

6. Mário de Andrade, "Mozart Camargo Guarnieri: Dança Brasileira," *Diário Nacional* (São Paulo), May 6, 1928.

7. Luiz Heitor Correa de Azevedo, *Música e Músicos do Brasil* (Rio de Janeiro: Casa do Estudante do Brasil, 1950), 19.

8. Andrade, "Mozart Camargo Guarnieri."

9. Manuel Diegues Junior, "Sugestões para Estudo Regional do Folclore Brasileiro," *Vozes, Revista de Cultura* LXIII, no. 10 (October 1969), 903.

10. Gerrit de Jong, "Music in Brazil," *Inter-American Music Bulletin,* no. 31 (September 1962), 1–15.

11. Nicolas Slonimsky, *Music of Latin America* (New York: Thomas Y. Crowell, 1945), 120.

12. De Jong, "Music in Brazil," 97.

13. França, *Música do Brasil,* 97.

14. Mário de Andrade, *Aspectos da Música Brasileira* (São Paulo: Martins, 1939), 17–18.

15. França, *Música do Brasil,* 30.

16. Mário de Andrade, *Ensaio Sôbre a Música Brasileira* (São Paulo: Martins, 1962), 16.

17. Ibid., 16, 20.

18. Andrade, *Aspectos,* 27.

3. COMPOSITIONAL STYLE

1. Renato de Almeida, *História da Música Brasileira,* 2nd ed. (Rio de Janeiro: Briguiet, 1942), 476.

2. Quoted in Lutero Rodrigues, "O Compositor Camargo Guarnieri," *Apollon Musagete—Periódico Musical IV-91* (Curitiba, no. 4), November 2, 1991.

3. Sidney Finklestein, *Composer and Nation* (New York: International Publishers, 1960), 10.

4. Eurico Nogueira França, "Camargo Guarnieri," *Correio da Manhã* (Rio de Janeiro), May 21, 1947.

5. Antônio Sá Pereira, "Mozart Camargo Guarnieri: Uma Esplendida Afirmação de Música 'Brasileira,'" *Diário de São Paulo,* September 8, 1929.

6. Mozart Araujo, "Mozart Camargo Guarnieri," typewritten address, Santos, n.p., n.d. (circa 1957).

7. Hans Joachim Koellreutter, "Camargo Guarnieri, O 'Lider' da Jovem Geração de Compositores Brasileiros," *Vida,* May 1943.

8. Cf. Lutero Rodrigues, "Camargo Guarnieri (I)," *Apollon Musagete—Periódico Musical* (Curitiba, no. 9), 1993.

9. Camargo Guarnieri, interview with author, São Paulo, December 20, 1969.

10. Wagner Carelli, "Camargo Guarnieri, a Magoa e o Exito de 70 Anos Dificeis," *O Estado de São Paulo,* January 30, 1977.

11. Claver Filho, "Guarnieri e o Dodecafanismo, Part II," *Correio Brasiliense,* March 1, 1977.

12. Mauricio Ielo, "Defensor do Nacionalismo Musical," *O Estado de São Paulo,* February 10, 1982.

13. Luiz Paulo Horta, "Da Originalidade dos Mestres," *Jornal do Brasil* (Rio de Janeiro), February 22, 1987.

14. Caldeira Filho, notes from record jacket, *Souza Lima, Perez Dworecki, Eudoxia de Barros Interpretam Camargo Guarnieri,* Ricordi Brasileira SRE-4.

15. Fernando Lichti Barros, "Guarnieri: Música dos 11 aos 70," *Diário de São Paulo,* February 6, 1977.

16. Horta, "Originalidade dos Mestres."

17. Camargo Guarnieri, *Depoimento.* (Note: Flávio Silva believed this had a 1959 date, but a typewritten copy that Guarnieri gave me had his handwritten 1975 with the "7" changed to an "8," thus, 1985.)

18. Quoted in Lutero Rodrigues, "O Compositor Camargo Guarnieri," *Apollon Musagete—Periódico Musical IV-91* (Curitiba, no. 4), November 2, 1991.

19. Abreu, "O Homen," 46.

20. Ibid., 52.

21. Ibid., 53.

22. Maria Abreu, "O Lirismo Impecável de um Pecador," *Zero Hora* (Porto Alegre), January 15, 1993.

23. Francisco Curt Lange, ed., *Latin American Art Music for the Piano* (New York: Schirmer, 1942), intro.

24. Ricardo Tacuchian, "O Sinfonismo Guarnieriano," in Silva, ed., *O Tempo e a Música,* 448.

25. Ludmila Ulehla, *Contemporary Harmony* (New York: Free Press, 1966), 509.

26. Belkiss Carneiro de Mendonça, "A Obra Pianistica," in Silva, ed., *O Tempo e a Música,* 401.

27. Paulo César Martins Rabelo, "The Cello and Piano Works of Camargo Guarnieri" (Ph.D. diss., Ohio State University, 1996), 24.

28. Mendonça, "A Obra Pianistica," 421.

29. Lais de Souza Brasil, "O Piano de Laís Recria os Ponteios de Guarnieri," *O Estado de São Paulo,* August 12, 1979.

30. Camargo Guarnieri, interview with author, São Paulo, November 1970.

31. Ibid.

4. MUSIC FOR SOLO PIANO

1. Mário de Andrade, "Canção Sertaneja," *Diário Nacional* (São Paulo), August 16, 1928.

2. Camargo Guarnieri, interview with author, São Paulo, October 1969.

3. Ibid.

4. Mário de Andrade, "Mozart Camargo Guarnieri," *Diário Nacional* (São Paulo), May 6, 1928.

5. Mário de Andrade, "Música," *Diário de São Paulo* (São Paulo), May 3, 1934.

6. Guarnieri, interview, October 1969.

7. Luís da Câmara Cascudo, *Dicionário do Folclore Brasileiro* (Rio de Janeiro: Edições de Ouro, 1969), vol. 2, 112.

8. Alvarenga, *Música Popular Brasileira,* 172–73.

9. Camargo Guarnieri, interview with author, São Paulo, December 1969.

10. Andrade Muricy, "Música," *Jornal do Comercio* (Rio de Janeiro), April 30, 1941.

11. João Itiberê da Cunha, "Correio Musical," *Correio da Manhã* (Rio de Janeiro), April 26, 1941.

12. Eurico Nogueira França, "Composições de Camargo Guarnieri," *Correio da Manhã* (Rio de Janeiro), March 17, 1956.

13. Eurico Nogueira França, "Música: Festival Camargo Guarnieri" *Correio Musical* (Rio de Janeiro), May 13, 1948.

14. Lange, ed., *Latin American Art Music,* intro.

15. Eurico Nogueira França, "Música: Novas Edições de Guarnieri," *Correio Musical* (Rio de Janeiro), February 4, 1948.

16. Guarnieri, interview, October 1969.

17. Osvaldo Lacerda, record jacket notes for Camargo Guarnieri, *Universo Tropical,* Cynthia Priolli, piano, São Paulo, Sul America Unibanco, 1985.

18. Ibid.

19. Belkiss Carneiro de Mendonça, "A Obra Pianistica," in Silva, ed., *O Tempo e a Música,* 420.

20. Muricy, "Música."

21. João Itiberê da Cunha, "Correio Musical," *Correio da Manhã* (Rio de Janeiro), May 9, 1941.

22. Os Irmaõs Tavares de Lima, "São Paulo no Tempo das Valsas," *Jornal de Música* 9, no. 53 (São Paulo: Grupo Vitale, 1986) (newsletter).

23. Mozart Araujo, record jacket notes for *Waltzes of Camargo Guarnieri,* Belkiss Carneiro de Mendonça, piano, Polygram, Rio de Janeiro, April 1984.

24. Guarnieri, interview, October 1969.

25. Ayres de Andrade, record jacket notes for *Ponteios: Camargo Guarnieri,* Isabel Mourão, piano, Ricordi SRE-8.

26. Camargo Guarnieri, interview with author, São Paulo, November 1969.

27. Gilbert Chase, "Music and Musicians: Inspired Young Brazilian Composer Wins Philadelphia Contest," *Inter-American Monthly* 2 (1943), 31.

28. Guarnieri, interview, November 1969.

29. Lange, *Latin American Art Music,* intro.

30. Otto Deri, *Exploring Twentieth Century Music* (New York: Holt, Rinehart & Winston, 1968), 40.

31. Edward T. Cone, *Musical Form and Musical Performance* (New York: W. W. Norton, 1968), 84.

32. Ulehla, *Contemporary Harmony,* 509.

33. Ibid., 405.

34. Mário de Andrade, "Camargo Guarnieri," *O Estado de São Paulo,* January 28, 1940.

35. Andrade, record jacket notes for *Ponteios: Camargo Guarnieri.*

36. Ney Fialkow, "The Ponteios of Camargo Guarnieri" (Ph.D. diss., Peabody Institute of the John Hopkins University, 1995), 109.

37. Frederick Moyer, quoted in Marion Verhaalen, compact disc notes for *Estudos,* Jupiter Recordings, Lee, N.H., 1997.

38. Ibid.

39. Maria Abreu, "Música," *Correio do Povo* (Porto Alegre), December 23, 1967.

40. Lacerda, jacket notes for *Universo Tropical.*

41. Eurico Nogeuira França, "Camargo Guarnieri," *Correio da Manhã* (Rio de Janeiro), May 21, 1947.

42. Antônio Sá Pereira, "Mozart Camargo Guarnieri: Uma Esplendida Afirmação de Música 'Brasileira,'" *Diário de São Paulo,* September 8, 1929.

43. Mário de Andrade, "Camargo Guarnieri: Sonatina," *O Estado de São Paulo,* October 22, 1929.

44. Mozart de Araujo, "Mozart Camargo Guarnieri" (manuscript of an address circa 1957).

45. Andrade, "Camargo Guarnieri: Sonatina."

46. Andrade Muricy, "Pelo Mundo da Música: Obras de Camargo Guarnieri em 1° Audição," *Jornal do Comercio* (Rio de Janeiro), April 30, 1942.

47. Anon., "Audição de Obras de Camargo Guarnieri," *O Jornal* (Rio de Janeiro), April 28, 1941.

48. Ibid.

49. João Itiberê de Cunha, "Composições de Camargo Guarnieri," *Correio da Manhã* (Rio de Janeiro), April 26, 1941.

50. Caio Pagano, compact disc notes for *Camargo Guarnieri Latin American: Choro and Other Works,* Czech National Symphony Orchestra, Caio Pagano, piano, Paul Freeman, conductor, Hallmark Classics.

51. Belkiss Carneiro de Mendonça, "A Obra Pianistica," in Silva, ed., *O Tempo e a Música,* 408.

52. Ibid.

53. Ibid.

54. Enio Squeff, record jacket notes for *Piano, Caio Pagano,* Fundação Nacional de Arte.

55. Ayres de Andrade, "Música," *O Jornal* (Rio de Janeiro), May 4, 1968.

56. Mendonça, "A Obra Pianistica," 410.

57. Ibid.

58. Acyr Castro, *Jornal do Brasil,* June 1972.

59. Lais de Souza Brasil, conversation with author, São Paulo, December 2001.

60. Caldeira Filho, "Sonata de Guarnieri em Estreia Mundial," *O Estado de São Paulo,* July 5, 1973.

61. Ibid.

62. Ibid.

63. Ibid.

64. Lea Vinocur Freitag, "Pianista Fiel e Vigorosa para a Arte de Guarnieri," *O Estado de São Paulo,* November 1, 1983.

65. Lacerda, jacket notes for *Universo Tropical.*

66. Cynthia Priolli, Commentary on the piano score *Improvisos,* Ricordi Brasileira #0798, 1988.

67. Lacerda, jacket notes for *Universo Tropical.*

68. Freitag, "Pianista Fiel e Vigorosa."

69. Lacerda, jacket notes for *Universo Tropical.*

5. MUSIC FOR PIANO AND ORCHESTRA

1. *Correio de São Paulo,* n.d. (circa 1936).

2. Andrade Muricy, *Caminho de Música,* vol. 2 (Rio de Janeiro: Editôra Guaira, 1937), 108.

3. Caldeira Filho, *O Estado de São Paulo,* December 19, 1944 (also *A Aventura da Música* [São Paulo: Ricordi, 1969], 67).

4. Filho, record jacket notes for *Souza Lima, Perez Dworecki, Eudoxia de Barros Interpretam Camargo Guarnieri.*

5. Lais de Souza Brazil, compact disc notes for *Camargo Guarnieri,* Repertôrio Rádio, MEC S008.

6. Eurico Nogueira França, "Música," *Correio Musical* (Rio de Janeiro) May 21, 1947.

7. Caldeira Filho, *O Estado de São Paulo,* October 25, 1947.

8. Sula Jaffe, *Diário de Notícias* (São Paulo), 27, May 1967.

9. Andrade Muricy, "Críticas de Andrade Muricy," *Jornal do Comercio* (Rio de Janeiro), June 4, 1967.

10. Antônio Hernandez, "Música Brasileira Foi Sucesso em 3 Dimenções," *O Globo* (Rio de Janeiro), May 26, 1967.

11. Edino Krieger, "Guarnieri em Primeira Audição," *Jornal do Brasil* (Rio de Janeiro), May 30, 1967.

12. Caldeira Filho, *O Estado de São Paulo,* November 7, 1973.

13. Camargo Guarnieri, interview with author, São Paulo, December 1969.

14. Caldeira Filho, "Concerto Reafirma Talento de Guarnieri," *O Estado de São Paulo,* July 24, 1975.

15. Antônio Hernandez, "Vanguarda não Deslumbra a Voz dos Velhos Mestres," *O Globo* (Rio de Janeiro), May 18, 1970.

16. Ibid.

17. Eurico Nogueira França, "O Festival de Música da Guanabara na Reta Final," *Correio da Manhã* (Rio de Janeiro), May 19, 1970.

18. Guarnieri's program notes on the piece, São Paulo, October 1969.

19. Ibid.

20. Ibid.

21. "Guarnieri: Apenas a Gênio Pode Fazer o Que Quiser," *O Globo* (Rio de Janeiro), May 14, 1970.

22. Caldeira Filho, "Dimençôes Emotiva na Música de Camargo Guarnieri," *O Estado de São Paulo,* October 22, 1972.

6. SONGS AND SMALLER CHORAL WORKS

1. Mário de Andrade, "Camargo Guarnieri," *O Estado de São Paulo,* January 28, 1940.

2. Mário de Andrade, "Os Compositores e a Lingua Nacional," in *Aspectos da Música Brasileira,* 86.

3. Eurico Nogueira França, "Canções de Camargo Guarnieri," *Correia da Manhã* (Rio de Janeiro), August 31, 1944.

4. Mário de Andrade, "Lembranças do Losango Caqui," *Diário Nacional* (São Paulo), July 18, 1928.

5. Andrade, "Os Compositores e a Lingua Nacional."

6. Vasco Mariz, *A Canção Brasileira* (Rio de Janeiro: Ministério da Educação e Cultura, 1948), 104.

7. Mário de Andrade, "Música," *Diário de São Paulo,* May 3, 1934.

8. Mário de Andrade, "Trovas de Amor," *Diário Nacional* (São Paulo), November 27, 1928.

9. Camargo Guarnieri, interview with author, São Paulo, November 1969.

10. Mariz, *Canção Brasileira,* 104–105.

11. Andrade Muricy, "Pelo Mundo da Música: Obras de Camargo Guarnieri em 1° Audição," *Jornal do Comercio* (Rio de Janeiro), April 30, 1942.

12. Hans Joachim Koellreutter, "Camargo Guarnieri, O 'Lider' da Jovem Geração de Compositores Brasileiros," *Vida,* May 1943.

13. Mariz, *Canção Brasileira,* 105.

14. Ayres Andrade, "Audição de Obras de Camargo Guarnieri," *O Jornal* (Rio de Janeiro), August 30, 1944.

15. Caldeira Filho, "Camargo Guarnieri," *O Estado de São Paulo,* March 30, 1938.

16. Mário de Andrade, "Camargo Guarnieri," *O Estado de São Paulo,* March 30, 1938.

17. Muricy, "Pelo Mundo da Música."

18. Lutero Rodrigues, program notes for *Camargo Guarnieri,* Symphonic Orchestra of the University of São Paulo, September 1988.

19. Caldeira Filho, "Camargo Guarnieri," *O Estado de São Paulo,* March 9, 1950.

20. Mariz, *Canção Brasileira,* 105.

21. Ibid.

22. Marlos Nobre, record jacket notes for *As Canções Brasileiras de Camargo Guarnieri,* Edmar Ferretti, soprano, Camargo Guarnieri, piano, Edições Fonográficas da Rádio Ministério da Educação e Cultura, Disco PRA 2–1004, 1968.

23. Luiz Heitor de Azevedo, *Canções Brasileiras* (Rio de Janeiro: Divisão Cultura do Ministério das Relações Exteriores, 1947).

24. França, "Composições de Camargo Guarnieri."

25. Filho, "Camargo Guarnieri," March 30, 1938.

26. Nobre, jacket notes for *Canções Brasileiras.*

27. Vasco Mariz, *História da Música no Brasil,* 5th ed. (Rio de Janeiro: Civilização Brasileiros, 1985), 229.

7. DRAMATIC CHORAL WORKS

1. Renzo Massarani, "Pedro Malazarte," *Jornal do Brasil* (Rio de Janeiro), June 4, 1952.

2. Eurico Nogueira França, "Novamente em Cena Pedro Malazarte," *Correio da Manhã* (Rio de Janeiro), April 9, 1952.

3. Ibid.

4. Mário de Andrade, "Music-Cultura Artistica," *Diário de São Paulo,* February 7, 1935.

5. Antônio Rangel Bandeira, "A Propósito de Pedro Malazarte," *Correio da Manhã* (Rio de Janeiro), February 18, 1952.

6. França, "Novamente."

7. Ibid.

8. Massarani, "Pedro Malazarte."

9. *Jornal do Brasil,* citing the journal *Buenos Aires Musical,* December 12, 1969.

10. Caldeira Filho, *Estado de São Paulo,* April 21, 1959.

11. Eurico Nogueira França, *Correio da Manhã* (Rio de Janeiro), November 23, 1962.

12. Ibid.

13. Camargo Guarnieri, program notes for Orquestra Sinfônica Municipal de São Paulo, September 10, 1971.

14. Celso Loureiro Chaves, "Música Brasileira," *Diário do Povo* (Porto Alegre) (circa 20 1974).

15. Caldeira Filho, record jacket notes for Camargo Guarnieri, *Missa Diligite,* São Paulo special recording, Coro de Câmara da Universidade Federal de Goiás, Camargo Guarnieri, 1972.

16. Ibid.

17. Ibid.

18. Ibid.

8. MUSIC FOR SOLO AND CHAMBER STRINGS

1. Caldeira Filho, *O Estado de São Paulo,* October 27, 1965.

2. Lais de Souza Brasil, compact disc notes for Camargo Guarnieri, *Sonatas 2, 3, 4,* Tânia Camargo Guarnieri, violin, Lais de Souza Brasil, piano, CD MixHouse M004, 1997.

3. Ibid.

4. Ibid.

5. Caldeira Filho, *O Estado de São Paulo,* November 25, 1960.

6. Brasil, CD notes for *Sonatas.*

7. Ibid.

8. Ibid.

9. Eurico Nogueira França, *Correio da Manhã* (Rio de Janeiro), June 11, 1965.

10. Dinorah de Carvalho, *Diário do Povo* (Porto Alegre), November 1965.

11. Caldeira Filho, record jacket notes for *Souza Lima, Perez Dworecki, Eudoxia de Barros Interpretam Camargo Guarnieri.*

12. Rabelo, "Cello and Piano Works," 78.

13. Ibid., 87.

14. Ibid., 89–90.

15. Camargo Guarnieri, personal notes, São Paulo (n.d.).

16. Mário de Andrade, "Uma Sonata de Camargo Guarnieri," *Diário de São Paulo* and *O Jornal* (São Paulo), April 24, 1935.

17. Rabelo, "Cello and Piano Works," 29.

18. Andrade, "Uma Sonata."

19. Ayres de Andrade, "Academie Brasileira de Música: Obras de Camargo Guarnieri," *Diário Carioca* (Rio de Janeiro), July 16, 1935.

20. João Itiberê da Cunha, "Composições de Camargo Guarnieri," *Correio da Manhã* (Rio de Janeiro), July 10, 1935.

21. Otávio Bevilacqua, "Música," *O Globo* (Rio de Janeiro), July 11, 1935.

22. Arthur Imbassi, "Instituto Nacional de Música, Camargo Guarnieri," *Jornal do Brasil* (Rio de Janeiro), July 12, 1935.

23. Caldeira Filho, *O Estado de São Paulo,* March 30, 1938.

24. Luiz Paulo Horta, "Concerto: Os 10 Melhoroso," *Jornal do Brasil* (Rio de Janeiro), December 27, 1987.

25. Rabelo, "Cello and Piano Works," 61.

26. Ibid., 69.

27. Eurico Nogueira França, interview with author, Rio de Janeiro, March 11, 1970.

28. Eurico Nogueira França, "Camargo Guarnieri," *Correio da Manhã* (Rio de Janeiro), May 21, 1947.

29. Adhemar Nobrega, record jacket notes for *Camargo Guarnieri—Claudio Santoro,* FESTA IG 79.012.

30. Luiz Heitor de Azevedo, n.p., n.d.

31. Andrade Muricy, "Pelo Mundo da Música: Obras de Camargo Guarnieri em 1° Audição," *Jornal do Comercio* (Rio de Janeiro), April 30, 1942.

32. "League of Composers Give Music by Guarnieri," *New York Sun,* March 8, 1943.

33. Alberto Ricardi, "Artes-Festival Camargo Guarnieri," *Jornal de São Paulo,* August 9, 1946.

34. Mozart Araujo, "Festival Camargo Guarnieri," *Folha de Noite* (São Paulo), August 9, 1946.

35. Mário de Andrade, "Música," *Diário de São Paulo,* May 28, 1935.

36. Caldeira Filho, "Música de Câmara de Camargo Guarnieri," *O Estado de São Paulo,* July 3, 1948.

37. Eurico Nogueira França, "Música: Camargo Guarnieri," *Correio da Manhã* (Rio de Janeiro), October 30, 1948.

38. Caldeira Filho, *Estado de São Paulo,* October 26, 1963.

39. Donald McCorkle, *Washington Evening Star,* May 10, 1965.

40. Theodore Strongin, *New York Times,* May 10, 1965.

41. Charles Crowder, *Washington Post,* May 10, 1965.

42. Ibid.

43. Caldeira Filho, *O Estado de São Paulo,* 1977.

44. Peter Baime, interview with author, Milwaukee, March 27, 2000.

45. Richard Freed, *Manuel Barrueco: 300 Years of Guitar Masterpieces,* VoxBox 3–CD3x 3007.

9. MUSIC FOR STRINGS WITH ORCHESTRA

1. Andrade Muricy, *Jornal do Comercio* (Rio de Janeiro), September 30, 1942.

2. Ayres de Andrade, "Camargo Guarnieri na Orquestra Sinfônica Brasileira," *O Jornal* (Rio de Janeiro), September 23, 1942.

3. Francisco Cavalcanti, "Orquestra Sinfônica Brasileira," *Jornal do Brasil* (Rio de Janeiro), September 22, 1942.

4. Caldeira Filho, *O Estado de São Paulo,* July 23, 1943 (also *A Aventura da Música,* 66).

5. Caldeira Filho, *O Estado de São Paulo,* March 24, 1956 (also *A Aventura da Música,* 78).

10. MUSIC FOR WIND INSTRUMENTS

1. Caldeira Filho, *O Estado de São Paulo,* November 30, 1941 (also *A Aventura da Música,* 65).

2. Eurico Nogueira França, "Música: Novas Edições de Guarnieri," *Correio Musical* (Rio de Janeiro), February 4, 1948.

3. Barbara and Frank Suetholz, interview with author, December 30, 1999.

4. Caldeira Filho, *O Estado de São Paulo,* March 17, 1959 (also *A Aventura da Música,* 80).

5. Maurício Alves Loureiro, "Chôro para Clarineta e Orquestra by Camargo Guarnieri" (Ph.D. diss., University of Iowa, 1991).

11. MUSIC FOR ORCHESTRA

1. Mário de Andrade, "Sinfônica," *Diário Nacional* (São Paulo), May 7, 1929.

2. Mário de Andrade, *Diário de São Paulo,* January 31, 1934.

3. Judith Cabette, program notes for Orquestra Sinfônica de Teatro Municipal, Rio de Janeiro, March 16, 1951.

4. Camargo Guarnieri, program notes for March 16, 1951.

5. Camargo Guarnieri, interview with author, São Paulo, January 29, 1970.

6. Antônio T. Corte Real, "Impressões de Arte: Camargo Guarnieri é Música Brasileira," *Correio do Povo* (Porto Alegre), November 14, 1940.

7. Caldeira Filho, "Três Concertos de Camargo Guarnieri," *O Estado de São Paulo,* December 4, 1977.

8. Luiz Heitor Correa de Azevedo, *Música Viva* (Rio de Janeiro), June 1940.

9. Andrade Muricy, "Pelo Mundo da Música: Camargo Guarnieri," *Jornal do Comercio* (Rio de Janeiro), June 5, 1940.

10. Hans Joachim Koellreutter, "Camargo Guarnieri, O 'Lider' da Jovem Geração de Compositores Brasileiros," *Vida,* May 1943.

11. Judith Cabette, program notes for Orquestra Sinfônica Municipal, São Paulo, October 11, 1964.

12. "Artes e Artistas," n.p., n.d.

13. Anonymous review of concert of March 26, 1943.

14. L. A. Sloper, "Three Novelties Heard at Symphony Concert," *Christian Science Monitor,* March 27, 1943.

15. Warren Storey Smith, "Noble Themes from Symphony: Schumann's Cantata and Brazilian Overture," *Boston Post,* March 27, 1943.

16. Rudolph Elie, Jr., "Schumann's Free Cantata," *Boston Herald,* March 27, 1943.

17. Caldeira Filho, *O Estado de São Paulo,* March 11, 1945 (also *A Aventura da Música,* 67–68).

18. Ibid.

19. Ibid.

20. Ibid.

21. Ibid.

22. Caldeira Filho, *O Estado de São Paulo,* March 9, 1950.

23. Ibid.

24. Ibid.

25. Flavia Toni, record jacket notes for *Camargo Guarnieri: Symphonies No. 2 & 3,* Orquestra Sinfônica de Estado de São Paulo, John Neschling, Sweden: BIS CD-1220 Digital, 2002.

26. Filho, *O Estado de São Paulo,* March 9, 1950.

27. Luiz Heitor de Azevedo, quoted in Mariz, ed., *História da Música no Brasil,* 222.

28. Ibid.

29. Herbert Elwell, *Cleveland Plain Dealer,* cited in Filho, *A Aventura da Música,* 73–74.

30. Marc Pincherle, "Les nouvelles littéraires," quoted in *Diário de Notícias* (Rio de Janeiro), February 24, 1953.

31. Eurico Nogueira França, "Camargo Guarnieri e Seu Prologo e Fuga," *Correio da Manhã* (Rio de Janeiro), December 1, 1948.

32. Eurico Nogueira França, "Duas Páginas Representativas," *O Estado de São Paulo,* May 11, 1969.

33. Camargo Guarnieri, program notes for Orquestra Sinfônica Municipal, Rio de Janeiro, March 16, 1951.

34. Anon., program notes for Orquestra Sinfônica Brasileira, Rio de Janeiro, January 1956.

35. Caldeira Filho, *O Estado de São Paulo,* September 29, 1954 (also *A Aventura da Música,* p. 76).

36. Ricardo Tacuchian, "O Sinfonismo Guarnieriano," in Silva, ed., *O Tempo e a Música,* 448.

37. Filho, *O Estado de São Paulo,* September 29, 1954.

38. Judith Cabette, program notes for São Paulo Orquestra Sinfônica Municipal, April 4, 1966.

39. Hans Joachim Koellreutter, "Música dos Maestros," *Diário de São Paulo,* September 9, 1955.

40. Eurico Nogueira França, "A Terceira Sinfonia de Camargo Guarnieri," *Correio da Manhã* (Rio de Janeiro), December 1, 1964.

41. Mariz, *História da Música no Brasil,* 223.

42. Caldeira Filho, *O Estado de São Paulo,* May 19, 1955 (also *A Aventura da Música,* 77–78).

43. Caldeira Filho, *O Estado de São Paulo,* March 17, 1959 (also *A Aventura da Música,* 77–78).

44. Judith Cabette, program notes, Orquestra Sinfônica Municipal, São Paulo, August 22, 1965.

45. Mariz, *História da Música no Brasil,* 223.

46. John Thornton, *Portland Press Herald* (Portland, Maine), December 6, 1967.

47. Caldeira Filho, record jacket notes for *Villa Lobos/Guarnieri,* Rio de Janeiro: Enir ECL-001.

48. Ibid.

49. Quoted in Filho, *A Aventura da Música,* 88–89.

50. Ibid., 89.

51. Caldeira Filho, *O Estado de São Paulo,* November 18, 1967.

52. Camargo Guarnieri, program notes for Orquestra Filharmônica de São Paulo, November 9, 1967.

53. Ibid.

54. Caldeira Filho, program notes, November 9, 1977.

55. Caldeira Filho, "Três Concertos de Camargo Guarnieri," *O Estado de São Paulo,* December 4, 1977.

56. Ibid.

57. Ibid.

58. Ibid.

59. Carlos Vergueira, review of recording, *O Estado de São Paulo,* February 29, 1984.

60. Filho, "Três Concertos."

61. Ricardo Tacuchian, "O Sinfonismo Guarnieriano," in Silva, ed., *O Tempo e a Música,* 461–62.

62. Ibid., p. 462.

63. Mário de Andrade, quoted in Lutero Rodrigues, "Camargo Guarnieri," *Apollon Musagete—Periódico Musical IV-91* (Curitiba, no. 4), April 1991.

64. Virgil Thompson, "Excellence from Brazil," *New York Herald Tribune,* March 8, 1943.

65. Rodrigues, "Camargo Guarnieri (I)."

66. Osvaldo Costa de Lacerda, "O Professor Camargo Guarnieri," quoted in ibid.

BIBLIOGRAPHY

Abreu, Maria. "O Homen e Episódios que Caracterizam Sua Personalidade." In Flávio Silva, ed., *Camargo Guarnieri: O Tempo e a Música.* Rio de Janeiro: Funarte, 2001.

Almeida, Renato. *Compêndio de História da Música Brasileira.* 2nd ed. Rio de Janeiro: Briguiet, 1958.

————. *História da Música Brasileira.* 2nd ed. Rio de Janeiro: Briguiet, 1942.

Alvarenga, Oneyda. *Música Popular Brasileira.* São Paulo: Livraria Duas Cidades, 1982.

Andrade, Mário de. *Aspectos da Música Brasileira.* São Paulo: Martins, 1939.

————. *Ensaio Sôbre a Música Brasileira.* São Paulo: Martins, 1962.

————. *Música, Doce Música.* São Paulo: Martins, 1963.

————. *Pequena História de Música.* 8th ed. São Paulo: Martins, 1968.

Appleby, David P. *The Music of Brazil.* Austin, TX: University of Texas Press, 1983.

Appleby, David P. *Heitor Villa-Lobos: A Life (1887–1959).* Lanham, Md.: Scarecrow Press, 2002.

Azevedo, Fernando de. *Brazilian Culture.* Trans. William Rex Crawford. New York: Macmillan, 1950.

Azevedo, Luis Heitor Correa de. *Canções Brasileiras.* Rio de Janeiro: Divisão Cultura do Ministério das Relações Exteriores, 1947.

————. *150 Anos de Música no Brasil (1800–1950).* Rio de Janeiro: J. Olympio, 1956.

————. *Music in Brazil.* Washington, D.C.: Pan American Union, 1948.

————. *Música e Músicos do Brasil.* Rio de Janeiro: Casa do Estudante do Brasil, 1950.

Behague, Gérard. *Music in Latin America.* Englewood Cliffs, N.J.: Prentice Hall, 1979.

Caetano, Pedro. *Meio Século de Música Popular Brasileira: O que Fiz, O que Vi.* Rio de Janeiro: Vila Doméstica, 1984.

Campos, Augusto de, *Balanço da Bossa, Antologia Crítica da Moderna Música Popular Brasileira.* São Paulo: Perspective, 1968.

Cascudo, Luís da Câmara. *Dicionário do Folclore Brasileiro.* 2 vols. Rio de Janeiro: Edições de Ouro, 1969.

Cone, Edward T. *Musical Form and Musical Performance.* New York: W. W. Norton, 1968.

Cosme, Luís. *Introdução á Música.* Rio de Janeiro: Edições de Ouro Culturais, 1967.

Deri, Otto. *Exploring Twentieth Century Music.* New York: Holt, Rinehart & Winston, 1968.

Enciclopédia da Música Brasileira Popular, Erudita e Folclórica. 2nd ed. São Paulo: Art Editora Publifolha, 1998.

Fialkow, Ney. "The Ponteios of Camargo Guarnieri." Ph.D. dissertation, Peabody Institute of the John Hopkins University, 1995.

Filho, Caldeira. *A Aventura da Música.* São Paulo: Ricordi, 1969.

Finklestein, Sidney. *Composer and Nation.* New York: International Publishers, 1960.

França, Eurico Nogueira. *Música do Brasil.* Rio de Janeiro: Edições de Ouro, 1968.

Freyre, Gilberto. *Interpretação do Brasil.* São Paulo: Livraria José Olympio, 1947.

————. *The Masters and the Slaves: A Study in the Development of Brazilian Civilization.* New York: Alfred A. Knopf, 1946.

Gerling, Cristina Capparelli, ed. *Três Estudos Analíticos: Villa-Lobos, Mignone, e Camargo Guarnieri. Série Estudos 5.* Porto Alegre: Federal University of Rio Grande do Sul, 2000.

Jong, Gerrit de. "Music in Brazil." *Inter-American Music Bulletin,* no. 31 (September 1962), 1–14.

Kiefer, Bruno. *História da Música Brasileira: Dos Primorios ao Inicio do Sec. XX.* 3rd ed. Porto Alegre: Movimento, 1982.

————. *Música e Dança Popular: Sua Influência na Música Erudita.* Porto Alegre: Movimento, 1979.

Lange, Francisco Curt, ed. *Latin American Art Music for the Piano.* New York: Schirmer, 1942.

Loureiro, Maurício Alves. "Chôro para Clarineta e Orquestra by Camargo Guarnieri." Ph.D. dissertation, University of Iowa, 1991.

Mariz, Vasco. *Camargo Guarnieri: Catálogo da Obra.* Brasilia: Ministério des Relações Exteriores, 1977.

————. *A Canção Brasileira.* Rio de Janeiro: Ministério da Educação e Cultura, 1948.

————. *Figuras da Música Brasileira Contemporânea.* 2nd ed. Brasilia: University of Brasilia, 1970.

————. *História da Música no Brasil.* 5th ed. Rio de Janeiro: Civilização Brasileiros, 1985.

Muricy, Andrade. *Caminho de Música.* Vol. 2. Rio de Janeiro, Editôra Guaira, 1937.

Neves, José Maria. *Música Contemporânea Brasileira.* São Paulo: Ricordi, 1981.

Preiss, Jorge Hirt. *A Música nas Missões Jesuíticas nos Séculos XVII e XVIII.* Porto Alegre: Martins, 1988.

Rabelo, Paulo César Martins. "The Cello and Piano Works of Camargo Guarnieri." Doctoral dissertation, Ohio State University, 1996.

Seeger, Anthony. *Os Indios e Nós, Estudos sobre Sociedades Tribais Brasileiras.* Rio de Janeiro: Campus, 1980.

Silva, Flavio, ed. *Camargo Guarnieri: O Tempo e a Música.* Rio de Janeiro: Funarte, 2001.

Slonimsky, Nicolas. *Music of Latin America.* New York: Thomas Y. Crowell, 1945.

Tinhorão, José Ramos. *Música Popular de Indios, Negroes e Mestiços.* Petropolis: Vozes, 1972.

————. *Pequena História da Música Popular: Da Modinha ao Tropicalismo.* 5th ed. São Paulo: Arts Editora, 1986.

Ulehla, Ludmila. *Contemporary Harmony.* New York: Free Press, 1966.

Universidade Federal de Rio Grande do Sul. *Aspectos do Modernismo Brasileiro.* Porto Alegre: Comissão Central da Publicações, 1970.

Vasconcellos Correa, Sergio. *Music in Brasil: Now.* Brasilia: Ministério das Relações Exteriores, Departamento de Educação e Cultura, 1974.

Vasconcellos, Gilberto. *Música Popular: De Olho no Fresta.* Rio de Janeiro: Graal, 1977.

Verhaalen, Marion. *Camargo Guarnieri: Expressões de Uma Vida.* São Paulo: University of São Paulo Press, 2001.

————. "The Solo Piano Music of Francisco Mignone and Camargo Guarnieri." Dissertation, Teachers College, Columbia University, 1971.

Wisnik, José Miguel. *O Coro dos Contrários, a Música em Torno da semana de 22.* São Paulo: Livraria Duas Cidades, 1977.

INDEX OF WORKS

GENERAL INDEX

MARION VERHAALEN teaches at the Wisconsin Conservatory of Music in Milwaukee. She is a composer and author as well, and has spent time in Brazil as a teacher and researcher, including a semester on a Fulbright Professorship at the Federal University in Porto Alegre. She has conducted pedagogy workshops throughout Brazil. Her work with Camargo Guarnieri, which spanned twenty-four years, resulted in *Camargo Guarnieri—Expressões de uma Vida* (2001) and in this new edition.

JOSÉ MARIA NEVES was Professor of Music at the University of Rio de Janeiro until his death in 2002. He held a Doctorate in Musicology from the University of Paris–Sorbonne.